THE DISJUNCTIVE LOGIC OF THE WORLD

TRANSMISSION

Transmission denotes the transfer of information, objects or forces from one place to another, from one person to another. Transmission implies urgency, even emergency: a line humming, an alarm sounding, a messenger bearing news. Through Transmission interventions are supported, and opinions overturned. Transmission republishes classic works in philosophy, as it publishes works that re-examine classical philosophical thought. Transmission is the name for what takes place.

THE DISJUNCTIVE LOGIC OF THE WORLD
THINKING GLOBAL CIVIL SOCIETY WITH HEGEL

Toula Nicolacopoulos
George Vassilacopoulos

re.press Melbourne 2013

re.press

PO Box 40, Prahran, 3181, Melbourne, Australia
http://www.re-press.org

© T. Nicolacopoulos & G. Vassilacopoulos 2013
The moral rights of the authors have been asserted

This work is 'Open Access', published under a creative commons license which means that you are free to copy, distribute, display, and perform the work as long as you clearly attribute the work to the authors, that you do not use this work for any commercial gain in any form whatsoever and that you in no way alter, transform or build on the work outside of its use in normal academic scholarship without express permission of the author (or their executors) *and* the publisher of this volume. For any reuse or distribution, you must make clear to others the license terms of this work. For more information see the details of the creative commons licence at this website: http://creativecommons.org/licenses/by-nc-sa/3.0/

National Library of Australia Cataloguing-in-Publication Data

Nicolacopoulos, Toula, author.

The disjunctive logic of the world : thinking global civil
society with Hegel
/ Toula Nicolacopoulos and George Vassilacopoulos.

9780987268280 (paperback)
9780987268297 (ebook)

Transmission. (Series)

Includes bibliographical references.

Hegel, Georg Wilhelm Friedrich, 1770-1831.
Civil society.
Philosophy, German--19th century.
Philosophy.

Other Authors/Contributors:
Vassilacopoulos, George, author.

320.01

Designed and Typeset by A&R

This book is produced sustainably using plantation timber, and printed in the destination market reducing wastage and excess transport.

CONTENTS

Acknowledgments	*vii*
1. Thinking Global Civil Society	9
2. Reading Hegel Systemically	41
3. The Sylllogistic Terms of the Concept of Civil Society	75
4. Civil Society as a System of Interdependence	89
5. Civil Society's Ethical Aspect and Global Significance	101
6. From The Hypothetical to the Disjunctive Syllogism and Civil Society's System Differentiation	129
7. The Logic of the Estates and Global Civil Society	149
8. The Corporation as an Aspect of Ethical Life in the Global Order	167
9. The Police, The Welfare State and Global Governance	181
Conclusion: The Transition to Objectivity and Hegel's Ethical State	199
References	205

To Paul Ashton
for making us think, and think again

ACKNOWLEDGMENTS

We would like to express our appreciation to re.press for supporting this publication and to La Trobe University for providing us with research leave to complete the manuscript.

1. THINKING GLOBAL CIVIL SOCIETY

This work is devoted to a detailed elaboration of the concept of 'Civil Society' that Hegel sets out in his *Philosophy of Right*.[1] Along with the 'Family' and 'The State' 'Civil Society' forms one of three aspects of the order of 'Ethical Life'.[2] Ethical Life elaborates the third and final stage in the logical development of Hegel's *Philosophy of Right* that in turn forms part of *The Philosophy of Mind* within the Hegelian system. Representing Hegel's 'mature' political philosophy, the *Philosophy of Right* has been the subject of a great deal of commentary motivated by a diversity of intellectual interests and approaches. These have ranged from setting aside Hegel's own purposes in order to extract useful insights, to uncovering Hegel's true intentions in developing his systematic social and political theory. Although we will be addressing some of this commentary, our main concern in this book is to offer a reading of Civil Society in response to the following question. What, if anything, can Hegel's philosophy tell us about the civil society/societies we encounter in the globalized world of the twenty-first century? To address this question we elaborate an account of Civil Society that relies on what we call 'the strict organization thesis'. This is the interpretive thesis according to which the logical categories of Hegel's system strictly organize those of empirical reality (hereafter 'the real categories') and, hence, of Ethical Life, which forms part of the domain of what Hegel calls 'Objective spirit'. On the basis of the strict organization thesis, we will be arguing that the standard readings of

---

1. G.W.F. Hegel, *Philosophy of Right*, trans. T.M. Knox, Oxford, Oxford University Press, 1967, (hereafter 'PR').
2. Throughout this book we use 'Civil Society', 'Family' or 'State' to refer to Hegel's concepts as he elaborates these in the text of the *Philosophy of Right*. When using the lower case we are referring simply to the social phenomena under discussion or to other theorists' conceptions.

Hegel are largely misplaced. Indeed a properly systemic reading of the concepts of Civil Society, the State and their relationship has the potential to shed new light on our understandings of the normative implications of global processes ranging from the effects of economic globalization to the global activism of non-governmental organizations ('NGOs') and social movements, to international relations and the question of global governance.

As such the book contributes to an emergent literature that sees Hegel's political philosophy as supporting a view of *global ethical community* of sorts and as offering principles that speak to the current demands of the global reality. Steven Hicks suggests that Hegel's theory of Ethical Life is relevant to the current global reality because

> the same political and juridical institutions, civic associations, and sub-political groupings that are central to unifying the ethical life of the [Hegelian] modern state [...] are those that are needed for the development of international cooperation and transnational unity as well.[3]

Hicks draws upon Hegel's theory of international relations to argue for its compatibility with an 'ethical cosmopolitanism' understood as 'a process of transnational / transcultural integration and global cooperation' that points to 'the formation of an "intercultural globality" and a higher-level ethical community of nations'.[4] By contrast we believe that the concept of Civil Society provides the proper basis for understanding significant aspects of territorial state relations in today's globalized world. These, however, go unnoticed when we focus discussion of this concept strictly on economic and civil life within the nation-state. As we hope to show, the concept of Civil Society provides a theoretical grounding for understanding the globalization processes that frame international relations issues today.[5]

---

3. Steven V. Hicks, 'Hegel on Cosmopolitanism, International Relations and the Challenges of Globalization', in Andrew Buchwalter (ed.), *Hegel and Global Justice*, New York and London, Springer, 2012, pp. 21-48 at pp. 30-31. See also the essays in Andrew Buchwalter (ed.), *Hegel and Global Justice*, New York and London, Springer, 2012.

4. Hicks, 'Hegel on Cosmopolitanism', p. 40.

5. We examine Hegel's treatment of the ethical State and international relations in a later work. The present book forms one of a series in progress, which elaborates the strict organization thesis and argues that it is a productive way of reading Hegel's concepts of Ethical Life. See also Toula Nicolacopoulos and George Vassilacopoulos, *Hegel and the Logical Structure of Love: An Essay of Sexualities, Family and the Law*, Melbourne, re.press, 2010.

GLOBAL REALITY AND NORMATIVE VISION

At the close of the twentieth century discussions of globalization processes were being framed against the background of the so-called triumph of capitalism, a triumph that was said to have consolidated the historical production of the world as *a single world* linked through relations of production and consumption.[6] For historians Jürgen Osterhammel and Niels Peterson, these processes are the product of 'the development, concentration and increasing importance of world-wide integration' that commenced with the emergence of the Portuguese and Spanish colonial empires in around 1500.[7] In its broadest rendition 'globalization' refers to 'a multidimensional process of change that involves increased connectivity across economies and societies creating a greater awareness of the world as a common point of reference'.[8] Yet, as one author of the new millennium puts it, 'the world left to us by the advent of globalization is a world of *logical* disconnections'.[9] In a similar vein, John Keane cautions against ignoring the growing awareness of the world as 'complex and vulnerable' and, from this perspective, 'to speak (as some do) of a "world order" or "one world" or a "global community"' is misleading.[10] To be sure, any sense of a 'necessary interdependence' that permeates the economic, environmental and communication cultures of the twenty-first century is offset by broader wide-ranging experiences of the *disconnectedness* that has come to be associated with exposure to a dangerous and endangered *world in transition*. This said, Keane's own study in *Global Civil Society?* (2003) takes off from the conviction that by the end of the last millennium:

> something new was born in the world—the unprecedented (if unevenly distributed) growth of the sense within NGOs and publics at large that civilians live in one world, and that they have obligations to other civilians living beyond the borders, simply because they are civilians.[11]

---

6. Roland Robertson, *Globalization: Social Theory and Global Culture*, London, Sage, 1992.

7. Jürgen Osterhammel and Niels P. Peterson, *Globalization: A Short History*, trans. Dona Geyer, Princeton, Princeton University Press, 2005, pp. 26-28.

8. Brian S. Turner and Habibul H. Khondker, *Globalization: East and West*, London, Sage, 2010, p. 36.

9. Mohammed A. Bayeh, *The Ends of Globalization*, Minnesota, University of Minnesota Press, 2000, p. ix.

10. John Keane, *Global Civil Society?*, Cambridge, Cambridge University Press, 2003, pp. 14-15.

11. Keane, *Global Civil Society?*, p. 36.

Andrew Buchwalter suggests that 'for Hegel, such consciousness of globality' takes shape through people's world-wide awareness 'that their identities are intertwined with the identities of others', their acceptance of 'the norms and values forged in increasingly obligatory processes of global interchange' and their growing awareness 'of the conditions for their shared commonality'.[12]

In the light of this growing awareness, there is today a fairly broad cross-disciplinary recognition of the need for a *fundamental normative reconceptualization* of the current global reality. This is a reality that, on the one hand, seems to call for the use of descriptive terms such as 'global governance', the 'global economy' and a 'global civic culture' and, on the other, is struggling to make manifest the true potential of its globality for humanity. Since the end of the previous century international relations theorists have been attempting to make sense of the world in the light of phenomena such as the growth of market capitalist economies and the movement towards a global economy; the end of political bi-polarity following the collapse of the Soviet Union; and the emergence of global civil society with the growth of the global labour market, increasing population movement and the dominance of the Internet and satellite communications more generally. With the so-called 'new internationalism' of the twenty-first century, we have witnessed a progressive extension of the reach and appeal of international human rights law and its imposition of greater restrictions on territorial states' sovereignty over their subjects in the name of granting protection against human rights violations. Yet we have also seen the emergence of transnational social movements, like the anti-globalization coalition, that oppose the democratic deficit linked to global developments and processes.[13] Globalization

---

12. Andrew Buchwalter, 'Hegel, Global Justice and Mutual Recognition', in Andrew Buchwalter (ed.), *Hegel and Global Justice*, New York and London, Springer, 2012, pp. 211-232 at p. 229.

13. Assessments of the effects of globalization vary greatly and in relation to different parts of the world. For an overview of the claims of critics and advocates of economic globalization see Turner and Khondker, *Globalization: East and West*, pp. 34-46. For a critical reading of the effects of globalization from an African perspective, see Anton Carpinschi and Bilakani Tonyeme, 'Cultural minorities and Intercultural Dialogue in the Dynamics of Globalization: African Participation', *Cultura: International Journal of Philosophy of Culture and Axiology*, vol. 8, no. 1, 2011, pp. 7-26. For a discussion of the impact of economic globalization on the lives of Indigenous peoples of Asia, which argues that the expansion of economic markets into what were previously subsistence economies combined with states' forced extraction of environmental resources that were previously within the control of the Indigenous peoples has produced increased marginalization and

analysts draw attention to transformations in temporality and social geography, giving rise respectively to 'a quasi-contemporaneity of [social] processes' and the emergence of 'supraterritoriality' through the transcendence of borders, distances, space and areas.[14] Some theorists have attempted to provide comprehensive explanations of such phenomena in terms of fundamental, even paradigm shifts. Most notably, Michael Hardt and Antonio Negri have argued that globalization brings with it the emergence of 'Empire' understood as a specific regime of global relations, which decisively combines sovereignty and capital to give rise to 'the police machine'.[15] As such, Empire 'is expressed as a juridical formation'; it is what regulates global networks of circulation through the enactment of an ordering function.[16] Observing that the world market is just such a decisive structure of hierarchy and command, the authors declare 'one simple fact: that there is world order'.[17] For Hardt and Negri then the order of Empire is that in relation to which 'the multitude' is called upon to respond in accordance with another vision of the global reality.[18] While Hardt and Negri's thesis is complex and debatable, in general we can say that international relations and political theorists acknowledge the role that *particular visions* of the world play in framing accounts of the dynamics that are shaping transnational forms of coercive authority as well as the possibilities for grass-roots endorsement of transnational governance networks within a recognizably global civil society.[19] Even those, like Keane who would avoid talk of a 'world order'

socio-economic deprivation, see Dev Nathan, Govind Kelkar and Pierre Walter (eds.), *Globalization and Indigenous Peoples in Asia: Changing the Local-global Interface*, London, Sage, 2004. For a defence of the view that the processes of globalization have generated new political and economic spaces in which the marginalized Maya peoples who constitute some 40-60% of Guatemala's population have developed the pan-Maya movement see Edward F. Fischer, *Cultural Logics and Global Economies: Maya Identity in Thought and Practice*, Austin, University of Texas Press, 2001.

14. Gunter Frankenberg, 'National, Supranational, and Global Ambivalence in the Practice of Global Civil Society', *Law Critique*, vol. 19, 2008, pp. 275-296 at p. 290.

15. Michael Hardt and Antonio Negri, *Empire*, Cambridge, Harvard University Press, 2001.

16. Hardt and Negri, *Empire*, p. 251.

17. See Hardt and Negri, *Empire*, p. 1: Hardt and Negri also make the point that Empire is 'neither the result of spontaneous heterogeneous forces or of a single rational centre that guides the phases of historical development'.

18. Michael Hardt and Antonio Negri, *Multitude: War and Democracy in the Age of Empire*, London, Hamish Hamilton, 2005.

19. See, for example, the essays in Randall D. Germain and Michael Kenny

or a 'global community', insist that a *'new world-view,* radically different from anything that existed before, has been born and is currently enjoying a growth spurt'.[20]

For Keane, this new world-view was signaled with the arrival of the 1990s neologism, 'global civil society'. Keane notes that 'talk of global civil society has become popular among, citizens' campaigners, bankers, diplomats, NGOs and politicians'.[21] Moreover, although the language of civil society originated in Europe, the terms 'civil society' and 'global civil society' have spread to every continent,[22] albeit with very little consensus as to their meaning.[23] Adam B. Seligman also makes the point that '[r]ight, left and centre, North, South, East and West—civil society is identified with everything from multiparty systems and the rights of citizenship to individual voluntarism and the spirit of community.[24] Seligman attributes the multiple usages of the term in current social and political practice to the concept's variously motivated revival after it had come to an end in the post-Marx nineteenth century.[25] For Seligman, however,

> [w]hat is ultimately at stake in this question [of civil society] is [...] the proper role of *normatively* constituting the existence of society—whether in terms of private individuals or in the existence of a shared public sphere.[26]

Here, it is worth noting that in some intellectual contexts the phrase 'global civil society' operates primarily as *an ideal* in that it connotes the ethical and political potential for social transformation towards a more just and humane world.[27] In these normative terms, the project of building a global civil society is itself subject

---

(eds.), *The Idea of Global Civil Society: Politics and Ethics in a Globalizing Era,* London, Routledge, 2005.
20. Keane, *Global Civil Society?,* p. 1, our emphasis.
21. Keane, *Global Civil Society?,* pp. 1-2.
22. Keane, *Global Civil Society?,* p. 35.
23. Keane, *Global Civil Society?,* p. 3.
24. Adam B. Seligman, 'Civil Society as Idea and Ideal', in Simone Chambers and Will Kymlicka (eds.), *Alternative Conceptions of Civil Society,* Princeton, Princeton University Press, 2002, pp. 13-33 at p. 13.
25. Seligman, 'Civil Society as Idea and Ideal', pp. 27-30.
26. Seligman, 'Civil Society as Idea and Ideal', p. 14.
27. For a review of the 'hype, gloom and exaggerated hopes that have tended to inform recent western analyses of global civil society' see Michael Kenny and Randall Germain, 'The Idea(l) of Global Civil Society' in Randall D. Germain and Michael Kenny (eds.), *The Idea of Global Civil Society: Politics and Ethics in a Globalizing Era,* London, Routledge, 2005, pp. 192-199 at p. 197. For a critique of global civil society's 'purism' see Keane, *Global Civil Society?,* pp. 57-88; p. 176.

to criticisms ranging from concerns about the ineffectiveness of NGO networks in the face of the overwhelming power of global capital, to claims that such a project ultimately furthers the imperialist expansion of Western values.[28]

By contrast, as a *descriptive* term 'global civil society' is not just used across the globe, but it also designates a broad and diverse range of civic actors operating transnationally.[29] The organizational and associational forms and networks referred to in this context are multiple, ranging from fluid social movements and mass membership organizations, to an ever-increasing number of national and international NGOs, as well as BINGOs and transnational private 'think tanks'.[30] Indeed along with a rapid increase in the number of globally operating NGOs, we have a blurring of the lines between not-for profit and business organizations.[31] As Keane notes, the processes of economic globalization have led to some NGOs modeling their operations on business corporations, for example, 'by developing commercial departments, headhunters, media sections and private fundraising and investment strategies'.[32] So the agents of global civil society, in the descriptive sense of the term, may be variously linked to the processes of economic globalization, that is, to global capital and the worldwide expansion of capitalist market economies, whether as advocates and regulators or as critics and opponents. Keane also makes

---

28. For discussion of these critiques see Andrew Gamble and Michael Kenny, 'Ideological Contestation, Transnational Civil Society and Global politics', in Randall D. Germain and Michael Kenny (eds.), *The Idea of Global Civil Society: Politics and Ethics in a Globalizing Era*, London, Routledge, 2005, pp. 20-21; and Turner and Khondker, *Globalization: East and West*, pp. 34-36. Claire Mercer objects that NGO analysts tend uncritically to endorse a normative view of the political role of NGOs as one of strengthening and democratizing civil society. Claire Mercer, 'NGOs, Civil Society and Democratization: A Critical Review of the Literature', *Progress in Developmental Studies*, vol. 2, no. 1, 2001, pp. 5-22. But see also Hardt and Negri, *Empire*, pp. 312-314, who distinguish between types of NGO and their differing relationships to global capitalism.

29. When speaking of 'global civil society' in this study, we do not distinguish, as some authors do, between the transnational reach of 'global civil society' and the narrower supranational reach of for, example, a European civil society in the sense of the civil society of the European Union. For a comparative discussion see Gunter Frankenberg, 'National, Supranational, and Global Ambivalence in the Practice of Global Civil Society'.

30. The acronym 'BINGO' refers to business-oriented international non-governmental organizations.

31. According to Keane at the start of the twenty-first century the number of NGOs had reached an estimated 50,000. Keane, *Global Civil Society?*, p. 5.

32. Keane, *Global Civil Society?*, p. 91

the point that whereas the term is used descriptively in explanatory accounts of the global reality, this should be distinguished not only from its normative sense but also from a third *strategic* sense that signifies a political campaigning criterion.[33] Bearing in mind these distinctions allows for the use of an inclusive descriptive definition of global civil society without also reducing the phenomenon to its current normative and strategic dimensions.[34] At the same time, however, as we will see in the course of this study, insisting on such a sharp distinction between descriptive/explanatory and normative usage may also inhibit a full appreciation of the meaning and significance of these variously related dimensions of global civil society.

GLOBAL CIVIL SOCIETY, THE DEMAND FOR NEW THEORY AND THE INTELLECTUAL TRADITION

Significantly for our purposes, it is as a normative ideal that global civil society has given rise to the demand for a new theoretical approach from which to view globalization processes. Michael Kenny and Randall Germain suggest that

> [d]ebates over the ideal of global civil society represent an important contribution to our understanding of global order in the contemporary period. Globalization, the end of the cold war, the 'retreat of the state', all suggest that traditional accounts of the global order need to be recalibrated.[35]

Brian Turner and Kabibul Haque Khondker agree that the social sciences 'need new methodologies, innovative theories, and almost certainly revised epistemologies to do good research on globalization processes'.[36] Similarly, in his major study of the concept and history of civil society, *The Civil Sphere*,[37] Jeffrey C. Alexander argues that after the late twentieth century re-entry of

---

33. Keane, *Global Civil Society?*, p. 3. For example, the conceptualization of civil society by the European Commission and the European Union's Economic and Social Committee in terms of functional participation and representation conforms to a strategic definition in Keane's sense. Stijn Smismans argues that, in being shaped by these institutions' interests, the EU discourse strategically downplays problems at the heart of European integration. Stijn Smismans, 'European Civil Society: Shaped by Discourses and Institutional Interests', *European Law Journal*, vol. 9, no. 4, 2003, pp. 473-495. We do not propose to examine such strategic uses of the concept of (global) civil society.

34. Keane, *Global Civil Society?*, pp. 57-65.

35. Kenny and Germain, 'The idea(l) of Global Civil Society', p. 15.

36. Turner and Khondker, *Globalization: East and West*, p. 7.

37. Jeffrey C. Alexander, *The Civil Sphere*, Oxford, Oxford University Press, 2006.

'civil society' into intellectual discourse, especially with Eastern European developments since the emergence of Poland's social movement, Solidarity,

> [t]here is a new theoretical continent to explore, a new empirical domain waiting to be defined. But we will not be able to make out this new social territory unless we can look at it through new theoretical lenses. Our old conceptual spectacles will not do.[38]

According to Alexander,

> we need a new concept of civil society as a civil *sphere*, a world of values and institutions that at once generates the capacity for social criticism and democratic integration. Such a sphere relies on solidarity, on feelings for others whom we do not know but whom we respect out of principle.[39]

Alexander lends support to the claim that we need a new concept by pointing to the history of the concept's emergence in the Western intellectual tradition. He notes that when the modern concept of civil society first entered into European social understanding via the intellectual achievements of the period from the seventeenth to the nineteenth centuries,

> "civil society" was a rather diffuse umbrella-like concept referring to a plethora of institutions outside the state. It included the capitalist market and its institutions, but it also denoted [...] private and public associations and organizations, and virtually every form of cooperative social relationship that created bonds of trust—for example, currents of public opinion, legal norms and institutions, and political parties.[40]

Significantly for Alexander, 'in this first period of its modern understanding, civil society was endowed with a distinctively moral and ethical force'.[41] As Seligman argues, in 'the early modern emergence and use of the concept', civil society was linked to the questioning and rejection of the idea that the social order was externally derived.[42]

> The image of civil society as an ethical model for conceiving the workings of the societal order [...] represents a critical new attempt to argue the moral sources of the social order from within the human world and without recourse to an external or transcendent referent. This challenge and, with it, that of

---

38. Alexander, *The Civil Sphere*, p. 24.
39. Alexander, *The Civil Sphere*, p. 4.
40. Alexander, *The Civil Sphere*, p. 24.
41. Alexander, *The Civil Sphere*, p. 33.
42. Seligman, 'Civil Society as Idea and Ideal', p. 13.

squaring the newly emerging interests of increasingly autonomous individuals with some vision of the public good provided the theoretical and ethical ground for the idea of civil society.[43]

It was not until market society was stripped of its positive moral and ethical rendition, in the early middle of the nineteenth century that

> "civil society" was transformed into a pejorative term whose meaning came to be identified with [the social ills of] market capitalism.[44]

For Alexander, this conflation of civil society and market capitalism had the regrettable effect of denying to theorists any opportunity 'to draw upon the idea of an independent civil sphere'.[45]

Alexander insists that neither of these two historical conceptions of civil society, which he labels 'CSI' and 'CSII' respectively, is adequate to current demands. On the one hand, 'to identify civil society with capitalism (CSII) is to degrade its universalizing moral implications and the capacity for criticism and repair that the existence of a relatively independent solidary community implies'.[46] On the other,

> social life at the beginning of the twenty-first century is much more complex and more internally differentiated than the early modern societies that generated CSI. The old umbrella understanding will not do. We need a much more precise and delimited understanding of the term. [...] Rejecting the reductionism of CSII, but also the diffuse inclusiveness of CSI, we must develop a third approach to civil society, one that reflects both the empirical and normative problems of contemporary life.[47]

What of Hegel's account of Civil Society? Hegel critics have pointed to a variety of different reasons to suggest the unsuitability of Hegel's theory for addressing current demands. Alexander suggests that any return to Hegel for the purpose of developing a new concept would be fruitless because Hegel's model of civil society also conforms to CSI[48] and 'civil society is not everywhere except the state', as this model implies.[49] Turner and Khondker fol-

---

43. Seligman, 'Civil Society as Idea and Ideal', pp. 13-15.
44. Alexander, *The Civil Sphere*, p. 33.
45. Alexander, *The Civil Sphere*, p. 33.
46. Alexander, *The Civil Sphere*, p. 33.
47. Alexander, *The Civil Sphere*, pp. 30-31.
48. Alexander, *The Civil Sphere*, p. 31.
49. Alexander, *The Civil Sphere*, p. 551.

low Alexander in endorsing the position that 'the reinvigoration of sociological theories of civil society cannot simply be a return to the classical political economy of Smith, Ferguson and Hegel'.[50] Seligman too locates Hegel's concept in a line of continuity with the classic idea that originated in the Scottish Enlightenment and subsequently responds to the modern problem of resolving the tensions between individualism and community.[51] He dismisses Hegel's concept on the basis of the popular argument that in Hegel 'its viability as a normative concept and model of social representation disappears [...] in the universal state'.[52] Keane would agree that Hegel's concept of Civil Society has little to offer us today given that one can draw only limited parallels with a concept belonging to 'a new theory of ethics beyond borders' that would speak to the demands of the global reality. For Keane, as for many Hegel commentators, because Hegel's concept of Civil Society is subordinated to that of the State, meaning the national or territorial state, it cannot accommodate resistance to state interventions in the case where states claim to act on behalf of the universal interest.[53] We will return to this question of interpreting Hegel's account of the State-Civil Society relation. For now, we should note that Keane's interpretation appears to be supported by modern states' treatment of Indigenous–colonizer relations, which often deny Indigenous sovereignty rights in the name of the interests of *all* citizens.[54] Finally, postcolonial critics reject Hegel's valorization of European achievements, seeing him as one of the intellectual figures of the West whose works have founded research

---

50. Turner and Khondker, *Globalization: East and West*, p. 216.
51. Seligman, 'Civil Society as Idea and Ideal', pp. 28-30.
52. Seligman, 'Civil Society as Idea and Ideal', p. 27.
53. Keane, *Global Civil Society?*, pp. 2-3; pp. 92-94; p. 196. For Keane's critique of Hegel's concept of Civil Society see John Keane, *Democracy and Civil Society*, London, Verso, 1988, pp. 46-48.
54. This has been the case with the Australian government. See Toula Nicolacopoulos and George Vassilacopoulos, 'Rethinking the Radical Potential of the Concept of Multiculturalism', in Tseen Khoo (ed.), *The Body Politic: Racialised Political Cultures in Australia*, University of Queensland, University of Queensland's Australian Studies Centre, 2005, pp. 1-13. In Australia, government policy frameworks, which are supposedly directed to the universal interest, also deny the preconditions for effective Indigenous participation in Australian civil society in so far as they operate within a legal system 'designed to undermine Indigenous cultures and collective rights': Victor G. Hart, Lester J. Thompson and Terry Stedman, 'The Indigenous Experience of Australian Civil Society: Making Sense of Historic and Contemporary Institutions', *Social Alternatives*, vol. 27, no. 1, 2008, pp. 52-57.

agendas, which, as Tina Chanter suggests, encourage 'a certain evasion of our own implication in empires built on slavery and colonization'.[55] As John and Jean Comaroff argue, such agendas tend to represent the establishment of civil order beyond Europe in terms of an imagined re-creation of stages of civilization grounded 'in a singular understanding of *"the* world historical spirit"'.[56] Clark Butler also observes that given Hegel's failure to anticipate developments in postcolonial societies, which resulted in increased poverty in the newly independent nations, 'we are no longer tempted like Hegel to celebrate global civil society as the key to solving the economic problems of Western nations'.[57] For different reasons, then, Hegel is taken to belong to an intellectual tradition that cannot supply a suitable theory of global civil society.

FORMULATING NEW MODELS OF CIVIL SOCIETY

Alexander responds to the demand for new theory taking into account that 'the articulation of an abstract ethics [such as Hegel's], and increased efforts to apply them to the regulation of social life, can never eliminate the dangers of moral violation, social contradiction and institutional constraint'. This is why he wants to focus on 'the [intellectual] territory *between* the abstract and the concrete'.[58] With this in mind, he replaces the two models he draws from the Western intellectual tradition, CSI and CSII, with a third model, CSIII, which he bases on the value of solidarity.

> Civil society should be conceived as a solidary sphere, in which a certain kind of universalizing community comes to be culturally defined and to some degree institutionally enforced. To the degree that this solidary community exists, it is exhibited and sustained by public opinion, deep cultural codes, distinctive organizations—legal, journalistic and associational—and such historically specific interactional practices as civility, criticism and mutual respect. Such a civil community can never

---

55. Tina Chanter, 'Antigone's Liminality: Hegel's Racial Purification of Tragedy and the Naturalization of Slavery', in Kimberly Hutchings and and Tuija Pulkkinen (eds.), *Hegel's Philosophy and Feminist Thought: Beyond Antigone?*, Basingstoke, Palgrave MacMillan, 2010, pp. 61-85 at p. 61.

56. John L. Comaroff and Jean Comaroff, 'Introduction', in John L. Comaroff and Jean Comaroff (eds.), *Civil Society and the Political Imagination in Africa: Critical Perspectives*, Chicago, University of Chicago Press, 1999, pp. 1-43 at p. 19.

57. Clark Butler, 'The Coming World Welfare State which Hegel Could Not See', in Andrew Buchwalter (ed.), *Hegel and Global Justice*, New York and London, Springer, 2012, pp. 155-176 at p. 170.

58. Alexander, *The Civil Sphere*, pp. 21-22, emphasis added.

exist as such; it can only be sustained to one degree or another. It is always limited by, and interpenetrated with, the boundary relations of other, non-civil spheres.[59]

These other 'non-civil spheres' include market relations and particularistic institutions such as religion, family and community. CSIII holds that the civil sphere inevitably confronts boundary problems with such non-civil spheres; as a sphere of justice it conflicts with other value demands generating what Alexander refers to as the struggles over civil repair that historically have defined social movements. So for Alexander civil society is a differentiated social sphere with its own value orientation, namely 'civil solidarity'. This is 'the real utopia' that 'lies beneath every particular demand for institutional reform, every historically specific demand for cultural reformation'.[60]

Although Alexander defends CSIII by drawing upon an extensive empirical study of social movements that have largely operated within nation-states or localized regions, he suggests that because the model's underlying 'theoretical reflections have been developed without reference to scale', 'it is possible, indeed, for the imagining and the organizing of civil society to go beyond the territory of the nation-state'.[61] This said,

> Even if we were able to establish a global civil sphere, and to extend the goalposts of civil society to the other side of the earth, the binary nature of civil discourse and the contradictions of time, place and function would not go away [...]. The spirit of civil society will always be restless. Its boundary relations will continue to be dynamic [...]. The contradictions would still be alarming, and struggles over civil repair would still be contingent and dramatic.[62]

Alexander appeals to the creative practices of social movement struggles in generating civil society. Others refuse to give up on the resources of the Western intellectual tradition and forego all appeals to 'abstract ethics', as Alexander advocates. For example, Andrew Gamble and Michael Kenny argue that the liberal intellectual tradition still affords 'invaluable resources' from which to develop 'an ethical account of the new global politics'.[63] Similarly,

---

59. Alexander, *The Civil Sphere*, p. 31.
60. Alexander, *The Civil Sphere*, p. 550.
61. Alexander, *The Civil Sphere*, p. 552.
62. Alexander, *The Civil Sphere*, p. 552.
63. Gamble and Kenny, 'Ideological Contestation, Transnational Civil Society and Global politics', p. 32.

Turner and Khondker respond to the demand for new theory by calling for the redirection of intellectual thought towards the development of a new *non-Kantian* 'cosmopolitan vision' that 'brings the West and East together in a common purpose'. To this end they appeal to the thought of G.W. Leibniz, who they suggest 'lays out the essential ethical ingredients for human rights not only as a juridical institution but also as a shared culture' that nevertheless preserves 'the notion of infinite cultural diversity'.[64]

Like Turner and Khondker, Keane argues for the move away from Kantian inspired notions of a 'world civil society' but also from traditional state-centred notions of an 'international society' because such normative conceptions cannot capture 'the latter-day emergence of a *non-governmental* social sphere'.[65] Instead, for descriptive and explanatory purposes global civil society is best understood

> as a vast, interconnected and multi-layered non-governmental space that comprises many hundreds and thousands of self-directing institutions and ways of life that generate global effects.[66]

There are five salient features of this definition, which together capture what Keane sees as the historical distinctness of the current phenomenon. Firstly, 'the term global civil society refers to *non-governmental* structures and activities'.[67] Like CSI, it excludes governmental institutions yet it does not face the objection that it too is diffusely inclusive given that it is not merely negatively defined in relation to governmental institutions. Although it excludes governmental structures and activities, it does not include all else. 'The truth is that in a descriptive sense global civil society is only *one* special set of 'non-state institutions'.[68] Keane makes the point that this set leaves out associations like tribal orders and *mafiosi* which, for different reasons, would be falsely described as *civil* society orders.[69] Notice, however, that on this definition, it is not only the activities of transnational governance organizations, such as the European Union, that fall outside the scope of the concept, but also of organizations engaging in transnational

---

64. Turner and Khondker, *Globalization: East and West*, pp. 207-208.
65. Keane, *Global Civil Society?*, pp. 22.
66. Keane, *Global Civil Society?*, pp. 22. For a more analytic statement of this definition see Keane, *Global Civil Society?*, p. 8.
67. Keane, *Global Civil Society?*, p. 8.
68. Keane, *Global Civil Society?*, p. 10.
69. Keane, *Global Civil Society?*, p. 10.

commercial activities if their members happen to be territorial states. Latin America's MERCOSUR—a network through which member states exchange goods and services in-kind depending on their respective needs, for instance, oil for doctors—is a case in point. Secondly, global civil society is 'a highly complex ensemble of differently sized, overlapping forms of structured social action' and as such is not exhausted by the aggregation of its various organizations but, instead, has 'a marked life or momentum or power of its own'.[70] Thirdly, global civil society is 'a space of non-violence' marked by civility. That is, global civil society 'encourages compromises and mutual respect' even as it contains pockets of 'incivility'. Its actors 'admire the peaceful' and 'enable civil society to be "civil" in a double sense: it consists of non-governmental (or "civilian") institutions that tend to have non-violent (or "civil") effects'.[71] Fourthly, it is a pluralistic system of inter-dependence that contains 'strong conflict potential' due to its heterogeneity.[72] Finally, it is global in the sense that 'its politically framed and circumscribed social relations [...] stretch across and underneath state boundaries and other government forms'. In other words, it is 'a special form of *unbounded* society'.[73]

Keane makes the point that the compilation of empirical data concerning the rise of global civil society is complicated by the fact that the phenomenon is constituted by the changing perceptions of global civil society's agents.[74] Borrowing a familiar phrase from Charles Taylor we might say that because global civil society's agents are *self-interpreting animals*, any descriptive account will face the difficulty of engaging with a changing phenomenon that cannot be neatly objectified. Keane's solution is to offer his analytic concept as an *ideal-type*, that is, as an intentionally produced mental construct that cannot be found in the social world but is useful for heuristic and explanatory purposes.[75]

Having elaborated this sort of concept to describe and explain the real-world phenomenon, Keane then limits his normative conception to the problem of providing civil society actors with sound moral grounds for endorsing and strengthening global civil

---

70. Keane, *Global Civil Society?*, p. 11.
71. Keane, *Global Civil Society?*, pp. 12-14.
72. Keane, *Global Civil Society?*, pp. 14-15.
73. Keane, *Global Civil Society?*, p. 17.
74. Keane, *Global Civil Society?*, p. 7.
75. Keane, *Global Civil Society?*, p. 8.

society as described.⁷⁶ Much like John Rawls' insistence on taking into account the so-called *fact of reasonable pluralism*, Keane sets aside all foundationalist justifications of global civil society in the name of what he calls 'the Law of Unending Controversy'.⁷⁷ He argues instead that the normativity of global civil society stems from its capacity to function as 'a condition of possibility of *multiple moralities*—in other words, as a universe of freedom *from* a singular Universal Ethic' whose practice insists upon correcting the perceived mistaken practices of others.⁷⁸ As an 'implied logical and institutional precondition of the survival and flourishing of a genuine plurality of different ideals and forms of life' the ideal of global civil society 'is anchored within the actually existing global civil society' which is now credited for functioning as this kind of plurality.⁷⁹ Moreover, its categorical force stems from its power to secure the conditions of its self-perpetuation.⁸⁰

HEGEL'S THEORY AND CONTEMPORARY CONCERNS AND DEBATES

In our view, the abovementioned theorists underestimate the potential of the Hegelian concept to satisfactorily address the sorts of issues their approaches seek to resolve. Hegel scholars have recently begun to explore the potential of Hegel's concept of Civil Society to inform our understandings of the current global reality, for example, by highlighting the links between Hegel's theory and the emergent reality of global civil society in his time. According to Butler,

> Hegel already recognized the emergence of global civil society. He saw three stages to the development of civil society: trade [...], the legal protection of property rights [...], and the provision of welfare in the case of poverty [...]. Global civil society in his time had advanced to world-wide trade and to the protection of property rights through the international customary law of civilized nations. But it had not advanced to a global public authority [for the provision of welfare]. This is what is beginning to happen today.⁸¹

However, most of this discussion and analysis takes the form of *drawing parallels* between the local and global levels on the

---

76. Keane, *Global Civil Society?*, pp. 175-176.
77. Keane, *Global Civil Society?*, p. 194.
78. Keane, *Global Civil Society?*, pp. 196-197.
79. Keane, *Global Civil Society?*, p. 202.
80. Keane, *Global Civil Society?*, p. 203.
81. Butler, 'The Coming World Welfare State which Hegel Could Not See', p. 169.

assumption that Hegel's substantive claims concerning the concept of Civil Society address the civic sphere operating within the confines of the territorial state.[82] For this reason they are unable to address the concerns of the theorists of globalization and global civil society who call for new theory in the light of the emergence of new social phenomena that take us beyond Hegel and the tradition.

By contrast, we want to suggest that a certain systemic reading of Hegel fills the intellectual gap the theorists of globalization and global civil society have identified. Such a reading points us in the direction of an appreciation of Hegel's theory that positions it to provide the requisite account of the global order, its processes, institutions and possibilities for ethical agency. It does this by offering a much-needed radically reconceived view of the concept's normativity. Here it is worth noting that Seligman's representation of the genesis of the *normativity* of the concept of civil society—the relationship of the individual to the community and the rejection of external authority—adopts and presumes the appropriateness of *the theorist's external reflection* upon the concept's emergence in the theory/world. The same can be said of Keane's way of differentiating between the normative and descriptive dimensions of the phenomenon. From the Hegelian perspective we will be elaborating, this standpoint of external reflection is limited to what Hegel calls the 'Understanding', a mode of engagement with normative ideas that lacks the appropriate ontological grounding. As we will see in the next chapter, the normativity of the Hegelian concept of Civil Society concerns the justifiability of its various aspects, not by reference to the particular theorist's judgements upon their worth or viability, but from the standpoint of the development of the speculative notion of the *Logic*. From this perspective, Alexander's relegation of Hegel's concept to CSI with its supposed outdated diffuse inclusiveness is mistaken, as is the concept's association by a number of Hegel scholars with a model that conforms to CSII. Moreover, as we will see, on the one hand, the common representation of Hegel's concept of Civil Society as subordinated to the State is seriously misinformed and, on the other, the dismissal of his theory due to a an irredeemable Eurocentrism is too premature.

From our Hegelian perspective, civil society theorists' attempts to produce a new theory are also misdirected. After dispensing with various levels of confusion and misunderstanding

---

82. See the essays in Buchwalter (ed.), *Hegel and Global Justice*.

surrounding the meaning, purpose and application of the Hegelian concept, we will be in a position to see that Hegel's ethical-(onto)logical system already anticipates the theoretical space in which Alexander locates his new model of civil society and in doing so confirms the unsuitability of CSIII as a model of civil society as a whole. We will also be able to appreciate the discursive limitations of an approach like Keane's, which sharply distinguishes between the descriptive and normative applications of the phrase 'global civil society'. Keane's reliance upon an ideal-type for explanatory purposes and a differentiated normative defence of global civil society turns out to be restrictively tied to the current condition of modernity. This, as we will explain in the next chapter, is constrained by the logic characterizing *the formal universality of particularity*. Finally, once we appreciate the explanatory power of Hegel's ethical-(onto)logical system, then we need not turn to alternatives such as Leibniz' monadology, which presupposes yet cannot articulate the absolute unity of multiplicity, or a reformulated liberal theory, which problematically presupposes an intrinsically private agency.[83]

GLOBAL CITIZENSHIP AND HUMAN RIGHTS

So far we have suggested that through the elaboration of Hegel's concept of Civil Society we will develop a response to the question of how precisely the concept might figure in an ethical theory that addresses the global world of the twenty-first century. Conversely, we may ask whether and in what sense it is possible and appropriate to offer an account of the existing global reality and its transformative potential in the light of Hegel's concept of Civil Society. But this investigation will also allow us to touch upon some more specific concerns and debates. Recent scholarship has sought to incorporate into analyses of the global reality the significance of individual agency and the nature of the norms that ground global citizenship and/or the global enforcement of human rights.

This raises the question of the meaning of the term 'global citizenship' and its analytic relationship to global civil society. In addressing this question the literature sometimes conflates the ideas of membership of a global civil society and citizenship of a world state or a world democratic order.[84] In this case 'global citizenship'

---

83. For a defence of the claim that liberalism problematically presupposes that agency is intrinsically private see Toula Nicolacopoulos, *The Radical Critique of Liberalism*, Melbourne, re.press, 2008.

84. For example, in attempting to offer a normative account of the transformative

may be understood, not as a privilege granted to individuals by an authoritative institution, such as a world state or the government of a cosmopolitan democracy, but more broadly in terms of active membership of the global political community. Such membership may be defined in terms of a visionary ideal, such as global democracy, or it may be defined in terms of participation in and acceptance of responsibility for what are recognized as world-wide goals, like environmental sustainability, elimination of poverty, or global justice and resource redistribution. In the course of this study we will examine three different senses of 'global citizenship', which according to Nigel Dower, arise in connection with discussions of the emergence of global civil society.[85] The first connotes an *individual ethic*:

> global citizens can choose whether to act through the institutions and networks that make up global civil society to further their global concerns or they can choose not to. They might engage in prayer for world peace, do their bit for the environment by recycling or not using their cars (reasoning on the basis of universalizability principles rather than on the basis of pre-existing solidarities or practice) or send aid to families on the other side of the world whom they have got to know about through personal happenstance, and in none of these cases are they acting through global civil society.[86]

Second, in a more complex sense of an *aspirational ideal*, global citizenship has a more limited application than in the first sense since it consists in the following two elements:

> (a) an idea of what the world would have to be like for us all—people generally—actually to be global citizens analogous to our being citizens of states as at present, and (b) a commitment by those who want us to become global citizens in the first sense and who work towards achieving this.[87]

Although global citizens in the aspirational sense may vary on the interpretation they give to (a) above—for example, they may

---

potential of global civil society, as embodied in the justice-oriented activities of transnational social movements, Iris Marion Young presupposes a related conception of global citizenship in the making. See Martha C. Nussbaum, 'Iris Young's Last Thoughts on Responsibility for Global Justice', in Ann Ferguson and Mechthild Nagel (eds.), *Dancing with Iris: The Philosophy of Iris Marion Young*, Oxford, Oxford University Press, 2009, pp. 133-145.

85. Nigel Dower, 'Situating Global Citizenship', in Randall D. Germain and Michael Kenny (eds.), *The Idea of Global Civil Society: Politics and Ethics in a Globalizing Era*, London, Routledge, 2005, pp. 100-118.
86. Dower, 'Situating Global Citizenship', p. 108.
87. Dower, 'Situating Global Citizenship', p.108.

envisage 'membership of a world state under world government' or of 'a form of cosmopolitan democracy' consisting of formal democratic institutions and a global legal framework of 'cosmopolitan law' that replaces the current international law between states—they share an instrumental relationship to global civil society in the descriptive sense using and developing it as a kind of 'stepping stone to something rather different'.[88]

Finally, in Dower's preferred sense, which he presents as a kind of middle way between the abovementioned conceptions, global citizenship is a matter of participating in democratic institutions and networks of the currently existing global civil society.

> [I]f the 'participation' aspect of citizenship is disconnected from the formal 'membership of a state' condition, we are free to recognize a wide range of co-operative activities as the activities of citizens. What is being retained is the element of deliberative engagement with others in the pursuit of the overall good of some community or other. That community might or might not be the state.[89]

For Dower, if we adopt this third sense of global citizenship, which we will refer to as the *community participation* sense, 'what happens in global civil society can be represented as the exercise of global citizenship and the expression of global democracy, even before any formalized citizenship or democracy at the global level has emerged'.[90] Moreover, Dower suggests that this view still accords with 'the core of global citizenship [which] is the assertion of a certain moral and legal status of all human beings through human rights law.[91] On Dower's preferred conception then 'global citizenship' refers to the mindful engagement of agents in their self-defined political community in ways that further the human rights of individuals.

All three of the abovementioned conceptions of global citizenship have some purchase on current experience. As we will see with the elaboration of the Hegelian concept of Civil Society and the clarification of its significance as an abstract moment of Ethical Life, the Hegelian system makes possible an explanation of the place and significance of each. From this perspective we should also be in a position to address the critics of global citizenship

---

88. Dower, 'Situating Global Citizenship', pp. 108-109.
89. Dower, 'Situating Global Citizenship', p. 111.
90. Dower, 'Situating Global Citizenship', p. 112.
91. Dower, 'Situating Global Citizenship', p. 113.

discourses who argue against the usefulness of this terminology in the current global reality and prefer instead to rely on an exclusively human rights discourse.

WEST-CENTRIC ASSUMPTIONS AND NON-WESTERN EUROPEAN TRADITIONS

Simone Chambers and Will Kymlicka point out that to date philosophical debate on conceptions of civil society 'lacks an appreciation for how traditions other than mainstream liberal ones might understand civil society and pose a challenge to liberal views'.[92] Recognizing that different traditions of thought may give rise to different conceptions of civil society, they suggest that engagement with a variety of traditions, including the Christian, Islamic, Judaic and Confucian traditions, leads to

> skepticism about whether any ethical tradition has the resources to develop a satisfactory ideal of civil society. [...] [T]he limits of existing approaches only highlight the need for further dialogue among the different ethical traditions that characterize our pluralistic world.[93]

Chambers and Kymlicka also observe that 'for some the very term *civil society* entails liberal presuppositions' given the historical association of civil society, both as a phenomenon and as a concept, with the rise of the liberal state and of liberalism as a tradition of thought.[94] They suggest that the absence of an explicit concept of civil society in one's own tradition

> implies that to think about ethical pluralism as structured and organized within a civil society framework is to presuppose that we are working within the broad framework of a liberal state. This clearly creates an imbalance between traditions.[95]

Moreover, talk of civil society

> implies that "civil society" is a different sphere from the state or family, one that operates according to its own logic of voluntary choice, a commitment that in turn is grounded in the value of individual autonomy. Or it is said that civil society operates according to a distinctive logic of undistorted communication grounded in the value of deliberative democracy. These sorts of assumptions about individual autonomy or deliberative democracy are said to reflect a distinctly Western,

---

92. Chambers and Kymlicka, 'Alternative Conceptions of Civil Society', p. 2.
93. Chambers and Kymlicka, 'Alternative Conceptions of Civil Society', p. 10.
94. Chambers and Kymlicka, 'Alternative Conceptions of Civil Society', p. 5.
95. Chambers and Kymlicka, 'Alternative Conceptions of Civil Society', p. 5.

or perhaps even distinctly liberal, conception of how society should be organized, one that is not a part of other traditions.[96]

In keeping with such Eurocentric conceptions of social organization empirical investigations of civil society in Latin America or sub-Saharan Africa tend to concentrate restrictively on processes like democratization, which play an important role within liberal conceptions of civil society. But such investigations are said to face problems when attempting, for example, to explain the activities of Indigenous communities within Latin America given the role played by factors such as kinship and ethnic relations.[97] Similarly, in postcolonial African contexts the application of a liberal discourse of civil society is said to marginalize or exclude indigenous approaches.[98] Turner and Khondker point out that globalization studies have also tended to rely on narrow 'West-centric assumptions' when attempting to explain the processes within civil society that contribute to the maintenance or contestation of the global order.[99] In summary, the concern is that to

---

96. Chambers and Kymlicka, 'Alternative Conceptions of Civil Society', p. 5. See also Keane, *Global Civil Society?*, p. 29; p.178. For a summary of different forms of the claim that (global) civil society lacks universal validity as an ethical ideal because it is historically specific to the West, see Keane, *Global Civil Society?*, pp. 182-186. See also Gideon Baker, 'Civil Society and Democracy: The Gap Between Theory and Possibility', *Politics*, vol. 18, no. 2, 1998, pp. 81-87. Baker draws attention to an Eastern European model of civil society to argue that the concept of civil society is based on Western liberalism and that failure to appreciate this, and the attribution of a putative universal application to the concept, obscures the realities of contextualized processes of democratization in non-western contexts. In a similar vein, having argued that the European notion of civil society is parochial, John and Jean Comaroff insist: 'if the impact on African realities of the idea of civil society is to be fully grasped [...] its terms must be read against the specificities of local histories; above all, once more, against the uncivil histories of colonial subjection': John L. Comaroff and Jean Comaroff, 'Introduction', pp. 27-28. For an extensive analysis of the racial underpinnings of civil society see David Theo Goldberg, *The Threat of Race: Reflections on Racial Neo-liberalism*, Madden MA, Wiley-Blackwell, 2009, pp.32-65.

97. See, for example, Tanya Korovkin, 'Reinventing the Communal Tradition: Indigenous Peoples, Civil Society and Democratization in Andean Ecuador', *Latin American Research Review*, vol. 36, no. 3, 2001, pp. 37-67 at pp. 39-43.

98. See the collection of essays in John L. Comaroff and Jean Comaroff (eds.), *Civil Society and the Political Imagination in Africa: Critical Perspectives*, Chicago, University of Chicago Press, 1999. Note, however, the editors' view that civil society discourse also has a positive dimension in that the concept opens up spaces for democratizing aspirations 'once relieved of the burden of its parochial roots in the European Enlightenment': John L. Comaroff and Jean Comaroff, 'Introduction', p. 22.

99. Turner and Khondker, *Globalization: East and West*, p. 8.

speak of non-Western or non-liberal civil society may be at best to place non-liberal traditions at a disadvantage in a dialogue over normative frameworks and at worst to contemplate a contradiction in terms.

One way to respond to this concern is to think of civil society as an already globally diversified concept, at least in terms of *trajectories*, if not origins. For example, Keane argues that in the twenty-first century 'the language of civil society is both pluralized and globalized' in that '*multiple* and *multi-dimensional* and *entangled* languages of civil society now contribute to the definition of the world of global civil society'.[100] He draws on Shalini Randiera's research into India to illustrate the claim.

> Randiera points out that the European language of civil society first travelled to India during the nineteenth century. With the founding of the colonial state, the civil sphere—often not named as such—took the form of spaces of social life either untampered with by colonial rulers or established through the resistance to their power by colonial subjects themselves. Randiera shows that the subsequent debates about civil society in India have come to interact with different European images of civil society, so highlighting not only their travelling potential but also the ways in which 'foreign' or 'imported' languages both resonate within local contexts, and are often (heavily) refashioned as a result. They then become subject to 're-export' back to the context from which they originally came.[101]

Randiera's analysis draws our attention to the fact that the concept of civil society has been globally diversified but Keane goes further in suggesting that where the descriptive/explanatory concept is concerned, we should read this pluralism in *exclusively* particularistic terms. This is why in an allusion to postmodern critiques of the Hegelian intellectual tradition, he comments:

> Western definitions of civil society are not universal in any simple sense. The plural understandings of civil society within the modern West [...] are to be seen as one *particular* approach, and not as a universal language that is thought to be synonymous with a world history that leads teleologically, smugly, triumphantly to the silencing or annihilation of other, 'residual' definitions of social order.[102]

---

100. Keane, *Global Civil Society?*, pp. 38-39.
101. Keane, *Global Civil Society?*, p. 38.
102. Keane, *Global Civil Society?*, p. 39.

In our view it is precisely its *universality* that is the strength of the Hegelian concept and, as long as we fully appreciate its significance as part of a certain teleological view of the modern world, it need not function as a colonizing concept.[103] We will return to Hegel's view of modernity in the next chapter. For now we should note that one of our aims will be to explore the extent to which our reading of Hegel's account of Civil Society can accommodate and inform the ethical pluralism characterizing the current global reality without risking the conceptual imperialism that has been attributed to universalist approaches like Hegel's. Interestingly, Keane thinks that his own approach to defining global civil society for descriptive purposes is not subject to the same criticism because a concept employed as *an ideal-type* 'does not aim to manipulate or to dominate others'[104] even though, as we noted above, he recognizes the categorical force of global civil society understood as a normative ideal and this in turn means that 'the ethic of global civil society does not tolerate its intolerant opponents'.[105] Here Keane overlooks the fact that the effects of conceptual imperialism tend to exceed the theorist's/analyst's stipulation of limited aims, however well-intentioned. Elizabeth Garland shows this to be the case in her assessment of anthropologists' efforts to analyze the situation of the Ju/'hoansi people of the Kalahari by reference to the dominant global civil society discourse.[106]

Nevertheless, one can agree with Keane that success will be a matter of 'how well the research questions and empirical findings elucidated by the concept of global civil society prove to be illuminating for others in the world'.[107] Of course, if we read the Hegelian concept primarily as an attempt to locate the source of moral authority in the autonomous or democratic individual, then it cannot accommodate the ethical pluralism characterizing our current global reality since it will be incompatible with intellectual

---

103. This, however, is not to deny, as David Theo Goldberg argues, that as our lived reality civil society (1) is currently the dominant domain of 'born again racisms', racisms operating in the name of the rejection of racism and (2) functions to displace race from the critical intervention of the state. David Theo Goldberg, *The Threat of Race*, pp. 32-65.

104. Keane, *Global Civil Society?*, pp. 29-33.

105. Keane, *Global Civil Society?*, p. 203.

106. Elizabeth Garland, 'Developing Bushmen: Building Civil(ized) Society in the Kalahari and Beyond, in John L. Comaroff and Jean Comaroff (eds.), *Civil Society and the Political Imagination in Africa: Critical Perspectives*, Chicago, University of Chicago Press, 1999, pp. 72-103 at pp. 74-81.

107. Keane, *Global Civil Society?*, p. 30.

traditions whose ethical grounds depend upon a conception of the transcendent good. But we propose to focus on Civil Society as a broader *ethical-ontological concept* in a sense to be explained in the next chapter. Also, rather than accepting a particularistic rendition of the globally pluralized concept of civil society, we will be considering whether Hegel's concept has the potential to supply a framework for developing a non-Eurocentric appreciation of modernity beyond the West, bearing in mind Sudipta Kaviraj's point that although 'to understand political modernity in the non-Western world is impossible without Western social theory; it is equally impossible entirely within the terms of that tradition'.[108] Whilst it is not our purpose in this book to undertake a comparative study of conceptions of civil society across different cultures and intellectual traditions, in the remainder of this chapter we will introduce just a few accounts of these intellectual traditions with a view to drawing upon them throughout the book to illustrate the potential of the Hegelian concept to accommodate and inform alternative discourses of global civil society. Because our discussion is restricted to a small sampling of non-Western intellectual traditions, we can do no more than illustrate this potential whilst acknowledging that a conclusive assessment depends upon an extensive exploration of the relationship of the Hegelian concept to a much broader range of non-Western frames of reference which would include the intellectual traditions of non-Europeans and Indigenous peoples in colonial and postcolonial contexts.

As Chambers and Kymlicka suggest, 'many authors from outside the liberal tradition acknowledge that there is no explicit conception of civil society within their own tradition'.[109] East Asia, or China in particular, is a case in point. For example, Richard Madsen observes that, in response to the challenges of globalization, today's Chinese intellectuals are under pressure to develop new theories of civil society amidst uncertainty as to how or even whether these might be linked with their own intellectual and cultural traditions.[110] To this end they invoke up to four different phrases that have come into use following the

---

108. Sudipta Kaviraj, 'In Search of Civil Society', in Sudipta Kaviraj and Sunil Khilnani (eds.), *Civil Society: History and Possibilities*, Cambridge, Cambridge University Press, 2001, pp. 287-321 at p. 287.
109. Chambers and Kymlicka, 'Alternative Conceptions of Civil Society', p. 5.
110. Richard Madsen, 'Confucian Conceptions of Civil Society', in Simone Chambers and Will Kymlicka (eds.), *Alternative Conceptions of Civil Society*, Princeton, Princeton University Press, 2002, pp. 190-206.

incorporation into the language of the term *shehui* or 'society', 'a neologism from the West introduced into China via Japan in the late nineteenth century'.[111] Accordingly, civil society might be referred to as:

> *shimin shehui*, which literally means "city-people's society"; or *gongmin shehui*, "citizens' society"; or *minjian shehui*, "people-based society"; or *wenming shehui*, "civilized society". These are all attempts to name phenomena and articulate aspirations that have arisen in an urbanizing East Asia linked to a global market economy.[112]

Madsen notes that whilst some advocate confronting the new challenges through 'all-out Westernization', others seek to reappropriate the Confucian legacy. To explain the two incompatible configurations of the social whole that underpin the fundamental differences in Confucian and Western ways of thinking, Madsen recalls two analogies that anthropologist Fei Xiaotong makes.

> In some ways Western society bears a resemblance to the way we bundle kindling wood in the fields. A few rice stalks are bound together to make a handful, several handfuls are bound together to make a small bundle, and several larger bundles are bound together to make a stack to carry on a pole. [...] In a society these units are groups [...]. The group has a definite demarcation line.[113]

By contrast, according to Fei Xiaotong, for traditional Confucian thought Chinese society is configured

> like the rings of successive ripples that are propelled outward on the surface when you throw a stone in the water. Each individual is the centre of the rings emanating from his social influence. Wherever the ripples reach, affiliations occur.[114]

The Confucian configuration of society as an internally related whole and its reliance upon a substantively universal principle of cosmic proportions raises some interesting questions of comparison with the Hegelian ethical State, which are the subject of the next volume in this series.

In this book we will explore some points of comparison between the Neo-Confucian and the Hegelian accounts as these relate to the internal differentiation of global civil society. The Neo-Confucian vision bases social order on the proper performance

---

111. Madsen, 'Confucian Conceptions of Civil Society', p. 190.
112. Madsen, 'Confucian Conceptions of Civil Society', p. 190.
113. Fei Xiaotong in Madsen, 'Confucian Conceptions of Civil Society', p. 191.
114. Fei Xiaotong in Madsen, 'Confucian Conceptions of Civil Society', p. 192.

of inter-dependent cosmically determined roles and attendant responsibilities with the potential to dissolve the appearance of competing demands.

> Sometimes it may appear that the roles one occupies in one sphere of life come into conflict with the roles in other spheres. For instance, one's role as a parent might seem to conflict with one's role as a loyal citizen or political subject. The Confucian position is that if one cultivates oneself fully enough and thus understands the responsibilities implicit in these roles deeply enough one will find that there is ultimately no contradiction.[115]

Interestingly for our purposes, Madsen maintains that neo-Confucianism is in need of creative adaptation to the demands of the global reality of the twenty-first century. Even drawing on what he sees as the 'relatively liberal strands of the Neo-Confucian tradition',[116] Madsen worries that

> without creative adaptation, the Confucian vision may fail to be attractive to modern mass societies, and be unable to inspire a civil society possessed of enough civility to sustain orderly forms of democracy.[117]

This is because

> Confucian self-cultivation requires slow, hard work, difficult to sustain in a frenetic market economy. It requires the development of moral discipline, difficult to accomplish in the face of the self-gratifications promised by consumer culture.[118]

In contrast to those intellectual traditions that face the challenge of making room for a suitable concept of civil society, Judaism and Islam are said to contain their own distinct conceptions. Suzanne Last Stone argues that even though Judaism 'lacks the building blocks, drawn largely from Christian conceptions of society and the individual and the experience of European Christendom, that gave rise to the idea of civil society in the West', the Jewish tradition can be understood to include its own conception of civil society in so far as it 'offers its own ethical perspective on the criteria necessary to establish trust, bonds of social solidarity and duties of association in a pluralistic world'.[119] Here, 'civil

---

115. Madsen, 'Confucian Conceptions of Civil Society', p. 200.
116. Madsen, 'Confucian Conceptions of Civil Society', p. 191.
117. Madsen, 'Confucian Conceptions of Civil Society', p. 200.
118. Madsen, 'Confucian Conceptions of Civil Society', p. 200.
119. Suzanne Last Stone, 'The Jewish Tradition and Civil Society', in Simone Chambers and Will Kymlicka (eds.), *Alternative Conceptions of Civil Society*, Princeton, Princeton University Press, 2002, pp. 151-170 at 151-153.

society' is taken to refer to an ethical vision 'concerned with the conditions for establishing bonds of social solidarity between diverse members of society and shaping rights of association to promote such bonds'.[120]

> The system of social solidarity that Judaism proposes is the product of a peculiar blend of particularism and universalism. Minimal obligations are owed to all humanity. Social solidarity is owed to civilized [non-Jewish] societies who adhere to universal criteria of morality. The deepest bonds of solidarity are owed to covenantal fellows.[121]

Due to the comprehensiveness of the law, the ideal Jewish social order consists of the particularistic covenantal community, which serves as the primary social unit from which individual members derive their rights and obligations in relation to one another.

Similarly, in Muslim societies a form of legally protected civil association predates European conquest.[122] Hasan Hanafi argues that although there are similarities between Islamic ethical theory and the key features of the concept of civil society that derives from the West, nevertheless, 'indigenous concepts of civil society from within Islamic culture [...] are more consistent and less opposed than the ingredients of civil society projected from Western culture onto Islamic societies in a misguided attempt to replicate the Western world'.[123]

On Hanafi's reformist, modernist reading of the role of an Islamic state in implementing the spirit of the law *(maqasid al shari'a)*, such a state would foster and protect many of the values underlying Western civil society.[124] But key aspects of the picture Hanafi paints also resonate strongly with the Hegelian ethical State, at least on our reading. According to Hanafi, 'Islamic theory contains within it the idea of an integrated politico-religious community, but with power dispersed among its constituent elements'.[125] The Islamic community of believers, the Muslim *umma*, is a 'nation without boundaries'.[126] Although the *umma* takes

---

120. Last Stone, 'The Jewish Tradition and Civil Society', p. 151.
121. Last Stone, 'The Jewish Tradition and Civil Society', pp. 157-158.
122. Keane, *Global Civil Society?*, pp. 32-33.
123. Hasan Hanafi, 'Alternative Conceptions of Civil Society: A Reflective Islamic Approach', in Simone Chambers and Will Kymlicka (eds.), *Alternative Conceptions of Civil Society*, Princeton, Princeton University Press, 2002, pp. 171-189 at pp. 172-173.
124. Hanafi, 'Alternative Conceptions of Civil Society', p. 172.
125. Hanafi, 'Alternative Conceptions of Civil Society', p. 175.
126. Hanafi, 'Alternative Conceptions of Civil Society', p. 173.

moral primacy over a range of religious, social and geographical groupings that are recognized within the ideal community of believers, 'these are intrinsically related to one another because they combine to form an integrated whole that is Islam's conception of human society'.[127] According to the Medieval theorists Hanafi draws upon, the legitimate human groupings that Islamic theory and practice sustain are 'endowed with their own sphere of autonomy free from government intrusion' and are supported by a range of relatively autonomous institutions—from the judicial authority of the *ulama*, to the supervision of the application of the law in the marketplace, the *hisba* performed by *muhtasib*, and the religious endowments for educational pursuits, the *awqaf*. These, Hanafi suggests, operationalize the concept of civil society.[128]

> While Islamic civil society is differentiated and contains many organizations and sub-groups, it forms a coherent society by virtue of a shared commitment to faith and brotherhood'.[129]

The Islamic ideal of the *umma* is thus grounded in the concept of unity, specifically the unity of God, on the basis of which it serves as a globally extended concept.

> The universal *umma* ideal may have little political significance today, but it is alive at the ethical and spiritual level, which unites individuals into a greater whole transcending their own often unrepresentative states.[130]

Non-Muslims are accommodated within the global society governed by the universal ideal of the *umma* in so far as

> [t]he Islamic *umma* is not composed exclusively of Muslims, but is a confederal *umma* composed of many [linguistically, culturally and legally autonomous religious] communities bound together by a treaty of non-belligerence and mutual respect.[131]

The universal aspect of the Islamic *umma* thus emphasizes a common human destiny as well as the universal community of humanity, as distinct from the particularistic actual community of believers.[132] As such,

> Islamic values applied properly in politics promote not a communal culture favoring the Muslim population, but a

---

127. Hanafi, 'Alternative Conceptions of Civil Society', p. 174.
128. Hanafi, 'Alternative Conceptions of Civil Society', pp. 174-175.
129. Hanafi, 'Alternative Conceptions of Civil Society', p. 177.
130. Hanafi, 'Alternative Conceptions of Civil Society', p. 177.
131. Hanafi, 'Alternative Conceptions of Civil Society', p. 177.
132. See also Keane, *Global Civil Society?*, pp. 40-43.

> pluralistic, "national" culture to which Muslims and non-Muslims belong.[...]
>
> [N]on-Muslims are assured a remarkable degree of communal autonomy aimed at preventing their independent identities and cultures from being overwhelmed by the Muslim majority. In their communal life they are autonomous from state regulation so long as they acknowledge the sovereignty of the Islamic state and the predominance of Islamic law as the regulatory mechanism across communities. At the same time they are essential components of the broader, what may be termed quasi-federal, "national" structures. In other words, the Islamic conception embraces a number of limited civil societies with the hope that each will promote the greater civil society of all.[133]

Hanafi argues that the above interpretation of the Islamic concept of civil society gives rise to certain values consistent with the United Nations Declaration of Human Rights, including the protection of life, the promotion of reason and the defence of honour and dignity, which incorporate universal liberties of speech, belief and movement and rights to privacy and which variously apply, to individuals and communities. Since these are 'values shared—in varying degrees of emphasis—by all cultures' it becomes possible to generalize this concept of civil society so that one can 'avoid taking the Western concept as a yardstick according to which all other concepts stemming out of other cultures are judged'.[134]

The analyses offered by Hanafi, Last Stone and Madsen enable consideration of the question of the extent to which the Hegelian concept of Civil Society can shed light on the issues raised from within non-Western European traditions. With this in mind, we turn next to the question of how one should read Hegel's social and political theory and, particular, the *Philosophy of Right* and its concept of Civil Society.

---

133. Hanafi, 'Alternative Conceptions of Civil Society', p. 179.
134. Hanafi, 'Alternative Conceptions of Civil Society', pp. 181-182.

2. READING HEGEL SYSTEMICALLY

A growing body of Hegel scholarship takes the view that the comprehension of the *Philosophy of Right* crucially depends upon reading it through the details of Hegel's *Logic*.[1] In the literature we find an increasing number of efforts to explain how various aspects of the *Logic* inform Hegel's elaboration of Ethical Life and the *Philosophy of Right* more generally.[2] Many would agree that

---

1. Unless otherwise indicated, we use '*Logic*' to refer both to *Hegel's Science of Logic*, trans. A.V. Miller, New York, Humanity Books, 1989 (hereafter '*SL*') and to *Hegel's Logic: Being Part One of the Encyclopaedia of the Philosophical Sciences*, trans. William Wallace, Oxford, Oxford University Press, 1975. For the purposes of this study we focus mainly on the Anglophone secondary literature while drawing selectively on German language secondary literature in translation. Brod suggests that there is a noteworthy difference in interpretive style between these. Whereas the former tends to take a pragmatic approach and examines Hegel's ideas on specific substantive issues while discounting questions concerning the Hegelian system, the latter tends to focus on broad generalizations about programmatic and meta-theoretical issues without enough attention to the specifics of Hegel's substantive political ideas: Harry Brod, *Hegel's Philosophy of Politics: Idealism, Identity and Modernity*, San Francisco and Boulder, Westview Press, 1992, pp. 1-2. As we will see from the discussions that follow, Brod's observation is probably less true of the more recently published literature, which tends to combine these two approaches.

2. David Kolb, *The Critique of Pure Modernity: Hegel Heidegger and After*, Chicago, The University of Chicago Press, 1988; Peter J. Steinberger, *Logic and Politics: Hegel's Philosophy of Right*, New Haven, Yale University Press, 1988, Ch.4; Henry S. Richardson, 'The Logical Structure in Sittlichkeit: A Reading of Hegel's *Philosophy of Right*', *Idealistic Studies*, vol. 19, 1989, pp. 62-78; Will Dudley, 'A Case of Bad Judgment: The Logical Failure of the Moral Will', *The Review of Metaphysics*, vol. 51, no. 2, 1997, pp. 379-405; Klaus E. Kaehler, 'The Right of the Particular and the Power of the Universal', *The Southern Journal of Philosophy*, vol. 39, no. 3, 2001, pp. 147-162; Thom Brooks, *Hegel's Political Philosophy: A Systematic Reading of the Philosophy of Right*, Edinburgh, Edinburgh University Press, 2007; Nathan Ross, *On Mechanism in Hegel's Social and Political Philosophy*, London, Routledge, 2008.

the *Logic* is indispensable to making sense of Hegel's understanding of his project, but they also take the view that such a project has become too difficult, irrelevant or unnecessary in our 'post-metaphysical' times, to borrow a phrase from Jürgen Habermas.[3] Nevertheless, in addressing broad interpretive questions, such as the tripartite structure of the *Philosophy of Right* as a whole and that of Ethical Life in particular or the nature of the State-Civil Society relationship and the role of the institutions contained within their respective domains, a number of scholars have attempted to develop a *systematic* reading of sorts. For example, Thom Brooks offers a 'weak systemic reading' of the *Philosophy of Right* in that he examines a range of topics, which support 'the necessity of the systemic account'.[4] Others, like Paul Franco, draw more selectively from the *Logic*. Although Franco takes the view that Hegel's political philosophy is not 'somehow "founded" on or "deducible" from his speculative philosophy', he appeals to the *Logic* to articulate Hegel's philosophical method as well as Hegel's account of the merits of philosophical explanation by comparison with empirical forms of explanation.[5] In this he exemplifies the approach that blends insights from the *Logic* with those from other aspects of Hegel's intellectual contribution.[6]

---

3. See, for example, Jürgen Habermas, *Philosophical Discourse of Modernity*, Oxford and Cambridge, Polity Press, 1992, pp. 23-44; Christopher J. Arthur, 'Hegel on Political Economy', in David Lamb (ed.), *Hegel and Modern Philosophy*, New York, Croom Helm, 1987, pp. 102-118; Z. A. Pelczynski, 'The Hegelian Conception of the State' in Z. A. Pelczynski (ed.), *Hegel's Political Philosophy Problems and Perspectives*, Cambridge, Cambridge University Press, 1971, pp. 1-29; Merold Westphal, 'The Basic Context and Structure of Hegel's *Philosophy of Right*' in Frederick C. Beiser (ed.), *The Cambridge Companion to Hegel*, New York, Cambridge University Press, 1993, pp. 234-269; Allen W. Wood, *Hegel's Ethical Thought*, Cambridge, Cambridge University Press, 1990; Axel Honneth, *The Pathologies of Individual Freedom: Hegel's Social Theory*, New Jersey, Princeton University Press, 2010.

4. Brooks, *Hegel's Political Philosophy*, p. 11.

5. Paul Franco, *Hegel's Philosophy of Freedom*, New Haven, Yale University Press, 1999: 140. See also Butler, 'The Coming World Welfare State which Hegel Could Not See', pp. 155-176. See, however, Kimberly Hutchings, 'Hard Work: Hegel and the Meaning of the State in his *Philosophy of Right*', in Thom Brooks (ed.), *Hegel's Philosophy of Right*, Oxford, Blackwell, 2012, pp. 125-141 at 125; and Brooks, *Hegel's Political Philosophy*, p. 5: Hutchings and Brooks read Franco as offering a non-systematic interpretation of Hegel given that Franco's account of the unfolding of the concept of freedom in the *Philosophy of Right* actually draws very little from his own account of the Hegelian method.

6. For example, Manfred Riedel examines the *Logic* in combination with Hegel's relationship to his own intellectual tradition: Manfred Riedel, *Between*

THE LIMITS OF READING THE *PHILOSOPHY OF RIGHT* WITHOUT THE *LOGIC*

Others offer a systematic reading without drawing upon the *Logic* in any substantial way. This approach takes a number of forms. One is to contextualize Hegel's development of his political theory with reference to the political culture, social phenomena and institutions of his time.[7] Another is to analyze the precise nature and assess the coherence of the dialectical movement of the categories of right.[8] In the literature we also find an increasing number of attempts to make sense of Hegel's claims concerning the concept of right by reference to other parts of the system, especially the *Philosophy of History*. For example, Harry Brod argues that because the *Philosophy of Right* serves dual programmatic and pragmatic purposes, in that it develops new standards for modern political philosophy and then seeks to apply them, Hegel relies on a philosophical reinterpretation of the historical forces that created the modern world to guide the first of these purposes and then treats the substantive issues that form the subject matter of his pragmatic purpose in the light of his programmatic conclusions. Brod thus reads Hegel's political philosophy as an attempt to reveal the 'hidden undercurrents of modern political life'.[9] He suggests,

---

Tradition and Revolution: The Hegelian Transformation of Political Philosophy, Cambridge, Cambridge University Press, 1984, pp. 31-56; pp. 129-158. More recently, Kevin Thompson seeks to establish the interdependence of Hegel's philosophical method and a certain view of the system's ontological foundation in terms of the role and function of the concepts of Objective Spirit, rationality and actuality: Kevin Thompson, 'Reason and Objective Spirit: Method and Ontology in Hegel's Philosophy of Right', *The Southern Journal of Philosophy*, vol. 39, no. 3, 2001, pp. 111-137. Angelica Nuzzo argues that in order to understand Hegel's concept of right, the speculative method of the *Logic* must be combined with history and practice: Angelica Nuzzo, 'Which Particulars Can Have a Right? Which Universal Can Exercise Power?' *The Southern Journal of Philosophy*, vol. 39, no. 3, pp. 2001, pp. 163-169. Similarly Kimberly Hutchings' approach is to take seriously Hegel's claim to have uncovered the immanent connection between logic, history and practice as a result of his time and place along with his self-identification as a child of his time: Hutchings, 'Hard Work'.

7. Terry Pinkard situates Hegel's philosophy in relation to his particular political outlook and response to the events/ideas of his day: Terry Pinkard, *Hegel: A Biography*, Cambridge, Cambridge University Press, 2000.

8. Klaus Hartmann, 'Towards a New Systematic Reading', in Z.A Pelczynski (ed.), *The State and Civil Society: Studies in Hegel's Political Philosophy*, Cambridge, Cambridge University Press, 1984, pp. 114-136; K-H. Ilting, 'The Dialectic of Civil Society', in Z.A Pelczynski (ed.), *The State and Civil Society: Studies in Hegel's Political Philosophy*, Cambridge, Cambridge University Press, 1984, pp. 90-110.

9. Brod, *Hegel's Philosophy of Politics*, pp. 3-6.

Hegel's analysis of historical developments, culminating in the French Revolution and its aftermath, enters into his philosophy in a much more fundamental way, shaping the basic structure and intent of his philosophical system.[10]

Within this framework the *Philosophy of Right* gives effect to 'a transformation of political philosophy whereby politics is situated in the context of a collective social consciousness', which Hegel sees as a product of his own epoch.[11] Although the *Philosophy of History* offers many valuable insights, as we will illustrate in the course of this study Brod overestimates its capacity to generate a full and adequate account of Hegel's concept of right.

Moreover, this approach underplays the concern that Hegel's view of history leads him to endorse a fundamentally imperialist and racist modernity. Critics have documented the claim that Hegel set out to ground his account of World History, the last moment in the elaboration of the concept of the Hegelian State, on a Eurocentric racial hierarchy, which at once positions (1) sub-Saharan Africans as dependent upon European colonization and enslavement in order to be brought into history and (2) American Indians as incapable of such inclusion.[12] One way of responding to the latter concern is to insist, as Richard Dien Winfield proposes, that 'because modernity's institutions of freedom do not depend on any particular culture for their legitimacy, they are inherently capable of global, not to mention intergalactic realization'.[13] Hegel's objectionable claims can be revised with this purpose in mind.

A common strategy amongst those who set aside Hegel's objectionable claims, as well as the *Logic*, is to focus more on making connections with Hegel's earlier writings in political and ethical theory and on elaborating the steps in the development of

10. Brod, *Hegel's Philosophy of Politics*, p. 6.
11. Brod, *Hegel's Philosophy of Politics*, p. 8.
12. See Robert Bernasconi, 'Hegel at the Court of the Ashanti', in Stuart Barnett (ed.), *Hegel after Derrida*, London, Routledge, 1988, pp. 41-63; Michael H. Hoffheimer, 'Hegel, Race, Genocide', *The Southern Journal of Philosophy*, vol. 39, no. 3, 2001, pp. 35-62. For some recent efforts to show how Hegel's racist and Eurocentric views are not inherent in his philosophical system see the essays in Buchwalter (ed.), *Hegel and Global Justice*. Characteristically, Buchwalter argues that Hegel's fundamental concepts 'can be instructively invoked to challenge racist and race-based modes of characterizing peoples and their relationships': Buchwalter, 'Hegel, Global Justice and Mutual Recognition', p. 220.
13. Richard Dien Winfield, 'Postcolonialism and Right', in Robert R. Williams (ed.), *Beyond Liberalism and Communitarianism: Studies in Hegel's Philosophy of Right*, Albany, State University of New York Press, 2001, pp. 91-110 at p. 93.

these ideas in response to problems posed by his intellectual tradition.[14] Although this strategy draws our attention to the intellectual problems Hegel was grappling with when developing his ideas, it either runs the risk or explicitly favours the adoption of a 'piecemeal approach', which as Kevin Thompson observes, gives rise to a basic choice: 'either we accept what we still find useful in some way or we reject the [Hegelian] project as a whole'.[15] Hegel commentators like Allen W. Wood and Frederick Neuhouser choose the former path arguing respectively that Hegel's description of modern Western European culture is independently insightful[16] and that Hegel's conception of social freedom is 'far less tied to distinctively Hegelian categories of thought than commentators assume'.[17] Other sympathetic readers of Hegel see his political philosophy as a rich source of selective insights that are useful to debates in contemporary liberal individualist and communitarian approaches. They usually detach the perceived illuminating details of Hegel's concept of Civil Society, not only from Hegel's general systemic approach, but also from the question of their relationship to his concept of the State. Here challenges associated with making sense of Hegel's claims regarding

---

14. Fred Dallmayr situates the *Philosophy of Right* in the wider context of Hegel's political writings: Fred Dallmayr, *G.W.F. Hegel: Modernity and Politics*, London, Sage, 1993. Michael O. Hardimon reads Hegel's social philosophy in terms of the project of reconciliation: Michael O. Hardimon, *Hegel's Social Philosophy: The Project of Reconciliation*, Cambridge, Cambridge University Press, 1994. Frederick Neuhouser reads Hegel's idea of social freedom primarily by positioning it in relation to the views of others in the modern Western intellectual tradition: Frederick Neuhouser, *Foundations of Hegel's Social Philosophy: Actualizing Freedom*, London, Harvard University Press, 2000. David James also concentrates on the idea of freedom: David James, *Hegel's Philosophy of Right: Subjectivity and Ethical Life*, London, Continuum, 2007. Joshua D. Goldstein offers a reading of the development of Hegel's conception of the good life from his early to his mature philosophy: Joshua D. Goldstein, *Hegel's Idea of the Good Life: From Virtue to Freedom, Early Writings and Mature Political Philosophy*, Netherlands, Springer, 2006. Rolf-Peter Horstmann proposes a genealogy of the concept of Civil Society: Rolf-Peter Horstmann, 'The Role of Civil Society in Hegel's Political Philosophy', in Robert B. Pippin and Otfried Hoffe (eds.), *Hegel on Ethics and Politics*, Cambridge, Cambridge University Press, 2007, pp. 208-240. See also David Peddle, 'Hegel's Political Ideal: Civil Society, History and *Sittlichkeit*', *Animus*, vol. 5, 2000, pp. 113-143; K. Kierens, 'The Concept of Ethical Life in Hegel's *Philosophy of Right*', *History of Political Thought*, vol. 13, no. 3, 1992, pp. 417-435.
15. Thompson, 'Reason and Objective Spirit', p. 112.
16. Wood, *Hegel's Ethical Thought*, p. 5.
17. Neuhouser, *Foundations of Hegel's Social Philosophy*, p. 3.

the transition from the concept of Civil Society to that of the State are largely set aside.[18]

As Thompson observes, however, the piecemeal approach ultimately sacrifices the most important aspect of Hegel's thought, namely the justificatory framework of its core claims, a framework that on Thompson's reading requires of the system that it satisfy criteria of completeness, consistency and comprehensiveness.[19] Wood, like others who adopt the piecemeal approach, implies that without such a 'sacrifice' Hegel would remain unpopular, but as Brooks argues, Hegel's popularity should not be the decisive factor in determining how to read him.[20] Neuhouser acknowledges that one cannot justifiably conclude that understanding Hegel's social and political philosophy in terms of the demands of the *Logic* is unrewarding until exhaustive attempts at explanation have been undertaken and failed.[21] However, his study, like that of Wood, serves to reinforce the concern that Thompson raises, namely that the piecemeal approach effectively reduces the ideas drawn from Hegel to 'mere conjecture'.[22]

In an attempt to overcome the perceived mismatch between contemporary concerns and systematic readings of the *Philosophy of Right* Axel Honneth has developed a new approach, effectively rewriting the text where necessary.[23] Agreeing that any appeal to Hegel's *Logic* to explain his political philosophy will be futile, Honneth advances the project of a 'systematic reactualization' of the *Philosophy of Right*.[24] For Honneth

> a productive understanding of both the intention and the fundamental structure of the text is still possible, even if neither

---

18. See, for example, Steven B. Smith, *Hegel's Critique of Liberalism: Rights in Context*, Chicago, The University of Chicago Press, 1989. In saying that the tendency within this approach is to disregard the question of the significance of the transition from Civil Society to the State we do not mean to suggest that readers who are interested in Hegel's relationship to liberal and individualist concerns inevitably do so. See, for example, Nathan Ross, who, despite seeking to position Hegel as an individualist in relation to contemporary liberal and communitarian discussions, elaborates his argument both via an interpretation of the role of a rehabilitated Hegelian state and via a reading of Hegel's social and political philosophy through the *Logic*. Ross, *On Mechanism in Hegel's Social and Political Philosophy*.
19. Thompson, 'Reason and Objective Spirit', p. 114.
20. Brooks, *Hegel's Political Philosophy*, pp. 6-10.
21. Neuhouser, *Foundations of Hegel's Social Philosophy*, p. 3.
22. Thompson, 'Reason and Objective Spirit', p. 112.
23. Honneth, *The Pathologies of Individual Freedom*.
24. Honneth, *The Pathologies of Individual Freedom*, p. 3.

the substantialist concept of the state nor the operative instructions of the *Logic* are given an explanatory role.²⁵

Although he is aware that this strategy runs the risk of 'sacrificing the true substance of the work to the objective of a bold clean up of the text', Honneth believes that this is the only way forward for a 'really productive reappropriation of the treatise' given that 'the *Logic* has become totally incomprehensible to us owing to its ontological concept of spirit'.²⁶

We take the view that the incomprehensibility that Honneth and others mention stems not from the relationship of the Hegelian system to the world of the twenty-first century but from the restrictedness of the limited range of reflective standpoints that theorists typically adopt when studying the power of the Hegelian onto(logical) system to inform the appreciation of our times. Angelica Nuzzo points us in this direction when, commenting on current processes of globalization, she concludes:

> what seems obvious to common sense [the contradictory nature of globalization processes] is not yet conceptually clear. In this situation the "need" for a logic of change, for a theory able to conceive contradiction and transformation in its fundamental and pure structures arises anew. [...] We should be ready to learn from Hegel's dialectic as logic of transformative processes.²⁷

Kimberly Hutchings is in broad agreement with the approach that sees value in drawing upon Hegel's *Logic* to work out the connections between the concepts of the *Philosophy of Right* and the demands of our own times, but she also shares with Honneth a desire to 'clean up' the Hegelian text. Acknowledging the postcolonial critiques of Hegel's political philosophy, she wants to develop a kind of middle ground between them and modernist defences of Hegel. Unlike Honneth, however, Hutchings proposes a strategy that aspires to a reworking of Hegel's system supported by an *immanent critique*. She argues that if we take seriously Hegel's own historicism—the fact that he identified as 'a child of his time' and that in recognizing this fact he enabled the development of his system—we find that the immanent connection between *Logic*, history and practice, not only 'opens up a distinctive

---

25. Honneth, *The Pathologies of Individual Freedom*, p. 5.
26. Honneth, *The Pathologies of Individual Freedom*, pp. 4-5.
27. Angelica Nuzzo, 'Dialectic as Logic of Transformative Processes' in Katerina Deligiorgi (ed.), *Hegel: New Directions*, London, Acumen, 2006, pp. 85-103 at p. 100.

understanding of the limitations on what political philosophy is and can do' but it also 'provides a route into an immanent critique of Hegel's argument'.[28] Hutchings suggests that this standpoint of immanent critique implies that universal meaning does not remain constant. This is because the audience changes over time. Moreover, if we follow Hegel and recognize the historical contingency of his own perception of history, we are free to ask what it was about Hegel's time that led him to reading history as he did.[29] By extension of this reasoning, which the space of immanent critique supposedly makes possible, we are also free to reformulate the Hegelian reading of history and so to purge it of its outdated racist and imperialist implications.

Hutchings' approach introduces an arguably unnecessarily arbitrary relativism into Hegel's system to the extent that it holds that different times will suggest different 'universal meanings'. But it is not our primary purpose in the present book to draw conclusions about this issue or to assess Hutchings' approach to reading the *Philosophy of Right* in any depth. Instead we want to focus on the question of where and precisely how one situates oneself in relation to the critical philosophical appropriation of the Hegelian system. This question is at the heart of this problem of generating a productive reading of the *Philosophy of Right* for the twenty-first century. In our view, Hegel's system does indeed allow for revision of the Hegelian text on the basis of immanent critique but, as we have tried to illustrate elsewhere, the identification of the standpoint of critique derives from an appreciation of the requirements of the relevant categories of the *Logic*, rather than from any general observation about Hegel's historicism.[30] We will be in a position to explain the sense in which the Hegelian system makes critique possible once we have outlined our understanding of the way in which the *Logic* informs the real categorial development.

At the same time as lending indirect support to the view that the presumption that the *Logic* has become unhelpful, unnecessary or unintelligible in our times is ultimately mistaken, we also hope to show that a reading that does indeed recognize the role of the *Logic* in the Hegelian system makes possible an appreciation

---

28. Hutchings, 'Hard Work', p. 128.
29. Hutchings, 'Hard Work', pp. 128-139.
30. For example, we argue that the *Logic* warrants certain systematic changes to Hegel's account of marriage and sexuality: Toula Nicolacopoulos and George Vassilacopoulos, *Hegel and the Logical Structure Love: An Essay on Sexualities, Family and the Law*, Melbourne, re.press, 2010, Chapter 10.

of the nature of the relationship between the concepts of Civil Society and State as well as the relevance of the former to the current global reality. Before outlining our position, however, let us review the various interpretations of these concepts and their relationship to reality.

CIVIL SOCIETY, STATE AND THE CURRENT REALITY

We have already suggested that many readers of Hegel take his concept of Civil Society to conform to the model we identified in Chapter One as CSII, which holds that Civil Society is limited to society's economy, rather than the model that Alexander attributes to Hegel, CSI, which holds that Civil Society deals with the whole of instituted society except for government. This seems to be the case irrespective of differences in their overall approach to reading the *Philosophy of Right* or indeed in their views about the relevance of the concepts of Civil Society and State to the current reality. For example, K-H Ilting suggests that we can make sense of the State as the perspective we, the participants in a modern liberal state, adopt for our critical observation of Civil Society when we take the latter to refer to early capitalist society. So his reading of Hegel's concept of Civil Society takes the concept to conform to CSII. Like Hartmann, who also analyzes Hegel's account of the transition from Civil Society to the State by reference to the dialectical movement of the categories elaborated in the *Philosophy of Right*, Ilting takes Civil Society to lack an explicitly ethical-political dimension that Hegel's State is called upon to supply.[31] Christopher J. Arthur is also amongst the commentators who take the view that Civil Society presents the economic sphere as abstracted from the ethical order so he too reads Civil Society along the lines of CSII but he takes the abstraction of the economy to accord with the nature of the economic sphere *as it is in reality*. He then claims that the move beyond the standpoint of Civil Society to that of the ethical State represents the imposition of a critical ethical perspective on the reality of civil life.[32] In this he is in broad agreement with Habermas' reading of Civil Society which objects to Hegel's account of the State and, in particular to

---

31. Ilting, 'The Dialectic of Civil Society', pp. 90-110; Hartmann, 'Towards a New Systematic Reading', pp. 114-136.

32. Arthur, 'Hegel on Political Economy', pp. 107-108. See also the accounts of the transition from Civil Society to the State offered by Pelczynski, 'The Hegelian Conception of the State', pp. 22-23; and Westphal, 'The Basic Context and Structure of Hegel's *Philosophy of Right*'.

'the primacy of the *higher-level subjectivity of the state* [which Hegel defines as a constitutional monarchy] over the subjective freedom of the individual'. Habermas attributes the need for the move to the State to the failure of Civil Society *to contain* its self-generated antagonisms.³³ David James follows Habermas in arguing that the State emerges in order to counter Civil Society's self-destructive tendencies, whether these arise due to confusions stemming from legal regulation within Civil Society or whether they arise due to the need for market expansion and colonization in response to overproduction.³⁴

Against the background of such readings one might insist that a weakness of the Hegelian concepts of Civil Society and the State is, as we noted in Chapter One, that they can be used to justify restrictions on individual freedom by appeal to the universal interest that Hegel supposedly identifies with the political / territorial state's executive power. In the twenty-first century against the perceived background of terrorism's global threat to human security, one can conceivably appeal to Hegel's account of the State-Civil Society relationship to supply the necessary conceptual framework for legitimating the West's extensive erosion of individual legal, civil and political rights the world over. From Australia's subjection of asylum seekers to indefinite detention, to France's ban on wearing the burqa in public, this sort of appeal to the merits of a subordinated conception of civil society, provides the rationale for a politically reactionary account of the place of individual rights in the global order of the twenty-first century. Brooks and Hutchings both suggest that this interpretation of the Hegelian State has been put to rest since the concept is now understood to integrate elements from different political traditions ranging from the liberal and republican to the social democratic and conservative.³⁵ But there is no reason to think that the current consensus cannot change, especially in the light of the prevalence of what we might call the 'standard view' of the transition from Civil Society to the State. The standard view represents the State as in some way completing Civil Society. The commentators who try to explain the move from Civil Society to the State typically argue that this move provides Civil Society with what it otherwise *lacks*. For example, highlighting a series of pragmatic considerations, Winfield suggests that the move from Civil Society to the State is a move to

---

33. Habermas, *Philosophical Discourse of Modernity*, pp. 23-44; esp. at pp. 39-40.
34. James, *Hegel's Philosophy of Right*, pp. 69-70.
35. Brooks, *Hegel's Political Philosophy*, p. 1; Hutchings, 'Hard Work', p. 125.

provide Civil Society with an otherwise absent political legitimacy.³⁶ Raymond Plant gives a similar impression when, in response to Civil Society's economic activity, he suggests that Hegel's account of the interventionist role of one of Civil Society's institutions, the Police, provides an early version of the 'legitimation crisis', the view that government intervention in a market economy lacks authority in the absence of a recognized political community with which citizens identify.³⁷ Plant reads Hegel's account of Civil Society as an attempt to re-describe economic interaction so that it yields a communitarian vision of society in preference to an individualistic one.³⁸ But he thinks that Hegel ultimately fails in this task given 'the residual but necessary role of individualism within the market' that hinders action for the common good within the state.³⁹ A. S. Walton is in agreement with Plant in so far as he takes Civil Society to be raising the question of the transcendence of market relations expressive of a utilitarian individualism in favour of relations that 'are mediated by the individual's sense of community and identity with others'.⁴⁰ Walton also notes that Hegel is in favour of a fundamental restructuring of the culture and organization of the community that operates according to an individualist ethic, but he attributes this restructuring role to the Police and the Corporations, that is, to institutions forming part of the account of Civil Society rather than to those belonging to the State.⁴¹ More recently, according to Hutchings, the State, which she takes to be 'an ideal type of the modern state' rather than a description of existing states or an identification of the ideal with a particular historical state, is indispensable to thinking Civil Society, the realm of

---

36. Richard Dien Winfield, 'Hegel's Challenge to the Modern Economy', in Robert L. Perkins (ed.), *History and System: Hegel's Philosophy of History*, Albany, State University of New York Press, 1984, pp. 217-253 at p. 248.

37. Raymond Plant, 'Hegel on Identity and Legitimation' in Z.A Pelczynski (ed.), *The State and Civil Society: Studies in Hegel's Political Philosophy*, Cambridge, Cambridge University Press, 1984, pp. 227-243 at p. 233.

38. Raymond Plant, 'Economic and Social Integration in Hegel's Political Philosophy', in Donald Phillip Verene (ed.), *Hegel's Social and Political Thought: The Philosophy of Objective Spirit*, New Jersey, Humanities Press, 1980, pp. 59-90 at p. 82.

39. Plant, 'Hegel on Identity and Legitimation', p. 243. See also Raymond Plant, *Hegel: An Introduction*, Oxford, Basil Blackwell, 1983, Ch. 9.

40. A. S. Walton, 'Economy, Utility and Community in Hegel's Theory of Civil Society', in Z.A Pelczynski (ed.), *The State and Civil Society: Studies in Hegel's Political Philosophy*, Cambridge, Cambridge University Press, 1984, pp. 244-261 at pp. 254-260.

41. Walton, 'Economy, Utility and Community in Hegel's Theory of Civil Society'.

production and trade, in terms of freedom.[42] This is because state mechanisms are needed to sustain this sphere.

> Precisely because there are no criteria inherent in the self-understanding of civil society as the sphere of particular free will, security has to be introduced and administered from elsewhere, by the state.[43]

But since citizens must already embrace the conditions for the existence of free individuality namely welfare, justice and policing as found in the analysis of Civil Society, if the state is to 'genuinely articulate the principle of self-determination', for Hutchings, the real issue in understanding the transition from Civil Society to the State is not the tension between individual and collective freedom but 'the possibility of the identification of the two'.[44]

So, on the standard view, regardless of differences in the interpretation of the rationale for the move from the concept of Civil Society to that of the State, (along with the Family) these concepts are taken to express different but synchronous dimensions of one and the same social whole. This is also the case, whether or not Civil Society and State are taken to refer to the empirical realities, respectively of a capitalist economy and a governmental system or whether they are taken to refer to merely possible and desirable or even necessary institutional arrangements of modernity. (This discussion of the claim that the *Philosophy of Right* aims to justify the necessity of the State takes various forms but in Chapter Three we will examine Horstmann's version of this argument in so far as it develops a noteworthy reading of the concept of Civil Society.)

A second less common way of understanding the respective domains of Civil Society and the State is to take the two concepts to express two different models of organization of the social whole. For example, Brod argues that the transition from Civil Society to the State is 'a transition from one category of organizational imperatives to another', that is, from an organizational state 'oriented toward the satisfaction of individual, economic needs' to one 'oriented toward the satisfaction of inter-subjective, political consciousness'.[45] On this view, far from providing Civil Society with a missing dimension, the concepts of Civil Society and State elaborate different organizational principles each of which defines the social whole. Regardless of differences in their interpretations,

---

42. Hutchings, 'Hard Work', pp. 129-130.
43. Hutchings, 'Hard Work', p. 132.
44. Hutchings, 'Hard Work', pp. 132-134.
45. Brod, *Hegel's Philosophy of Politics*, p. 91.

none of the abovementioned commentators view the State in this way, seeing it at most as adding an account of the *political dimension* to the organization of the social whole.

By comparison, although we agree with Brod that Civil Society and the State manifest distinct organizational principles, we also want to argue that these concepts are manifested by the politically organized social whole in its differentiated, but overlapping, *temporal* being. Thus we are in agreement with David Macgregor's view that Civil Society manifests a mode of social life and organization that is distinguishable from the 'new form of civilization' that Hegel envisaged with his concept of the State and in relation to which Civil Society is 'a point of transition'.[46] Along with MacGregor, Nicholas Onuf is one of the few Hegel commentators to interpret the concept of Civil Society as an all-inclusive set of social arrangements.[47] As we will see in some detail in Chapter Five, his interpretation supports the view that we wish to defend by reference to the demands of the *Logic*, namely that the concept of Civil Society is manifested by the current global reality and, in particular, by the emergence of what is now the recognizably global civil society. In order to explain why we claim that the current world (dis)order manifests the logic of the concept of Civil Society we will comment briefly on the relationship of Hegel's system to the problem of making critical sense of the modern world.

THE CONCEPT OF CIVIL SOCIETY AND MODERNITY'S SELF-DENIAL

As Gareth Stedman Jones points out, twentieth century Marxists, sociologists and critical theorists generally saw Hegel as attempting to make new predictions about the sociological reality of the modern world.[48] Using Keane's terminology (Chapter One) we might say that the tendency here was to concentrate on the descriptive / explanatory uses of the concept. Moreover, as we saw in connection with our review, above, of approaches to reading

---

46. David MacGregor, *The Communist Ideal in Hegel and Marx*, Toronto, University of Toronto Press, 1984, pp. 195-196 at p. 254.

47. Nicholas Onuf, 'Late Modern Civil Society', in Randall D. Germain and Michael Kenny (eds.), *The Idea of Global Civil Society: Politics and Ethics in a Globalizing Era*, London, Routledge, 2005, pp. 47-64 at pp. 54-55. See also Noberto Bobbio, 'Gramsci and the Concept of Civil Society', in John Keane (ed.), *Civil Society and the State*, London, Verso, 1988, pp. 73-100 at p. 81.

48. Gareth Stedman Jones, 'Hegel and the Economics of Civil Society', in Sudipta Kaviraj and Sunil Khilnani (eds.), *Civil Society: History and Possibilities*, Cambridge, Cambridge University Press, 2001, pp. 105-130.

the Civil Society-State relationship, this tendency is typically combined with the practice of taking the meaning of normativity for granted and either treating the question of Civil Society's normative dimension as secondary or displacing it to the realm of the State. To be sure, a focus on the predictive and diagnostic potential of Civil Society avoids the charge that Hegel's approach ultimately rationalizes the given order of reality. Nevertheless, as we hope to illustrate throughout this book, within a sociological orientation understood in the above terms, the true significance of the abstractness of this concept is misunderstood.

So what is the significance of the fact that Civil Society is an abstract moment of Ethical Life for our understanding of its relationship to the current reality and to the problems of the justification and critique of this reality? To begin with, as Thompson explains, Hegel's systematicity is not just a *procedure* for investigating the structure of reality, it is also this structure itself, since the Hegelian methodology is 'nothing less than the conceptual articulation of the process in and through which things come to be what they intrinsically are'.[49] Moreover, as Thompson suggests, from this perspective justification involves the practice of demonstrating the proper place of something within reality as a whole.[50] On our reading, the process of becoming concerns the emergence of the *mode of being* of things, as distinct from causal origins and relations. This is why the ontological conception of justification does not reduce normativity to the categorical force of the ethical reasoning of particular subjects but instead, in demonstrating the proper place of things within the whole, it creates a vantage point from which to critically review the reality of one's experience. To this extent Neuhouser is correct in claiming that Hegel's social philosophy supplies standards from which to assess the institutions of modernity.[51] But what Neuhouser and others ignore is that Hegel's account of Civil Society is addressed to the problem of elaborating a distinctively *ethical-ontological* ideal, in the abovementioned sense, within a certain teleologically conceived relationship to the ethical State. This is an ideal that simultaneously explains, justifies and enables critique of the modern world in so far as, on the one hand, the concept that is relied upon properly *belongs* to the modern world itself and, on the other, modernity conforms or fails to conform to its own principle. So to appreciate

---

49. Thompson, 'Reason and Objective Spirit', p. 115.
50. Thompson, 'Reason and Objective Spirit', pp. 115-116.
51. Neuhouser, *Foundations of Hegel's Social Philosophy*, p. 8.

the full significance of what the *abstract* moment of Civil Society claims for our own times we must view the concept as expressing modernity's denial of its own principle. Let us explain briefly what this denial refers to.

Elsewhere we have argued that we should take our world, the world of modernity, to be an essentially self-determining whole whilst also denying that its self-determining power can be fully realized in modernity's current condition.[52] For, if we suppose that in order to be genuinely self-determining modernity must achieve, rather than take as given, its inescapable self-referentiality and that this requires it to undergo an appropriate kind of development, then the process towards achieving its own immanent determining activity must include the moment of its as yet unrealized self-referentiality. This negative moment marks the current condition of modernity, which is the moment of its self-denial given that modernity denies its own principle of self-determination. Significantly for our purposes, in modernity's current condition every unit of agency manifests modernity's as yet unrealized principle of self-determination, in one of three ways: (1) as an affirmation of modernity's negative moment; (2) as signaling the immanent collapse of modernity's negative moment, that is, modernity's transitional movement towards the actualization of its principle; or (3) as the visionary anticipation of the conditions of the actualized principle of modernity, that is, modernity as fully self-determining. On this teleological account of modernity Hegel's concept of the ethical State is manifested by the global order of modernity as fully self-determining, an order whose various features are at best only capable of being anticipated in the current global reality, a reality which is, in turn, the manifestation of the Hegelian concept of Civil Society.

For reasons that we need not develop here, we take the view that the current global reality is related to the concepts of Civil Society and State in the abovementioned way because under the current conditions of modernity every unit of agency unavoidably conforms to 'the formal universality of particularity' on some level of its existence.[53] In brief, modernity is defined by the rejection of the conflation of the being of any substantive particular with the universal as such. In requiring every individual unit of

---

52. Nicolacopoulos and Vassilacopoulos, *Hegel and the Logical Structure of Love*, Part I.

53. Nicolacopoulos and Vassilacopoulos, *Hegel and the Logical Structure of Love*, p. 35.

agency—the human being, the collective, the organization—to manifest its particular substantive being as *not being* the universal on at least some level of its interactions, in the current conditions of modernity the universal (all-encompassing) framework of the being of particulars is unavoidably restricted to a universal *form* that is abstracted from any and all substantive universal values.

Even though this remains largely unacknowledged, contemporary discussions of the current global reality typically presuppose the formal universality of particularity in the abovementioned sense. Keane's account of global civil society as a *universal ethic* illustrates this tendency well. As we observed in Chapter One, Keane represents the normative dimension of global civil society as a condition of possibility of the infinite variety of moralities that exist within it or, conversely, as the freedom from an all-encompassing substantive principle. To see how Keane presupposes the formal universality of particularity we need to look more closely at his claims. Keane claims that, as a haven of moral pluralism, civil society nevertheless 'celebrates social diversity' by 'asking after the universal preconditions of dynamic social diversity' and finding that 'durable co-existence of many moral ways of life requires each to accept unconditionally the need for the institutions of a civil society'.[54] It is, therefore,

> an ethical ideal that is universally applicable—in China no less than in Chile, in Afghanistan as well as Andorra—precisely because it is the only ethic capable of recognizing and respecting a genuine plurality of social differences.[55]

Keane's conception of the framework that governs the interrelations between particular moralities, that is, between beings whose moral outlooks are taken in their capacity as *substantive particulars*, is both *universal* and purely *formal*. As an ethical ideal then, global civil society accords with the formal universality of particularity. One can see this even more clearly in the detail of Keane's reasoning.

> Global civil society is not a 'Universal Principle' that subordinates and stifles all particularities. Global civil society is rather to be interpreted as an implied logical and institutional precondition of the survival and flourishing of a genuine plurality of different ideals and forms of life. This precondition is anchored within the actually existing global civil society, whose functioning relies upon the more or less unuttered inference

---

54. Keane, *Global Civil Society?*, pp. 201.
55. Keane, *Global Civil Society?*, pp. 201-202.

that it is a space of many ideals and ways of life, and that civil society for that reason is a good thing. It is as if global civil society requires each of its participants or potential members to sign a contract: to acknowledge and to respect the principle of global civil society as a *universal* ethical principle that guarantees respect for their moral differences. [...] In order for its differences to be recognized and contested as such, global civil society must be present as a common framework of intelligibility that encompasses the principles, means, modes and substance of disagreement. Understood in this way, global civil society is a universal ethical ideal. But it is a universal principle with a difference. It is the universal precondition of the open acceptance of difference.[56]

If the notion of the formal universality of particularity implicitly informs otherwise insightful theoretical discussions of global civil society, in our view this is because the formal universality of particularity fundamentally frames and constrains relations in the current conditions of modernity. Moreover, if, as we will explain in some detail in Chapter Five, Hegel's concept of Civil Society manifests the being of modernity in its moment of self-denial and the current conditions of modernity manifest this moment of self-denial, then we should expect to find clear links between the formal universality of particularity as a constraining framework, the current global reality and Hegel's concept. It is in these terms that Hegel's abstract concept of Civil Society offers us a logically informed ethical-ontological account of the current global reality. From this it also follows that an appreciation of normative issues, like the conditions for making economic globalization fair and just, are not within the parameters of the Hegelian concept of Civil Society in the light of its abstractness.[57] For such an appreciation we must look forward to the conditions under which civil society is incorporated into the organization of the ethical State. But, according to our reading, these conditions manifest a different logical structure, namely the logic of Objectivity. In order to explain

---

56. Keane, *Global Civil Society?*, pp. 202-3.
57. For some recent discussions of the question of an Hegelian account of global justice see Andrew Buchwalter, 'Hegel and Global Justice: An Introduction', in Andrew Buchwalter (ed.), *Hegel and Global Justice*, New York and London, Springer, 2012, pp. 1-20; Buchwalter, 'Hegel, Global Justice and Mutual Recognition', pp. 211-232; Steven V. Hicks, 'Hegel on Cosmopolitanism', pp. 21-48; Thom Brooks, 'Between Statism and Cosmopolitanism: Hegel and the Possibility of Global Justice', in Andrew Buchwalter (ed.), *Hegel and Global Justice*, New York and London, Springer, 2012, pp. 65-84.

our reasons for making these connections between Hegel's categories and our reality, we will turn next to the question of how we approach the complex task of developing this logical-systemic reading of the Hegelian concepts of Ethical Life and the concept of right more generally.

HEGEL'S SYSTEM AND THE STRICT ORGANIZATION THESIS

We have already suggested that the logical categories of Hegel's system strictly organize those of Ethical Life. Indeed one of our aims in this book is to demonstrate the explanatory power of what we have termed 'the strict organization thesis'. This thesis consists of two fundamental claims: firstly, that the formal categorial progression of the *Logic* strictly organizes the subject matter of Hegel's *Philosophy of Mind* of which the *Philosophy of Right* forms a part; and, secondly, that the development of this subject matter, which deals with the real categories, in turn, proceeds as the work of that which Hegel calls 'the Idea'. In this context, 'the Idea' refers to what one can call 'the logical Idea', that is, the logical concept that is elaborated at the end of the *Science of Logic* along with the process of its logical categorical development, but not just to the logical Idea. It also refers to the Idea *in its becoming* pursuant to the movement of the real categories. Hegel explains in the *Philosophy of Right* that in the course of its actualization the Idea has two essential moments: the first is 'its form, [...] its mode of being as concept alone' and the second consists of 'the shapes which the concept assumes in the course of its actualization [that] are indispensable for the knowledge of the concept itself'.[58]

We suggest that whereas the first of these moments is realized in the *Logic* with the emergence and development of the logical Idea to its conclusion as 'Absolute Idea', the second is progressively realized in the rest of the Hegelian philosophical system after the systemic treatment of the *Philosophy of Nature*, with the aid of the already developed logical categories and the retrospective knowledge of their systemic progression. Accordingly, the work of 'the Idea' that comes into play in analyzing the concept of Civil Society is not merely that of the logical concept that is elaborated at the end of the *Science of Logic*. Here we are in agreement with Angelica Nuzzo in so far as she argues that even though the dialectical-speculative method of the *Logic* comes into play in the

---

58. Hegel, *PR*, §1Remark.

logical process that develops the concept of right, this latter process is not identical with that of the logical concept. However, to distinguish the logical Idea and the Idea of right Nuzzo asserts the identity of the Idea of right and history: 'history is precisely the "real" element that modifies the concept into a *"realphilosophische"* logic'.[59] In our view, the Idea that we encounter at the beginning of the *Philosophy of Right*, like the Idea we encounter at the beginning of the *Philosophy of Mind*, is the logical idea in its *anticipatory readiness* to actualize its notion through the process of organizing the real categories. For this reason, the logical unfolding of the categories of right does not require an *additional supportive* ontology drawn from history.[60]

This is not, however, to advocate the sufficiency of a mere repetition of the logical categories in the process of thinking the categories of spirit. Against a strict organization thesis, Nuzzo maintains that 'the logical categories alone are not sufficient to define real categories' and that when the real categories are taken up by the method of the *Logic*, 'the method actually redefines or modifies the meaning of the logical categories instead of merely repeating them'.[61] But to argue, as we do, for the necessity of the strict organization thesis is not to deny that there is more at stake than the mere repetition of a logical categorial progression that has already been achieved within the Hegelian system. Rather our linear correlation of the categories of the *Logic* with those of spirit forms part of a certain interpretation of the completeness of the Hegelian system. On this interpretation the anticipation, unfolding and completion of the Hegelian system is informed throughout by thought's awareness of its 'pure self-recognition in absolute otherness'.[62] Let us explain this claim very briefly.[63]

---

59. Nuzzo, 'Dialectic as Logic of Transformative Processes', p. 167. Nuzzo bases this claim on the suggestion that with the inclusion of 'World History' as the conclusion and truth of right, 'the systemic succession of the determination of the idea is necessarily identical with the temporal succession of the figures of its historical reality'. She maintains not only that for Hegel 'this identity between logical and temporal determination of spirit' constitutes Hegel's notion of history but also that history plays a *necessary*, methodological role in shaping the concept of right: Nuzzo, 'Dialectic as Logic of Transformative Processes', p. 168.

60. Simon Lumsden argues this point against Kevin Thompson in Simon Lumsden, 'Beyond and Ontological Foundation for the *Philosophy of Right*', *The Southern Journal of Philosophy*, vol. 39, no. 3, 2001, pp. 139-145.

61. Nuzzo, 'Dialectic as Logic of Transformative Processes', p. 165.

62. G.W.F. Hegel, *The Phenomenology of Spirit*, Oxford, Oxford University Press, 1970, § 26.

63. For extensive discussion of these claims see Toula Nicolacopoulos and

To begin with, the bearer of the abovementioned awareness is the speculative philosopher. His or her awareness functions as the horizon for the development of philosophy as the thinking that both belongs to the world and is unavoidably systemic. That is, the thinking in question belongs to the world since, in so far as it is informed by *self-recognition in otherness* it articulates the condition of modernity, namely the self-denial that we discussed above. At the same time, it is unavoidably systemic since the modern world's self-denial, its negation of itself, gives rise to the unconditional and hence all-inclusive division of notion (the very principle of self-determination) and being (the world). It is the explicit revealing of this division (spirit 'looking the negative in the face, and tarrying with it'[64]) that posits the speculative being of the human collective, uniquely rending it as completely denaturalized. Only the human collective can and must actively fail to be what it is at the same time as sustaining itself in and as such failing. Everything else in nature simply is what it is, and where it fails to be what it is, it merely ceases to be. Ultimately the being / becoming of the human collective *as otherness* or self-denial is a state of gathering intensity for a holistic overcoming of the achieved moment of denaturalization and the passing over to the achievable stage of spiritualization that would posit the collective as the project of appropriating its principle of self-determination.

In this teleological account, in order to move forward, so to speak, the human collective must first move backwards into the depth of its self-denial, the depth of its absolute otherness. This depth is at once the dwelling place of the philosopher and the philosopher as the dwelling place of the world itself. It is thus the moment of *pure* self-recognition. This kind of recognition expresses the very principle of self-determination *as denied*. Recognition of this principle, and this principle as self-recognition, is pure in the sense that its purity is abstraction itself, the purely inner, denied, notion of self-determination that is without world. This in turn leads thinking to the state of *absolute otherness*. If the world negates its notion, the notion, in turn negates the world in thinking it.

Two things follow from the above. Firstly, in so far as the notion or principle of self-determination becomes accessible, it

---

George Vassilacopoulos, 'The Ego as World: Speculative Justification and the Role of the Thinker in Hegel's Philosophy', in Paul Ashton, Toula Nicolacopoulos and George Vassilacopoulos (eds.), *The Spirit of the Age: Hegel and the Fate of Thinking*, Melbourne, re.press, 2008, pp. 259-291. See also Nicolacopoulos and Vassilacopoulos, *Hegel and the Logical Structure of Love*, Part I and Part II.

64. Hegel, *The Phenomenology of Spirit*, § 32.

makes sense of itself as *purely inner* or *abstract*. In Hegel's system this task of pure thinking is activated and articulated in the *Logic*. Secondly, with the development of the notion or principle of self-determination through the articulation of its various manifestations and degrees of freedom in the inner realm of pure thought, the very element in which this notion unfolds must also be explicitly recognized. This is the element of abstractness or denial that implicates the world. Its recognition involves the thinking of the world in all the relevant manifestations and degrees of the notion's freedom, in a manner that strictly registers *both* the principle of the world that *does the thinking*, or necessitates the movement of thought, and the very thinking of this principle *as denied*. In other words, the real categories must be thought in a way that progressively makes them recognize the denial of that which they themselves deny. It is precisely this relation between the categories of thought and the thinker (as the bearer of the denied principle of self-determination) that gives rise to the need for the strict organization thesis. With this in mind we will turn next to give a brief account of the principle of self-determination at work in the development of the categories of the *Logic* followed by our understanding of the relevant categorical correlations.

LOGIC AS SELF-DETERMINATION

The *Logic* constitutes the systematic and comprehensive elaboration of the fundamental formal categories of philosophical thought. This process involves a cyclical progression from the most abstract to the most concrete of forms via three main developmental cycles. It begins against the background that although speculative thinking takes its notion or principle to be the unity of three moments, the Universal, the Particular and the Individual, it must think this unity in and as pure thought. The demand, as Hegel puts it, is that thought must verify itself to itself and this is what governs the progression of the categories. It follows that no point of the process can rest on mere assertion. Thought must create its concepts immanently. In other words, thought acquires the status of objectivity by determining its content as the mediated result of the thinking process. The outcome of the categorial development establishes thought as the unity of its two aspects, unity and difference. Thought thus determines itself as the concrete unity of subject and object through the unity of form and content. Thought acquires this status pursuant to the full investigation of the formal categories and their diverse modes of interrelating. This investigation explores the dynamic of categorial interrelations that exhibit alternative configurations of thought's differentiated unity, that is, of the notions of unity, difference and their relationships.

The form of this cycle of categorial interrelations is produced as the result of a movement through categories that are thought, firstly, in their immediate presence, in abstraction from all relatedness (the categories of being), and, then, as pairs of correlatives exhibiting relatedness externally (the categories of essence). As the truth, in the sense of justified presupposition, of these preceding configurations of differentiated unity, the differentiated unity of universality, particularity and individuality emerges in what Hegel conceives as thought's 'self-evolved determination'.[65]

Whereas the first two cycles of development in the *Logic* function as prerequisites for the notion's readiness to tackle the question of its realization, in the third and final main developmental cycle of the *Logic*, 'The Doctrine of Notion and Idea', it is the notion that explicitly enacts its self-determining activity. That is, in this third cycle of development the notion fully determines its otherwise indeterminate differentiated unity. As the references to both notion and idea in the title of this third cycle suggest, at this point the notion undertakes a developmental process that eventually gives rise to the objectified notion that Hegel calls the 'Idea'. Here we encounter 'thought in its return into itself, and its developed abiding by itself' that corresponds to 'the Notion in and for itself'.[66] Significantly, as self-determining, the notion 'must itself posit what it is'. In other words, the notion which is a positedness because it 'has come to be' through the development of its moments of unity and differentiation, must now develop itself as this differentiated unity.[67]

For Hegel the requirement that the notion determine its differentiated unity amounts to the requirement that it engage in a process whose result will be to develop the moments of its truth, namely the Universal, the Particular and the Individual, from the perspective of this truth.[68] When the self-determining notion constructs its differentiated unity from the perspective of its truth it

---

65. Hegel, *SL*, p. 596.
66. Hegel, *Hegel's Logic*, §83.
67. Hegel, SL, p. 596.
68. In what follows we use the upper case when referring specifically to Hegel's concepts of the Universal / Universality, the Particular / Particularity and the Individual / Individuality.

first develops the 'Notion of the Notion'.[69] This refers to the principle of the notion understood as that which makes it the notion at its most abstract level. Hegel refers to this as the 'universal Notion'.[70] In this process of self-determination the notion is 'universal' because it presents itself as the truth of every step making up the process. The claim that 'each of these moments is no less the *whole* Notion' means that each moment must incorporate the others. According to Hegel,

> the universal is the self-identical, with the express qualification, that it simultaneously contains the particular and the individual. Again, the particular is the different or the specific character, but with the qualification that it is in itself universal and is as an individual. Similarly the individual must be understood to be a subject or substratum, which involves the genus and species in itself and possesses a substantial existence.[71]

The process in question takes the Universal, the Particular and the Individual to be stages that are 'determinations' of the notion. At the same time each one of these categories is a form of the 'determinate' notion, that is, one form of the notion's differentiated unity. In other words, the justified notion is the differentiated unity that aims at determining itself as this unity.

The rationale underlying this development can be put as follows. Precisely because it is merely self-determining, as distinct from already self-determined, the notion both anticipates the realization of its self-determination and is ready to realize what it anticipates.[72] In its attempt to realize its self-determining power, the notion enters a developmental process whose principle is the differentiated unity of the Universal, the Particular and the Individual. (For ease of reference one can simply refer to the differentiated unity of these three categories as 'the categorial differentiated unity'.) The abstract unity of Universality corresponds to the notion that, in anticipating its realization, is not yet and, so, is as otherness expressed by the Particular. In transcending its otherness the notion reflectively knows itself as self-determining and is

---

69. Hegel, SL, p. 582.
70. Hegel, *SL*, p. 600.
71. G.W.F Hegel, *Hegel's Logic*, §164.
72. J. M. Fritzman argues that the dialectical movement of the logical categories involves a two-fold movement such that 'what is [retrospectively] counted as first already has been prepared and anticipated'. Interestingly, he maintains that the movement thus involves 'a moment of irreducible contingency' by which 'Hegelian necessity is catalyzed': J. M. Fritzman, 'Return to Hegel', *Continental Philosophy Review*, vol. 34, 2001, pp. 287-320 at pp. 312-314.

thereby the Individual. Given that the notion is the categorial differentiated unity that anticipates its determination, it begins with the moment of Universality that becomes the abstract expression of the differentiated unity. In this way, the Universal is 'the whole Notion' and at the same time, a moment of the notion's development. The same holds for the Particular and the Individual, the first of which expresses the differentiated unity in its determinate otherness whilst the second expresses the accomplished categorical differentiated unity.

So the notion must begin with the moment of Universality in which it is abstractly self-related in a way that includes both determinateness (particularity) and awareness (individuality) since it is the as yet unrealized truth. From Universality the notion moves to Particularity. According to Hegel, 'the particular is the universal itself but it is its difference or relation to an other, its *illusory reference outwards*'.[73] It eventually realizes 'the return into itself' in the moment of individuality which is 'the notion reflecting itself out of the difference into absolute negativity'.[74] The difference expressed by the fact that the notion is related to the Particular as its other is transcended when the notion reflectively knows that the essence of the Particular is to embody the Universal. The reflective awareness expressed by individuality reveals that the notion is not simply immersed in its determinateness; it knows itself to be its own creation. The truth of the notion's embodiment (the truth of its Particularity) is the fact that in it and through it the universal is united with itself as both the determinate universal and the universal that is responsible for its determination. This is why Hegel calls the Individual the absolute determinateness. The absolute negativity initially expressed in universality is explicitly shown in individuality to be that which determines the differentiated unity of the notion. In the categorial differentiated unity formulated by the moment of Individuality the notion returns to the absolute negativity of Universality through Particularity and it is in this regard retrospective. The notion is an Individual that has accomplished its anticipated self-reflective determination.

THE CYCLICAL DEVELOPMENT OF THE LOGICAL CATEGORIES

If the rationale offered above is sound, then the movement from the moment of Universality that is itself a categorial differentiated

---

73. Hegel, *SL*, p. 606.
74. Hegel, *SL*, p. 601; p. 621.

unity (hereafter 'the U-moment') through the unity of Particularity (hereafter 'the P-moment') to that of Individuality (hereafter 'the I-moment') exhibits the principle of the notion's process of becoming. Referring to this kind of movement, from the U-moment through the P-moment to the I-moment, as a 'U, P, I progression', one can say that a U, P, I progression characterizes the developmental logic of 'The Doctrine of the Notion and Idea'. Accordingly, on this interpretation the development in 'The Notion', the beginning of 'The Doctrine of the Notion and Idea', is (at least part of) the U-moment of the doctrine's cycle of development. The last section, 'The Idea' is (at least part of) its I-moment. Indeed in this scheme the notion's I-moment is fully constituted by this stage whereas the notion reaches this stage through the P-moment that is developed as 'The Objective Notion' in the stage of 'Objectivity'.

Moreover, one can make sense of the transition from one developmental stage to the next, whether between developmental cycles or within a cycle, having regard to whether, and in what combination, the notion is positioned as a U, P or I-moment and is consequently (a) anticipatory and, hence, abstract relative to its end (U-moment); (b) in otherness, in so far as it has yet to determine its being (P-moment); or (c) retrospectively aware of itself as whatever it has determined itself to be (I-moment). For example, if we consider the movement within the U-moment of the most comprehensive cycle of development within the *Logic*, we find three stages, 'The Notion', 'The Judgement' and 'The Syllogism', which are equally stages of abstractness given their anticipatory role in the most comprehensive cycle of development within the *Logic*. On the other hand, they are also related to each other as the three moments of a U, P, I progression. The U-moment of abstractness, 'The Notion', expresses the notion's absolute indeterminacy. The P-moment of abstractness, 'The Judgement', expresses the notion's complete loss in externality given the otherness of this moment in abstractness. That is, the notion immanently introduces itself into otherness by establishing its inner identity in otherness. However, in doing so, it posits the determinateness of its abstractness and thereby moves to the I-moment of abstractness, which is its reflective moment.

The I-moment of abstractness, 'The Syllogism', expresses the notion's opposition of its mediating unity to its externality due to its formality. The notion thereby exhibits its full determinateness as abstractness. Through this relation of opposition its inner abstract unity (the absolute indeterminacy of the accomplished notion's differentiated unity) is reflectively equated with externality (the being to which the syllogistic form is related as the mere form). As a result of this equation in 'The Syllogism' the notion is posited as the essence of its other and thereby moves to 'Objectivity', the P-moment of the most comprehensive cycle of development within the *Logic*.

As the P-moment of its developmental cycle, 'Objectivity' incorporates the determinateness of its U-moment which is made explicit in the latter's reflective I-moment, that of 'The Syllogism'. The determinateness of the notion as the essence of otherness is thus exhibited with the emergence of the objective notion. The task of 'Objectivity' is then to become the self-determining identity of externality. Since it is not yet this identity the movement to objectivity gives rise to a new developmental cycle with its own anticipatory and retrospective moments.

In this way the notion develops through its first reality, that of the development of the subjective notion to objectivity, and, then through its second reality, that of the development of the objective notion's subjectivity. At the completion of the development through these two realities the notion becomes the self-determining identity of its externality from which externality it is thus distinguished. It thereby passes into 'The Idea', the I-moment of the most comprehensive developmental cycle within the *Logic*, in which the idea as the unity of notion and being becomes the truth of the preceding movement retrospectively.[75]

This reading of the development of the notion's first and second realities implies three things about the nature of any particular point in the developmental process. Firstly, such a point constitutes one moment of a U, P, I progression. Secondly, it is also part of the U, P, or I-moments of the cycles of development from 'The Notion' to 'The Syllogism' or from those within 'Objectivity'. Finally, the particular point of the developmental process is an aspect of either the U-moment or the P-moment constituting the most comprehensive logical cycle. On this view any particular point in the system is not merely to be understood as manifesting

---

75. Nuzzo presents a discussion of the similarities and differences between the absolute Idea that results from the logical development up until the point of its emergence and the subsequent development of this Idea into method or absolute form at the completion of *Logic*, which is 'to be used in cognition and action by speculative thinking': Angelica Nuzzo, 'The End of Hegel's Logic: Absolute Idea and Absolute Method', in David Gray Carlson (ed.), *Hegel's Theory of the Subject*, New York, Palgrave Macmillan, 2005, pp. 187-205 at p. 190. In what follows we are invoking the latter when referring to 'the logical idea'.

features that belong to it in virtue of its position in the notion's developmental process. Such a position should not be taken as *one* point in a single cycle of development but rather as a point in a number of cycles operating at different levels and these different levels need to be taken into account in order to understand the features manifested at any particular point in the system.

THE CORRELATION OF LOGICAL AND REAL CATEGORIES

As we will see, awareness of the subtleties of the system's multi-layered developmental cycles enables a very rich reading of Hegel's concept of Civil Society. But how precisely does the development of the logical categories strictly organize the development of Civil Society and the other real categories? In other words, following Hegel's terminology, how does the form of thought correlate to the intellectual work of 'mind' or spirit as elaborated in the *Philosophy of Mind*? In Hegel's system, spirit manifests itself to itself through a three stage developmental process from 'Mind Subjective' through 'Mind Objective' to 'Mind Absolute'.[76] The *Philosophy of Right* deals specifically with the categories of Objective spirit. Franco suggests that Hegel's procedure in the *Philosophy of Right* models that of the logical movement from 'Being' and 'Essence' to 'The Notion'.[77] That is, the movement in the *Philosophy of Right* from the categories of 'Abstract Right' and 'Morality' to 'Ethical Life' mirrors that in the *Logic* from the immediacy of being, though 'a moment of mediation in which the immediate is related to another' to its conclusion with the sublation of otherness in the self-determining notion. The same pattern of movement is also repeated in the movement within 'Ethical Life' from the 'Family' and 'Civil Society' to the 'State'.[78] Klaus Kaehler advances the view that the determinations of Objective logic, especially the logic of Essence, inform the realm of Objective spirit, albeit in accordance with the supersession of their relations of division so that the various shapes of Objective spirit follow the ordering of the notion's moments of Universality, Particularity and Individuality.[79] Butler argues that the movement is shaped in accordance with a seven phase dialectical method, that 'begins with the *abstraction* of some

---

76. G.W.F. Hegel, *Hegel's Philosophy of Mind: Being Part Three of the Encyclopaedia of the Philosophical Sciences*, trans. William Wallace, Oxford, Oxford University Press, §385.
77. Franco, *Hegel's Philosophy of Freedom*, p. 145.
78. Franco, *Hegel's Philosophy of Freedom*, pp. 152-153.
79. Kaehler, 'The Right of the Particular and the Power of the Universal', p. 152.

x apart from an inseparable y, which is the specific other of x' and ends 'negating the absolutization of x in the negation of y'.[80] As we will argue in the course of this study, the identification of such general patterns of movement is too broad to assist with the interpretation of the logic of Objective spirit.

In contrast to the above, on the reading we propose, the logical idea's progressive development through the *Logic* strictly organizes the development of the three stages of the *Philosophy of Mind* as follows. 'Mind Subjective' corresponds to the development from 'The Doctrine of Being' to the completion of 'The Judgement'.[81] 'Mind Objective' corresponds to the structure of relations developed in 'The Syllogism' and 'Objectivity'.[82] Finally, 'Mind Absolute' is informed by the logical development of 'The Idea'.[83] It follows from this correlation, that we must read the concept of Civil Society in the light of the logic of 'The Syllogism'.

SYLLOGISTIC REASONING

Earlier we suggested that 'The Doctrine of the Notion and Idea', the third part of the *Science of Logic* that includes the treatment of the syllogistic forms, explores thought's differentiated unity and addresses the question of the notion's realization and that this part elaborates the interplay between the basic categories of Universality, Particularity and Individuality. More specifically, the role of syllogistic reasoning is to unite the abstract categories of Universality, Particularity and Individuality and to overcome their immediacy (unmediatedness). It achieves this by bringing the categories into definite relations that give them their objective meaning. The most important of these relations are those of differentiation and mediation. In syllogistic reasoning thought's unity takes on the form of explicit mediation as represented by one of three terms that is positioned as a middle term between two extremes. Its difference is exhibited as the middle term's differentiating activity. Both these aspects characterize each of the three categories at various points in the syllogistic process. This process gives rise to forms exhibiting increasingly more adequate ways of conceiving the differentiated unity of the categories. Differentiation and mediation are exhibited to varying degrees, with varying effects and measures of success. All this depends on precisely where and

---

80. Butler, 'The Coming World Welfare State which Hegel Could Not See', p. 156.
81. Hegel, *SL*, pp. 663-667.
82. Hegel, *SL*, pp. 664-754.
83. Hegel, *SL*, pp. 755-844.

how the categories are positioned both in the complex relation of each to the other two at any given moment, as well as in the whole process of syllogistic development. This latter is the process that begins with the abstract forms that represent mere existence ('The Syllogism of Existence' that constitutes the Syllogism's U-moment). It moves to the external reflection upon the categories ('The Syllogism of Reflection', the Syllogism's P-moment) and ends when the categories become necessarily interrelated ('The Syllogism of Necessity', the Syllogism's I-moment).

For present purposes, it is enough to bear in mind that, for Hegel, the totality of syllogistic forms, their respective dynamics and limits are rendered fully visible in this elaborate way. His treatment of the syllogism purports to represent all the conceivable modes of differentiating and uniting the three categories. These modes begin with the case in which the categories are in their respective self-subsistence. That is, they are mutually indifferent to their respective determinations and their indifference exhibits various oppositions and external relatedness. The syllogistic cycle culminates in the full integration of the categories that have become necessarily (non-contingently) interrelated and each category reflects all three within it, as the result of effective differentiation and mediation by the category of Universality. The Syllogism of Necessity, which on one level constitutes the Syllogism's I-moment, also consists in a U, P, I progression from the Categorical Syllogism through the Hypothetical Syllogism to the Disjunctive Syllogism. Within this developmental cycle we encounter a totality, in the sense of an *achieved* internal categorical differentiated unity (hereafter 'a comprehensive categorical differentiated unity') but initially this totality is only relative given that the Categorical Syllogism does not also manifest an internal categorial *differentiation*. It is only with the Disjunctive Syllogism, which manifests the completed syllogism, that the middle term determines both aspects of the complex process of differentiation *and* mediation. Indeed, this syllogistic structure is related to its preceding formulations in much the same way as a geometric circle is related to the process of its construction prior to its completion.

THE LOGICAL CATEGORIES AND THE ORDER OF ETHICAL LIFE

The abovementioned scheme suggests that a full account of the logical categories, which includes the features of the process of their construction at any point prior to its completion, must include reference to two kinds of features: firstly, those that can be found in the completed construction; and, secondly, those that must be transcended since they would undermine the would-be qualities of the completed construction were they to be retained. It follows from this that in so far as Hegel's account of Ethical Life is developed in strict accordance with its corresponding logical progression, one part of the work of reading the *Philosophy of Right* involves identifying the status of the various textual claims and, in particular, where they are positioned within relevant developmental cycles and whether they are to be transcended. The other has to do with correlating the logical and real categories systematically.

On our reading, the categories of Ethical Life are informed by those of the Syllogism of Necessity as follows. As we have argued elsewhere in some detail, the form of the Categorical Syllogism strictly organizes the development of the concept of the Family.[84] Whereas the form of the Hypothetical Syllogism informs the features of Civil Society *in its initial appearance as a system of interdependence*, the form of the Disjunctive Syllogism informs *the differentiation* of Civil Society into its three moments, the System of Needs, the Administration of Justice and the Police-Corporations. Finally, as already suggested, the categories of Objectivity strictly organize those of the Hegelian State. This means that in order to read Hegel's abstract concept of Civil Society systemically, we must at once appreciate both the internal and transitional logic relating to two syllogisms, the Hypothetical and the Disjunctive Syllogism.

How does one make and confirm the above-mentioned correlations? Unlike H.S. Richardson, who proposes a scheme that, whilst similarly linking Civil Society to the logic of the Hypothetical Syllogism, nevertheless takes the Disjunctive Syllogism to inform the concept of the State, we do not engage in comparing possible 'hypotheses of correlation' and testing them for 'structural fidelity, intuitive appeal and textual basis'.[85] Richardson's methodology seeks to arrive at the best explanation through a process of *elimination* of hypotheses of correlation. Taking for granted that the Hypothetical Syllogism correlates to Civil Society as a whole, Richardson's methodology leads him to suggest that the State cannot but conform to the consecutive logic of the Disjunctive

---

84. Nicolacopoulos and Vassilacopoulos, *Hegel and the Logical Structure of Love*, Part III.

85. Richardson, 'The Logical Structure in Sittlichkeit', pp. 64-66.

Syllogism and Objectivity.[86] But Richardson cannot adequately explain the implications of this suggestion for our understanding of the transition to the State, which on our analysis is informed by the logic of the transition from the Syllogism to Objectivity. In contrast, the specific correlations we have proposed derive, not just from the identification of comparative similarities between the claims of the *Philosophy of Right* and the *Logic*, but from reading the details of Hegel's real philosophical categories through the developmental cycles of the *Logic* and its multilayered U, P, I progressions. Indeed, the limitations of a methodology like Richardson's become evident at the very points where only a close scrutiny of the categorical interplay in the light of the notion's precise point of development can settle deeply puzzling interpretive issues. We will be addressing these issues in the course of elaborating our position and demonstrating the potential explanatory power of our interpretive framework.

Let us sum up the major concerns of Hegel scholars in relation to the problem of how to read the concept of Civil Society in terms of the following broad questions. First, given that Hegel acknowledges the devastating effects that life in Civil Society has on some people(s), whether as poverty stricken or as colonized, why does he present this form of association as a stage of Ethical Life and does this acknowledgement suggest dependence upon a problematic Eurocentrism? In other words, in what sense can Civil Society be recognized as a moment of *ethicality* of universal significance? Second, why does Hegel include the concept of the Corporation as part of the account of the concept of Civil Society even though the internal logic of the former does not match the instrumental logic that seems to define relations within the latter? Third, given Hegel's differentiation of Civil Society from the State, why does he include within the former the realms of legal administration and government that on the face of it fall within the domain of the State? Fourth, given that Civil Society, the abstract moment, does not manifest the final stage of Ethical Life, what precisely is it about this form of organization that renders it *incomplete*? Fifth, what is the best way to understand the relationship between the latter two stages of Ethical Life, Civil Society and the State? Finally, how is the *immanent* transition to the State possible? As we will see, the answers to these questions depend upon a careful analysis of the Hypothetical and Disjunctive Syllogisms

---

86. Richardson, 'The Logical Structure in Sittlichkeit', p. 72.

and of their transitional movement in the light of their positioning as moments within U, P, I progressions at different levels of the logical categories' cyclical development.

3. THE SYLLLOGISTIC TERMS OF THE CONCEPT OF CIVIL SOCIETY

We have suggested that even though Hegel's concept of Civil Society forms part of his attempt to incorporate the socially instituted ethical-ontological conditions of modern life within a philosophical system whose methodology is guided by the movement of the categories of the *Logic*, most commentators try to make sense of his claims without recourse to a strict organization thesis. At the same time readers of Hegel who still seek to engage with Hegel's ideas systematically but with priority on bringing his philosophy into line with current demands take quite a different stand on the question of the importance of remaining true to Hegel's own thought and intentions. As we have already noted in Chapter Two, in seeking to reactivate Hegel's political philosophy by creatively reconstructing it Honneth rejects the aspiration to read Hegel *with Hegel*. By contrast, Hutchings, who also wishes to rehabilitate Hegel by purging the racist and imperialist overtones of his work, argues that this can be achieved whilst remaining true to Hegel's central insights regarding the historicity of ideas.[1] Rolf-Peter Horstmann offers a detailed reading of the concept of Civil Society, which similarly attempts to remain true to Hegel's own intellectual trajectory even as he too sets the *Logic* aside.[2] This is not to say that Horstmann denies the general relevance of Hegel's *Logic* in understanding Hegel's system, but that he does not draw upon it for the purposes of situating Hegel's concept of Civil Society within his system.[3] Agreeing, moreover,

---

1. Hutchings, 'Hard Work'.
2. Horstmann, 'The Role of Civil Society in Hegel's Political Philosophy', pp. 208-240.
3. Elsewhere Horstmann defends the claim that the *Logic* is decisive in relation to the exposition of the Hegelian system's leading concepts: Rolf-Peter

that 'the key to understand the political intentions of [... Hegel's] theory lies precisely in the appropriate interpretation of the relationship between [Hegel's concept of] the state and civil society', Horstmann maintains that to grasp 'the full intention of Hegel's political philosophy' one must read the concept of Civil Society genealogically or, in his words, one must read 'the mature theory' 'as the result of a development that consists in the elaboration and exposition of various original approaches'.[4] Before going on to develop the argument based on the *Logic*, Horstmann's analysis is worth investigating since it promises to explain Hegel's concept of Civil Society. By identifying the limitations of Horstmann's detailed explanation we will also be indicating the limits of analysis of the Hegelian concept that does not draw upon the *Logic*.

For Horstmann the problem Hegel confronts in the *Philosophy of Right* is that of 'mediating the ideal articulated in the classical tradition with the actual conditions of modernity', that is, the ancient concept of the ethical state with the social conditions that have called forth subjective particularity, understood as autonomous individuals or free subjective conscience, along with a sphere of social life in which such individuals pursue their desires without regard to a universal end or purpose.[5] This 'program of uniting the contributions of antiquity and modernity in a systematic fashion' turns out to be a serious challenge for Hegel in so far as he seeks to unite two opposed concepts: ethical life, understood as a living, organic unity, and civil society which manifests the very incapacity to express this unity.[6]

Horstmann argues that Hegel's early work already establishes two goals that ultimately inform the direction of the later work. Firstly, Hegel needs to make the distinction between civil society and the ethical state in response to the natural law view of civil society which, in deriving all ethical relationships from the concept of the isolated singular individual, denies a space for the idea of a universal ethical life that constitutes the ground of its own determinations.[7] Secondly, he needs to assign priority to 'the people as the universal, represented as a living organism, over against the

---

Horstmann, 'Substance, Subject and Infinity: A Case Study of the Role of Logic in Hegel's System', in Katerina Deligiorgi (ed.), *Hegel: New Directions*, London, Acumen, 2006, pp. 69-84.

    4. Horstmann, 'The Role of Civil Society in Hegel's Political Philosophy', pp. 210-1.
    5. Horstmann, 'The Role of Civil Society in Hegel's Political Philosophy', pp. 211-2.
    6. Horstmann, 'The Role of Civil Society in Hegel's Political Philosophy', p. 212.
    7. Horstmann, 'The Role of Civil Society in Hegel's Political Philosophy', pp. 217-8.

individual interests of particular social formations within the totality of ethical life'.[8] Accordingly, once Hegel re-articulates the foundations of his political philosophy, which Horstmann describes in terms of a transition 'from a philosophical model oriented toward the concept of life and organism to one conceived in terms of the structure of consciousness' it becomes possible to view the unity of individuality and universality 'as the very ground of the possibility of a relationship in general' and, hence, to view all social and political relations in terms of this unity.[9] For Horstmann Hegel is thus in a position to demonstrate: firstly, the difference between the universal interest and purpose and the aggregate of individual interests and purposes and, hence, the one sidedness of the approach of the natural law tradition; and, secondly, that the logical unfolding of the unity of individuality and universality determines the various manifestations of different forms of the ethical whole, like the estates or government, and this, in turn, necessitates the adoption of a systematic approach.

On Horstmann's genealogical reading then the conceptual problems that Hegel's mature philosophy elaborates 'had been effectively resolved by the categorical means elaborated in *Realphilosophie II*'.[10] At the same time, this reading generates a puzzle as to why Hegel would decide to use the term 'civil society' to introduce a relatively new category by the time he comes to write the *Philosophy of Right*. Horstmann observes that if his reading is correct, however, Hegel's decision seems strange since such a move implicates him in a departure from a presentation that had developed the particular forms of ethical life out of the concept of 'society as state' in favour of one that is focused on the constitution and on 'determining the specific difference between the universal and the particular, namely between the state and civil society'.[11] Horstmann must therefore offer a further explanation for why Hegel decided to introduce the concept of Civil Society in the *Philosophy of Right*. Let us consider this explanation.

Horstmann notes, firstly, that although the term is new for Hegel the concept itself is only 'relatively new' since he had previously developed a conception of 'the sphere of needs and labour' 'where particularity prevails'. Horstmann then reduces the question concerning 'the new presentation' of Civil Society in

---

8. Horstmann, 'The Role of Civil Society in Hegel's Political Philosophy', p. 221.
9. Horstmann, 'The Role of Civil Society in Hegel's Political Philosophy', p. 223.
10. Horstmann, 'The Role of Civil Society in Hegel's Political Philosophy', p. 223.
11. Horstmann, 'The Role of Civil Society in Hegel's Political Philosophy', pp. 223-4.

the *Philosophy of Right* to the question of 'why Hegel should have *changed the exposition* of a theory that remained largely unchanged with respect to its essential foundations'.[12] His answer is that, in distinguishing Civil Society systematically, Hegel was thus able to defend his monarchical ideal of the state against the charge that he was a mere apologist for the status quo at the same time as distancing his position from the restorationist views that were circulating amongst his contemporaries.[13]

As to the effect of the inclusion of the concept of Civil Society on the development of Hegel's system, Horstmann has this to say.

> The purpose of Hegel's mature political philosophy [...] also lies in demonstrating the necessity for a universal that can exercise power over all that is merely particular, that is, of the necessity of the state. The doctrine of civil society as a domain defined by the principle of particularity performs the systematic function, within the Hegelian theory, of providing precisely this demonstration.[14]

On Horstmann's genealogical reading then Hegel's systemic incorporation of the concept of Civil Society is 'simply a means to an end' even as it also had the beneficial effect of contributing to our understanding of modern social and political relations in the light of 'the resultant overcoming of the traditional identification of the state and civil society'.[15] Nevertheless, Horstmann concludes critically that this achievement, the *overcoming of the intellectual practice of conflating* civil society and state, does little to resolve the question of their *relationship* with which Hegel is also concerned. On Horstmann's reading and analysis it follows that Hegel falsely infers the rationality of the state from his demonstration of 'the irrational potential that attaches to civil society'.[16] For Horstmann, the concepts of Ethical Life therefore remain unjustified.

So, Horstmann objects to Hegel's account of the logic of Ethical Life via an explanation of the systemic positioning of the concept of Civil Society that he formulates through a meticulous study of Hegel's own intellectual trajectory. This is a study that nonetheless by-passes Hegel's own logical-systemic reasoning on the grounds that 'the precise relationship of this logic to existing

---

12. Horstmann, 'The Role of Civil Society in Hegel's Political Philosophy', p. 224, our emphasis.
13. Horstmann, 'The Role of Civil Society in Hegel's Political Philosophy', p. 229.
14. Horstmann, 'The Role of Civil Society in Hegel's Political Philosophy', p. 231.
15. Horstmann, 'The Role of Civil Society in Hegel's Political Philosophy', p. 231.
16. Horstmann, 'The Role of Civil Society in Hegel's Political Philosophy', p. 231.

reality is one that has always remained quite unclear, in spite of Hegel's assurances to the contrary'.[17] This is the case even though Horstmann acknowledges that

> in the overall context of Hegelian philosophy, that which decides whether something should count as rational or not, is not what one generally calls reality, but rather speculative logic.[18]

Admittedly, Horstmann's interpretation is partly motivated by a desire to dispense with suggestions that Hegel might be read as some kind of advocate of political liberalism, given that such an interpretive approach must ultimately ignore the full implications of the system's subordination of civil society to the state. Even so, it is curious that Horstmann can acknowledge the role that the *Logic* is meant to play and yet ignore it completely when pointing to Hegel's supposed failure to justify his account of the relationship of Civil Society to the State, a failure that Horstmann thinks he has rendered visible by exposing the specific intellectual history leading Hegel to invoke the two concepts. We want to suggest that in order to agree that Hegel implicates himself in an unfortunate false inference from the demonstrated irrationality of civil society to an 'ideal of universal ethical life [...] as the existing manifestation of reason',[19] one must first dispense with the attempt to make sense of the *Philosophy of Right* in the light of a strict organization thesis of the sort we are proposing. Otherwise, the question remains whether the methodology of the interpretive approach that avoids appealing to the *Logic* is not after all responsible for imposing the supposed 'failures' of the system that this approach identifies. Indeed, as we will see in this and the next volume, the strict organization thesis provides the key to a precise appreciation of the relationship between Civil Society and the State and not merely of their differentiation. With these concerns in mind, let us turn now to the task of explaining the emergence of the concept of Civil Society within Ethical Life and the logic that underpins it.

CIVIL SOCIETY AS AN 'EXTERNAL STATE'

In Civil Society we encounter a process of categorial development that combines two previously established embodiments of freedom into a social system. The first two stages of the *Philosophy of Right* respectively establish the right of property-owning persons to commodity production and exchange relations ('Abstract Right')

---

17. Horstmann, 'The Role of Civil Society in Hegel's Political Philosophy', pp. 231-2.
18. Horstmann, 'The Role of Civil Society in Hegel's Political Philosophy', pp. 231-2.
19. Horstmann, 'The Role of Civil Society in Hegel's Political Philosophy', p. 231.

and the right of particular subjects to the satisfaction of their desires ('Morality'). Accordingly, Civil Society emerges as a system of productive and exchange relations through which particular subjects with property-owning power realize the right to the satisfaction of their desires. As to the form that this structure of relations takes, the *Philosophy of Right* explains that since Civil Society is ethical mind 'passed over into division, and into the phase of relation', property relations take the form of 'an association of members' in an 'abstract universality'.[20] In Civil Society we encounter

> an association of members as self-subsistent individuals in a universality which, because of their self-subsistence, is only abstract. Their association is brought about by their needs, by the legal system [...] and by an external organization for attaining their particular and common interests (PR §157).

In other words Civil Society takes the shape of a *formal* association that is at best *co-operative* or 'a unity of different persons [...] which is only a partnership'.[21] The members of this association exist as 'self-subsistent individuals' in the sense that, quite apart from whether they appreciate the social influences upon their formative identities, they do not recognize the necessary place of other individuals or social institutions in the definition of their identity *as individuals*. Indeed, given that they need not take each other or their social organizations to be integral to their own or each other's identity, in their capacity as units of agency functioning within Civil Society individuals are externally related to each other. Even their *'common* interests' are initially understood as an aggregation of their 'particular' interests rather than the manifestation of any non-reductive universal end or purpose. Their unity is an 'abstract universality' in that it is only grounded in the abstract determinations of the right of private property-ownership.

But Civil Society does not just accommodate individuals who are externally related to one another in the abovementioned sense. Instead it is a wholly 'external state' (PR §157). This means that within Civil Society *all* units of agency are externally related to one another *on some level*. That is, they manifest relations of externality even when on another level their relations within and amongst sub-groups or categories of units also happen to be internally related to one another. Regardless of their specific internal dynamics then, by comparison with the internal, organic differentiated unity that defines Hegel's concept of the State as a whole, Civil

---
20. Hegel, *PR*, §157.
21. Hegel, *PR*, §182 Addition.

Society's units of agency ultimately conform to the externality defining the formal universality of particularity that we sketched in Chapter Two.[22]

It follows from this understanding of Civil Society's externality that Civil Society does not simply represent the economic sphere that is externally related to the state understood as the institutions of government and associated agencies. MacGregor argues that Civil Society elaborates the capitalist economic system of bourgeois society along with its institutions of law and public authority, which constitute 'the modern representative state' that Marx described as 'a committee for managing the common affairs of the whole bourgeoisie'.[23] Hegel's Civil Society does indeed appear as such an 'external state'. It is thus a complete *externally combined system* of social—economic, legal and political—units. According to Hegel,

> Civil society contains three moments:
> (A) The mediation of need and one man's satisfaction through his work and the satisfaction of the needs of all others—the *System of Needs*.
> (B) The actuality of the universal principle of freedom therein contained—the protection of property through the *Administration of Justice*.
> (C) Provision against contingencies still lurking in systems (A) and (B), and care for particular interests as a common interest, by means of the *Police* and the *Corporation*.[24]

Following Onuf we can add here that Civil Society is thus an 'inclusive set of functional relations'.[25] As Onuf suggests, these relations consist in both vertically structured functional sectors and laterally structured 'ascending levels of institutional development'.[26] But what precisely is the status of these relations? Observing that Civil Society contains institutions whose universality is not reducible to that characterizing the economic sphere, Wilfried ver Eecke concludes that Civil Society therefore includes

---

22. For a discussion of Hegel's concept of organic unity see Sally Sedgwick 'The State as Organism: The Metaphysical Basis of Hegel's *Philosophy of Right*', *The Southern Journal of Philosophy*, vol. 39, no. 3, 2001, pp. 171-188; Michael Quante, '"Organic Unity": Its Loose and Analogical and its Strict and Systematic Sense in Hegel's Philosophy', *The Southern Journal of Philosophy*, vol. 39, no. 3, 2001, pp. 189-195.
23. David MacGregor, *The Communist Ideal in Hegel and Marx*, p. 195.
24. Hegel, *PR*, §188.
25. Onuf, 'Late Modern Civil Society', p. 54.
26. Onuf, 'Late Modern Civil Society', pp. 54-55.

its own conception of the political sphere.[27] Brod suggests instead that Hegel differentiates between higher and lower order governmental regulatory functions and Brod reserves the term 'political' for the former. According to Brod, in including legal administration and public regulatory bodies in his elaboration of the concept of Civil Society, Hegel's purpose was precisely to challenge the conflation of the *economic* regulatory functions of government, which Hegel treats under the concept of Civil Society, and the political legislative functions of government, which he addresses under the concept of the State.[28]

Despite their differences, the abovementioned readings by Brod and ver Eecke support the conclusion that it is a mistake to assign Hegel's concept of Civil Society to one or other of the two models of civil society that Alexander attributes to the history of the development of the concept—CSI, which incorporates everything but government, and CSII, which restricts civil society to capitalist market relations—that are admittedly of limited use in making sense of today's global reality. However, neither interpretation gives an explanation for why Hegel treats the differentiation that he makes as a matter of systemic necessity. If it is the case that Civil Society contains its own conception of the political, why must it do so? If the concept contains its own conception of economic regulation to the exclusion of governmental political legislative functions why is this necessary within the system?

On our analysis although in its abstractness Civil Society manifests the very being of modernity, because it is this being in its negative moment, it must be socially instituted in a way that affirms a *developing process* from its *as yet unrealized internally differentiated* unity of its various moments. As we will see in Chapter Six, Civil Society's three moments constitute its differentiation into its three distinct systems in accordance with their own degrees of externality, which form the economy or system of needs; the legal system; and the political system in the limited sense of a system for the provision of security and welfare or what Hegel calls the 'external organization for attaining [...] interests' which, in addition to the Police-Corporation, includes the system of the Estates as occupational divisions.[29] Significantly, this differentiation is

---

27. Wilfried ver Eecke, 'The Relation Between Economics and Politics in Hegel', in Donald Phillip Verene (ed.), *Hegel's Social and Political Thought: The Philosophy of Objective Spirit*, New Jersey, Harvester Press, 1980, pp. 91-101 at pp. 99-100.

28. Brod, *Hegel's Philosophy of Politics*, pp. 90-92.

29. Hegel, PR, §§188-256. Throughout this discussion we will be using the

achieved through the interplay of the logically preceding principles of Particularity and Universality. In other words, as we will demonstrate in Chapter Four, in the logical progression these two moments of the notion inform the initial appearance of Civil Society and give rise to the differentiated system.[30] As we indicated in Chapter Two, at this point in the notion's logical categorial progression the notion is in the process of *constructing* its comprehensive categorial differentiated unity. Even though it has already determined itself into a mutually informing *unity* of the categories of Universality, Particularity and Individuality, the same cannot yet be said of their differentiation. Consistently with their positioning within the P-moment characterizing the Syllogism of Necessity, here Particularity and Universality have lost their positive unity just in order to regain it through a self-determining process. Once we understand the specifics of the process of self-determination at this point in the logical categorial progression we will be in a position to identify the rationale underlying the details of Hegel's account of Civil Society as well as its usefulness for making sense of today's global reality. Horstmann points to the latter when he suggests that the concept of Civil Society manifests not only a 'moment of difference in relation to the true unity of Ethical Life, but *actually exists*, as it were, as this difference'.[31] In the remainder of this chapter we will turn to an examination of the categorial interplay defining the logic of the Hypothetical Syllogism.

THE HYPOTHETICAL SYLLOGISM

The terms of the Hypothetical Syllogism constitute an implicit unity, like the terms of the Categorical Syllogism that precedes it. (As we pointed out in Chapter Two, the Categorical Syllogism is the first of the three syllogistic forms that make up the Syllogism

---

term 'Estates' in preference to 'classes' to refer to the particular occupational systems Hegel has in mind in order to retain a clear distinction between occupational divisions and divisions in wealth and power. As Allen Wood explains, 'Estates rest on "concrete distinctions" between functionally different and complementary social positions and roles. Class distinctions rest on mere "inequalities" of birth, wealth, education, social status and self-valuation': Wood, *Hegel's Ethical Thought*, p. 251. On the significance of this distinction see also Bernard Cullen, 'The Mediating Role of Estates and Corporations in Hegel's Theory of Political Representation', in Bernard Cullen (ed.), *Hegel Today*, Aldershot, Gower Publishing Company, 1988, pp. 22-41 at p. 36, f.5.

30. Hegel, *PR*, §§182-187.
31. Horstmann, 'The Role of Civil Society in Hegel's Political Philosophy', p. 214, our emphasis.

of Necessity and its identity of content or substantial unity organizes the familial bond in accordance with the concept of the Family as the first moment of Ethical Life.) Their difference lies in the fact that the Hypothetical Syllogism's implicit unity is the identity of content that 'is also *posited* as such'.[32] According to Hegel, what we have here is a '*necessary relation*' of immediate beings.[33] This 'necessary relation' is formulated explicitly as the hypothetical judgement: "'If A is, then B is"; or, the being of A is equally the being of *another*, of B', whereas the syllogistic relation of the terms supplies the '*immediacy* of being':

If A is, then B is,
But A is,
Therefore B is.[34]

It is important to note here that the immediacy of being that the Syllogism introduces (A is) brings together the terms so that this immediate being is also affirmed as the mediating middle term:

> The syllogism contains the relation of subject and predicate, not as the abstract copula, but as the pregnant *mediating* unity. Accordingly, the being of A is to be taken *not as a mere immediacy*, but essentially as the *middle term of the syllogism*.[35]

In the same manner, 'B is in the form of *immediate* being, but equally has its being through an other, or is *mediated*'.[36] So this Syllogism expresses the contradictory relation in which both middle term and that which is mediated are also immediate beings. According to Hegel,

> A is the *mediating* being insofar as first it is an immediate being, an indifferent actuality, and secondly, insofar as it is no less an *intrinsically contingent*, self-sublating being.[37]

The 'necessary relation' that the Hypothetical judgement expresses has already determined that A has this double-sided character:

> the relation of the hypothetical judgement is *necessity* or inner *substantial identity* associated with external diversity of Existence, or mutual indifference of being in the sphere of Appearance—an identical *content* which forms the internal basis. The two sides of the judgement therefore do not appear

---

32. Hegel, *SL*, p. 701.
33. Hegel, *SL*, p. 698.
34. Hegel, *SL*, p. 698.
35. Hegel, *SL*, p. 699.
36. Hegel, *SL*, p. 700.
37. Hegel, *SL*, pp. 699-700.

as an immediate being but as a being held within the necessity and thus at the same time as *sublated* being or being only in the sphere of Appearance.[38]

The structure of the Hypothetical Syllogism thus exhibits immediacy of being and mediation in such a way as to reveal the split between the 'substantial identity' of being, its 'identical content', and the *form* of being. The former is taken to be an *inner* necessity in contrast to the objectively Universal, immediate substantial identity that defines the logically preceding Categorical Syllogism. As inner necessity the being in question is a substantial unity held together of necessity but this unity is not also characteristic of the *apparent* form of being. Accordingly, from the standpoint of the notion's categorial progression in the structure of relations defining the Hypothetical Syllogism, being 'sublates' itself; it is an *apparent* being and its way of appearing is as contingent.

Contrary to its substantial identity, the form of being that the Hypothetical Syllogism expresses appears as immediate yet mediating *and* mediated. In other words although A and B are, on one level, identical in terms of their content they do not appropriate this substantial identity. At the level of 'Appearance'—the level at which there is mere existence in diversity—A and B do not exhibit their intrinsic relatedness and they appear as mutually indifferent. However, the being of A is shown not to be exhausted in its apparent immediacy given its relation to B. Furthermore, the move beyond the Hypothetical *judgement* to a concern with actual being renders it explicit that we have a *contingent* being—a being that is not unconditional or fully self-determining. In the Hypothetical Syllogism immediacy is exhibited (*A is*) together with its sublation (*A's* being is necessarily related to *B's* being) and this is made explicit in the kind of mediating activity in which A is engaged.

As terms of the Hypothetical judgement A and B exhibit Universality and Individuality:

> as sides of the judgement they [A and B] stand to one another as *universality* and *individuality*; one of them, therefore, is the above content [the inner substantial identity] as *totality of conditions*, the other as *actuality*. It is however, indifferent which side is taken as universality and which as individuality.[39]

As the 'totality of conditions' Universality and Individuality are interchangeable since in the Hypothetical judgement the conditions are universal in so far as they 'are still the *inner, abstract* side of an

---

38. Hegel, *SL*, p. 699.
39. Hegel, *SL*, p. 699.

actuality' or the conditions are *'separated, scattered,* Appearance' (Individuality) that obtains a 'universally valid existence' in 'actuality'.⁴⁰ The Universality of the totality of the conditions is thus abstract and dependent upon the conditions being brought together as an actuality out of their external diversity of existence. The Syllogism exhibits this actuality in the being of Particularity (*B* is) since it is the conditioned being of the Particular that renders explicit the mediating activity of the Universal. At the same time, the Particular's actuality is not just its own but the actuality of the Universal as well. (By way of contrast, compare the conclusion of the Categorical Syllogism that strictly organizes the concept of the Family. There the predicate expresses the totality of specific difference whereas the subject, the Particularized Individual, expresses the actuality of the totality qua member of the totality and so Individuality exhibits only *the principle* of specific difference.⁴¹)

According to Hegel, in the Hypothetical Syllogism the conditions that we have just outlined become an actuality through *'individuality* as self-related *negative* unity'.⁴²

> The conditions are a scattered material that waits and demands to be used; this *negativity* is the mediating element, the free unity of the Notion. It determines itself as *activity* since the middle term is the contradiction of the *objective universality* or the totality of the identical content, and the *indifferent immediacy.* This middle term is therefore no longer an inner necessity, but a *necessity* that is; the objective universality contains self-relation as a *simple immediacy,* as being.⁴³

In that it mediates, the Universal contradicts the 'identical content' that characterizes the totality of conditions (and the Notion's moments) as well as the indifference that characterizes its apparent immediacy. In this way it exhibits the 'free unity of the Notion'. However, the Universal also exhibits the *negative* unity of the moments of the Notion since the contradiction exhibits the identical content as involving a relation of necessity rather than freedom. Since the middle term exhibits the *necessity* of relatedness in this kind of unity, objective Universality 'contains self-relation as a simple immediacy' in the sense that although the Universal does

---

40. Hegel, *SL*, p. 699.
41. For an elaboration of the significance of this for appreciating the concept of the Family see Nicolacopoulos and Vassilacopoulos, *Hegel and the Logical Structure of Love*, Part III.
42. Hegel, *SL*, p. 700.
43. Hegel, *SL*, p. 700.

indeed mediate it does not *incorporate* mediation in its self-relation. The mediation characteristic of the Hypothetical Syllogism amounts to a negation of the kind of mediation that the Categorical Syllogism exhibits. This is because in the Categorical Syllogism the being of the middle term is its positive substantial unity in its 'determination of the extremes' even though the extremes effect mediation. In the Hypothetical Syllogism even though it does the mediating, 'the middle term itself in its objectivity is now also being', a being that is characterized by simple immediacy and so does not thematize itself but rather *is as necessity*.[44]

Accordingly, this Syllogism exhibits objective Universality—the identical content of the moments of the notion that is not as yet identical form—as the appearance of immediate being in its contradiction. At the level of appearance the unconditional unity of the notion is a negative unity of an indifferent abstract Universality and a Particularity that is the actuality of, yet equally indifferent to, the Universal. This state of affairs posits the implicitness of the unity of the Syllogism.

---

44. Hegel, *SL*, p. 700.

4. CIVIL SOCIETY AS A SYSTEM OF INTERDEPENDENCE

How might the analysis of the Hypothetical Syllogism assist in making sense of Civil Society? The *Philosophy of Right* attributes three noteworthy features to Civil Society's initial appearance. Firstly, it presents the characteristics of subjective Particularity and formal Universality as they appear in isolation from each other. Secondly, it identifies the nature of the contribution of each of these to their relation in 'division' and, thirdly, it links their underlying unity to the shape that the Idea gives to Civil Society.[1] How then does the form of the Hypothetical Syllogism shed light on the meaning and rationale underpinning these aspects of the order of Civil Society? To begin with, note that on the face of it the two principles of Civil Society, the principles of Particularity and Universality, are presented as related to each other in terms similar to the moments of the Hypothetical Syllogism's notion. If the unity that the Hypothetical Syllogism manifests characterizes that of Civil Society, then following the analysis of the previous section, we should expect the two principles of Civil Society to *appear* as immediacies that are nevertheless *necessarily* related. Furthermore, we should expect their reality to amount to *the positing of the implicitness of the principle of inter-subjectivity* as the existential expression of the notion's self-determination.

To lend support to this interpretive claim we will draw upon two strategies concurrently. The first is to appeal to those statements in the *Philosophy of Right* that refer to the *Logic* and indeed seem to be alluding to the form and reasoning that define the Hypothetical Syllogism and the second is to draw upon our analysis of the Hypothetical Syllogism itself in order to fill in what

---

1. Hegel, *PR*, §§182-187.

appear to be some of the gaps in the presentation of Civil Society in the *Philosophy of Right*. Together these strategies will hopefully result in a coherent account of the nature of the unity of Civil Society in its initial appearance.

CIVIL SOCIETY'S TWO PRINCIPLES: PARTICULAR PERSONS AND THE FORM OF UNIVERSALITY

The *Philosophy of Right* introduces the two principles of Civil Society as follows:

> The concrete person who is himself the object of his particular aims, is, as a totality of wants and a mixture of caprice and physical necessity, one principle of Civil society. But the particular person is essentially so related to other particular persons that each establishes himself and finds satisfaction by means of the others, and at the same time purely and simply by means of the form of universality, the second principle here.[2]

The principle of Particularity manifests as the self-interested concrete person, a 'totality of [whimsical and physical] wants' who is only instrumentally related to others. For Hegel, this combination of characteristics represents the 'singularity' of the concrete person but Hegel does not explain why this should be so in Civil Society.[3] As part of a philosophical anthropology the qualities in question are familiar enough but Hegel cannot take them for granted. To be sure, in the context of the development of the abstract right to welfare, the *Philosophy of Right* establishes that in the sphere of Morality the subject is constituted as desiring but this does not explain why the concept of the person should emerge in Civil Society as a totality of wants. Why should the self-interested person define subjectivity in what is considered to be Ethical Life? Nor does Hegel explain why the principle of Universality should be only formal except to say that it is still only the 'inward principle' of Particularity and that the 'characteristic embodiment' of each of the principles is the one given to them as moments of the Idea in its stage of division.[4]

James argues, without drawing upon the *Logic*, that the self-interest of Civil Society's individuals emerges as an unintended consequence of the multiplication of needs and the means of their satisfaction whereas the universal element arises through their co-dependence. This explanation forms part of James' account of the

---
2. Hegel, *PR*, §182.
3. Hegel, *PR*, §187.
4. Hegel, *PR*, §181 and §184.

various aspects of Civil Society's subjective particularity, which draws on a reading of the *Philosophy of Right* in terms of the progressive development of a notion of subjectivity whose increasing self-awareness gives rise to weak and strong forms of ethical subjectivism that must be countered.[5] But notice that within such a broadly conceived interpretive framework one could just as easily reverse the order of explanation that James offers. For example, in the present context one could equally plausibly argue that it is the multiplication of needs and their means of satisfaction that emerge as an unintended consequence of persons' self-interest, rather than the reverse. By contrast, David Kolb tries to explain Hegel's characterization of the two principles of Civil Society by appeal to 'The Notion', an earlier point in the logical categorial progression than that of the Syllogism.[6] In this context Kolb proposes a rather neat formulation of the division between the Universal form and Particular content of Civil Society. On his analysis the organization of Civil Society manifests its categorial unity in terms of particular differences and formally universal institutions that together bring about a new kind of unity emphasizing the difference between Universality and Particularity. For Kolb, on Hegel's view 'modernity entails both individual rights and formal institutions' because form and content have been divided between Universality and Particularity respectively and their separation means that there is no internal connection between them, 'no principle in the formal institutions and no pre-adaptation in the particular content to account for the unity between them'.[7] Kolb's discussion of the *Logic* remains fairly general so it is not evident from this perspective that the form-content division he identifies manifests only *a single aspect* of the operative categorial interplay. However, a different picture emerges once we take into account the relatively more sophisticated relations of the syllogistic terms. From this perspective the recourse to an earlier stage in the logical categorial progression will not suffice to explain the nature of the form-content relations that obtain with Civil Society's two principles.

Developing the syllogistic analysis of Civil Society's two principles we should note that following the transition to the Hypothetical Syllogism from the Categorical Syllogism, the identical content (objective Universality) that is the principle of the moments as extremes of the Categorical Syllogism is still only 'inner'

---

5. James, *Hegel's Philosophy of Right*, pp. 64-71.
6. Kolb, *The Critique of Pure Modernity*, pp. 65-69.
7. Kolb, *The Critique of Pure Modernity*, pp. 67-68.

in the sense that it captures their implicit principle but not their concrete being as a whole. Moreover, even though their categorial interrelation is not an element of the self-definition of each—they appear as self-subsistent—each *has being* to the extent that the other has being. We have already seen that the Hypothetical judgement renders explicit the necessity of this relation and that the Hypothetical Syllogism as a whole exhibits a reality consisting of an 'inner substantial identity' held together of necessity and existing only in 'the sphere of Appearance'. In the sphere of appearance or 'external diversity of Existence' the notion's moments do not exhibit their intrinsic relatedness since they fail to appropriate their substantial identity and thus sublate their (substantial) being.

As the manifestation of the unity of the Hypothetical Syllogism's middle term, Civil Society is

> the system of the Ethical order, split into its extremes and lost, which constitutes the Idea's abstract moment, its moment of reality. Here the Idea is present only as a relative totality and as the inner necessity behind this outward appearance.[8]

The 'relative totality' of the Idea is present through its moments since the Ethical order is here 'split into its extremes' and it is this 'split' that renders the totality relative. At this point in the logical unfolding of the notion and its corresponding real manifestation, the notion is a *totality* in that it has achieved its internal categorial *unity* but it is nevertheless only relative because the affirmation of this identity is secured through the being of its moments that have come apart and therefore do not also exhibit internal categorial *differentiatedness*.

Moreover, as the other of 'the immediate unity of the family [that] has fallen apart into a plurality', Civil Society exhibits the notion's moment of differentiation that was not properly accounted for previously.[9] The 'outward appearance' of Civil Society is the appearance of 'its moments which have now won their freedom and their determinate existence' in the sense that their determinate existence as self-subsistent has made explicit the notion's moment of differentiation.[10] Recall however that the notion's moment of differentiation is exhibited in the structure of relations constructed from the standpoint of the unconditional middle term and as such is the negation of the mediation characterizing the Categorical Syllogism. Accordingly, the differentiatedness of the principles

---

8. Hegel, *PR*, §184.
9. Hegel, *PR*, §184 Addition.
10. Hegel, *PR*, §184 Addition.

of Civil Society is of a kind that *does not recognize mediation*. Civil Society's principles must thus appear as immediate and therefore mutually indifferent. This indifference is not to be understood in terms of the obliviousness of each to the presence of the other but rather in terms of the *irrelevance* of the other to one's self-definition since all are related in a way that exhibits and affirms their respective immediacy. This is why it is a mistake to represent the Hegelian concept of Civil Society as diffusely inclusive. (This, as we saw in Chapter One, is the view of contemporary theorists of civil society.) The Hypothetical Syllogism exhibits a negative unity, or *relation as the lack of unity*, as distinct from the lack of relation. Each principle is what it is in the sphere of Appearance *irrespective* of the other, even though it can only affirm its being *through* the other. This also explains why the concrete person appears as self-interested. Since the principles are self-grounded (because self-subsistent) they have also acquired their 'characteristic embodiment' as a matter of 'right'. Next we will go on to consider how this characteristic embodiment of Civil Society's principles of Universality and Particularity takes shape within a system of interdependence pursuant to the Hypothetical Syllogism's form of necessity.

THE SYSTEM OF INTERDEPENDENCE

We have been tracing the unconditionality of Civil Society's two principles in the light of their conformity with the logic characterizing the Hypothetical Syllogism. Notwithstanding our observations so far, the unconditionality of the Universal and the Particular is at best *formal* given that neither principle can produce its self-determined realization alone. The being of one principle can only be affirmed through that of the other. As we saw when analyzing the Hypothetical Syllogism, the Universal appears as 'negativity', as a 'scattered material waiting and demanding to be used', while Particularity is this material as actuality 'gathered into an individuality'. Similarly, the one actuality of Civil Society's two principles emerges as follows.

> In the course of the actual attainment of selfish ends—an attainment conditioned in this way by universality—there is formed a system of complete interdependence, wherein the livelihood, happiness and legal status of one man is interwoven with the livelihood, happiness and rights of all. On this system, individual happiness etc., depend, and only in this connected system are they actualized and secured.[11]

---

11. Hegel, *PR*, §183.

In this way the sociality of the concrete person is exhibited as *necessity* that is the *enabling condition* for the subjective attainment of formal freedom. (Necessity also underpins the limitedness of this kind of freedom but we will return to this point in Chapter Five.)

Because each principle must affirm its being through the other while retaining its immediate appearance, the *other* can only have instrumental significance for it. The sense in which this is the case for the Universal as well as for the Particular appears from the way in which each principle exhibits its contradictory form. As manifestations of the categorial interplay characterizing the Hypothetical Syllogism, the principles of Particularity and Universality must also exhibit their respective contradictory forms as *mediated immediacy* and *mediating immediacy*. That is, they must show themselves to be mutually indifferent and contradicting their immediacy in so far as they are intrinsically contingent, self-sublating and thus dependent on the other for their being. This is the rational ground for Hegel's description of the respective 'right' of each principle:

> to particularity [... the Idea] gives the right to develop and launch forth in all directions; and to universality the right to prove itself not only the ground and necessary form of particularity, but also the authority standing over it and its final end.[12]

THE LOGIC OF PRIVATE PERSONS' SELF-INTEREST AND THE INHERENT DIVERSITY OF LIMITED NEED SATISFACTION

The principle of Particularity has the 'right' to pursue its own unrestrained satisfaction because the concrete person of Civil Society manifests the characteristics of a mediated immediacy. Let us consider briefly the specific details of this requirement. As already suggested, in so far as the person of Civil Society is a totality, his or her self-sense is not inter-subjective but an immediate self-relation that is self-grounded and requires embodiment as such. (Call this 'the requirement of subjective unconditionality'.) Still, as a *relative* totality the affirmation of his or her being can only be secured through the being of another. Accordingly, the self-affirmation of the concrete person (the way in which he or she 'establishes himself [or herself] and finds satisfaction') is not yet self-grounded or absolute. In order to exhibit both the unconditionality of the person's immediate self-relation and the reality that

---

12. Hegel, *PR*, §184.

this self-relation is as yet not unconditionally realizable, the concrete person—Civil Society's principle of Particularity—must exhibit *limited self-affirmation*.

This limited self-affirmation takes the shape of the limited satisfaction of needs. In the present context the term 'need' is preferable to 'desire' in order to emphasize that the Particular takes satisfaction to be a matter of a socially instituted 'right' and that irrespective of their specific character—Civil Society treats 'needs, accidental caprices and subjective desires' in the same terms—the desires and needs in question are taken up as *self-grounded need*.[13] Indeed, the requirement of subjective unconditionality takes the shape of the satisfaction of one's own privately defined needs.[14] The reason is that only *particular satisfaction* can exhibit completeness in this structure of relations and thereby give expression to the person's self-grounded self-relation. At the same time, while the Particularity of the satisfied needs exhibits satisfaction in its completeness, this kind of satisfaction of Particularity is always also only *an instance* of satisfaction. In this sense it is also limited. Limited need satisfaction thus manifests the principle of Particularity as the concrete person whose subjective unconditionality (immediacy) is simultaneously not absolutely realizable. This manifests the contradictory form of mediated immediacy.

According to Hegel,

> the satisfaction of need, necessary and accidental alike, is accidental because it breeds new desires without end, is in thoroughgoing dependence on caprice and external accident, and is held in check by the power of universality.[15]

The satisfaction of need gives rise to infinite need that takes the form of an inherent diverse multiplicity. Need functions like the repetition of mirror images that is produced when two mirrors face each other; it is 'carried on to the false infinite'.[16] On our analysis the rationale underlying this claim about the generation of infinite need out of satisfaction also has to do with the relativity of the person as a totality. Infinite need is presented as arising from particular satisfaction in order to exhibit limited satisfaction that, as already suggested, involves two conditions: the presence of particular satisfaction and the lack of infinite satisfaction. Because

---

13. Hegel, *PR*, §185.
14. Hegel, *PR*, §187.
15. Hegel, *PR*, §185.
16. Hegel, *PR*, §185 Addition.

the affirmation of the person's self-relation as such can never be complete in this kind of categorial relation, the satisfaction of one need inevitably gives rise to other needs.[17] Moreover, since infinite need cannot be satisfied, and since the reality of the non-satisfiability of need as such manifests the limitedness of satisfaction, Hegel presents needs as only finite and 'accidentally' satisfiable; needs are dependent upon 'caprice and external accident'.

A final point to note is that limited satisfaction manifests the dependence of the Particular's subjective unconditionality on the Universal for the affirmation of its being. Satisfaction is also 'accidental' and limited in that it is 'held in check by the power of universality' since the relation exhibits the relativity of the person's totality. If the self-subsistent concrete person were able to achieve satisfaction without reliance upon an external Universal he or she would not be *merely subjectively* self-determining.

Given the logical structure of limited satisfaction, the concrete person's outlook is characterized by an apparent openness to social influences without loss of the person's sense of himself or herself as the self-grounded source of his or her needs. This is why Civil Society presents the concrete person as no more than a 'totality of wants'. It follows from the conception of need in the terms already discussed that need is understood in abstraction from inter-subjectively generated content. As a combination of needs the person himself or herself appears as the adequate source of needs. Wanting something is on the face of it a sufficient ground for the demand to satisfaction since as subjective unconditionality the person takes himself or herself to be the only legitimate source of content. Furthermore, the nature of specific needs—their precise source and determinate content—is unimportant to the rational aspect of need satisfaction. (This is not to say however that the *rational result* of satisfaction emerges from the satisfaction of wants whatever their source and content.) The mediated immediate person is intrinsically contingent and self-sublating and as such does not invoke an objectively Universal substantive being to provide an absolute ground for the formation of specific needs.

---

17. Observing similarities in the views of Hegel and Rousseau on the 'pathological tendencies of modern expansive desires', Jeffrey Church explains Hegel's references to the multiplication of desires in terms of the desire of particularity to 'assert oneself as different from and superior to others': Jeffrey Church, 'The Freedom of Desire: Hegel's Response to Rousseau on the Problem of Civil Society', *American Journal of Political Science*, vol. 54, no. 1, 2012, pp. 125-139 at pp. 127-130. But Church leaves unexplained Hegel's reasons for treating this phenomenon within his account of the system of right.

'Individuals in their capacity as burghers in this state are private persons whose end is their own interest'.[18]

THE LOGIC OF PUBLIC ACTIVITY AND INTER-SUBJECTIVE RELATIONS

The logical categorial interrelation that constructs the Particular as a mediated immediate, and hence the person of Civil Society as a singularity, also explains the conception of inter-subjective relations operating within Civil Society. If the conceptions of the person and inter-subjective relations are similarly based on the construction of Particularity in terms of the Hypothetical Syllogism's mediated immediacy, then mirroring personal activity, public activity must also be defined solely in terms of self-interested desire and instrumental relations. As Hegel puts it, the self-interested end of private persons 'is *mediated* through the universal which thus *appears* as a *means* to its realization'.[19] So the very same instrumental orientation characterizes both the singular person who is needful in the ways already discussed, and the public activity that defines inter-subjective relations.

This conception of inter-subjectivity finds its place in 'the system of complete interdependence' that is 'prima facie regarded as the external state, the state based on need, the state as the Understanding envisages it'.[20] This state of external Universality also exhibits its contradictory form as a mediating immediate. Recall that Universality is given 'the right to prove itself not only the ground and necessary form of particularity but also the authority standing over it and its final end'.[21] Through its mediating activity the Universal secures satisfaction and in this way affirms its own being as 'the ground and necessary form of particularity'.[22]

As well as mediating, the Universal exhibits its immediacy in that it appears as a formal association *irrespective of Particularity*. The external state is not formed through the agreement of participating individuals. Given the free play and infinite multiplication of needs and given that the Universal's affirmation of its being depends upon the satisfaction of these needs, the Universal exhibits the affirmation of its being in its perpetual capacity to cater

---

18. Hegel, PR, §187.
19. Hegel, PR, §187.
20. Hegel, PR, §183.
21. Hegel, PR, §184.
22. Hegel, PR, §184.

for whatever needs arise. From the standpoint of the Universal, the person's treatment of the Universal as a means is *the means* through which the Universal shows itself to be the person's 'final end'.[23] This is because, irrespective of the person's intentions, the person's activity results in the enhancement of the Universal's capacity to satisfy needs. This discrepancy between subjective willing and the results of this willing constitutes the Universal's 'proof' that it is indeed Particularity's *final end*.

At the same time the Universal depends for its own being on the concrete subject. According to Hegel,

> it is from this particularity that the universal derives the content which fills it as well as its character as infinite self-determination.[24]

So the affirmation of its being is also not complete but relative. In its mediating activity the (formal) Universal reveals that the Universal cannot realize itself unconditionally. Although the formal association appears to be unconditional, it realizes this unconditionality only to the extent that it is *the form* that the Particular fills with content.

A final point to note is that the activity that the Universal depends on to affirm its being (though not consisting of a conscious decision or agreement between participants) must involve persons' willingness to postpone the satisfaction of their needs.[25] For in the absence of the postponement of need satisfaction, needs would be either unsatisfiable or *immediately* satisfiable. In both cases the externally related Universal would have no role to play in securing their satisfaction. Although Hegel does not explicitly refer to the activity of postponing the satisfaction of one's needs, he implies as much in his description of the individual's liberation from his or her singularity.

---

23. Hegel, *PR*, §184.

24. Hegel, *PR*, §187 Remark: Hegel claims that 'particularity itself is present in ethical life as infinitely independent free subjectivity'. The 'principle of subjective freedom' is 'the principle of the self-subsistent inherently infinite personality of the individual': Hegel, *PR*, §185 Remark. The reality of Civil Society accounts for the 'inherent infinity' of both the Particular and the Universal in that these principles appear as immediacies that retain their appearance as immediate even as they are mediating/mediated. Recall the analysis of the Hypothetical Syllogism regarding this point.

25. Niklas Luhmann discusses the relevance of the postponement of need satisfaction to the economic sphere. See Niklas Luhmann, *The Differentiation of Society*, trans. Stephen Holmes and Charles Larmore, New York, Columbia University Press, 1982, pp. 190-225.

In the individual subject, this liberation is the hard struggle against pure subjectivity of demeanour, against the immediacy of desire, against the empty subjectivity of feeling and the caprice of inclination.[26]

This 'hard struggle', the postponement of satisfaction, is not only indispensable for the affirmation of the Universal's being but it also alerts us to the temporality of the interaction between the concrete person and the Universal. Together, the Particular's activity of postponement and the Universal's activity of securing need satisfaction manifest a form of mediation that generates a shared time. But, here, time appears as part of the means through which need satisfaction is capable of being secured and postponed. So this combination of mediating and mediated activity gives effect to time that is instrumental in character.

---

26. Hegel, PR, §187 Remark.

5. CIVIL SOCIETY'S ETHICAL ASPECT AND GLOBAL SIGNIFICANCE

We have been tracing some of the features of the emergence of a form of mediation between instrumentally related Particular subjects and the Universal ends to which their inter-subjectively mediated, self-interested actions give rise. But for Hegel there is a further, ethically significant, consequence flowing from the resulting unity of the Universal and the Particular. For, at this point Civil Society also exhibits the 'interest of the Idea', an interest that is not reducible to the instrumental external reflection of Particularity. When the principle of Particularity 'passes over into' Universality as an outcome of the employment of means-end rationality, this form of rationality ceases to characterize the unity.[1] That is, in so far as the instrumental aspect of the relationship of Particularity to formal Universality is overcome through the necessity of their relation, the situation gives rise to the possibility of the ethical development of subjective Particularity.[2]

Hegel scholars typically interpret the ethicality of Civil Society in terms of the provision of structures of mutuality for the free individual. For example, Terry Pinkard suggests that

> what makes civil society "ethical" *sittlich*, what makes it a common enterprise, has to do in the first place with the way in which the structures of the market compel individuals to take account of the particular needs and wants of others, so that the individual's pursuit of his private interests turns out to require a mediated form of mutuality in order for that pursuit to be successful.[3]

Thomas Wartenberg suggests that in compelling individuals to work together the market builds wealth and thereby enables the

---
1. Hegel, *PR*, §186.
2. Hegel, *PR*, §187.
3. Pinkard, *Hegel: A Biography*, p. 483.

realization of human freedom.⁴ However, such explanations do not suffice since, as Wartenberg recognizes, Hegel also makes the point that given this very compulsion, the unity of subjective Particularity with the Universal 'is present here [in Civil Society] not as freedom but as necessity'.⁵ Wartenberg reads this as a reference to measures, such as taxation, which individuals perceive to be against their own interests despite their being taken in the universal interest.⁶ But there is no reason to think that the members of Civil Society will respond in this way only to a select range of their experiences. It follows that engaging in collaborative activity as such, although necessary, is not sufficient to explain the ethicality of Civil Society.

Furthermore, at the same time as explicitly presenting Civil Society as an aspect of Ethical Life, Hegel also acknowledges the devastating effects that life in this associational form will have on sections of the population. He speaks in terms of both a 'physical *and* ethical degeneration'.⁷ Famously, Hegel draws attention to the social cost of overproduction, the creation of poverty, and the need to expand Civil Society's (labour) markets as a consequence.⁸ He also observes that unimpeded Civil Society not only produces poverty and surplus labour, but it may also lead to the creation of a 'rabble of paupers', that is a class of unemployed poor whose exclusion from the benefits of Civil Society has given rise to an attitude of 'inner indignation against the rich, against society, against the government'.⁹ Hegel presents the Police and the Corporations as the appropriate institutions for addressing poverty.¹⁰ But, as Wood points out, Hegel introduces these measures as 'mere palliatives' rather than as solutions.¹¹ These references raise the interpretive question of their significance for the development of the concept of right.

In Chapter Two we noted the postcolonial critiques of Hegel's view of history and its implication in racist ideologies. Applied to the present context such critiques take Hegel's references to the expansion of markets, including the establishment of new labour

---

4. Thomas E. Wartenberg, 'Poverty and Class Structure in Hegel's Theory of Civil Society', *Philosophy and Social Criticism*, vol. 8, 1981, pp. 169-182 at p. 171.
5. Hegel, *PR*, §186.
6. Wartenberg, 'Poverty and Class Structure in Hegel's Theory of Civil Society', p. 174.
7. Hegel, *PR*, §185, our emphasis.
8. Hegel, *PR*, §244 and §246.
9. Hegel, *PR*, §244 and §244 Addition.
10. Hegel, *PR*, §248-§249; §253-§253 Remark.
11. Wood, *Hegel's Ethical Thought*, p. 248.

markets through 'colonizing activity' as legitimating *imperialist* colonization.[12] For example, Robert Bernasconi argues that when combined with his account of Africa 'as a land without history and without *Bildung*' and hence as benefiting from the transformative effects of European slavery on the relatively inferior forms of slavery practiced by Africans, these references in the *Philosophy of Right* 'provided a potent justification for the exploitation of a continent'.[13] According to Hegel, Civil Society's colonizing activity provides it with 'a new demand and field for its industry' and at the same time the unemployed poor, who lacking membership in a Corporation cannot receive such support, have the opportunity to resettle in the colonies and thus 'return to life on the family basis in a new land'.[14] But, not only did Hegel mistakenly assume that the newly independent colonies would have the purchasing power to create new markets.[15] As Neuhouser comments, if the Hegelian account of Civil Society is taken to treat 'the earth as a whole as the unit that aspires to self-sufficiency, then poverty amongst one social group seems to be addressed at the expense of the rights of 'the original inhabitants of the colonized lands'.[16]

Neuhouser himself does not favour such a reading. He argues instead that Hegel's discussion of poverty shows that his account of the modern social world ultimately fails to meet its own criteria of rationality. This is because in proposing colonization as a solution to the problem of poverty Hegel's account of Civil Society 'relies on something outside itself to achieve its ends'.[17] On Klaus Hartmann's systemic reading, however, the treatment of poverty points instead to the necessity of the state as a 'higher categorical structure'.[18] Wood believes that Hegel's discussion of poverty rather suggests an indictment against the state, which, however, Hegel was never inclined to make.[19] Schlomo Avineri maintains that although Hegel's treatment of poverty represents an anomaly within the system, his intellectual honesty leads Hegel to raise an issue he implicitly admits he cannot solve.[20] But sympathetic

12. Hegel, PR, §248 and §248 Addition.
13. Bernasconi, 'Hegel at the Court of the Ashanti', p. 62.
14. Hegel, PR, §248; §248 Addition.
15. Butler, 'The Coming World Welfare State which Hegel Could Not See', p. 170.
16. Neuhouser, *Foundations of Hegel's Social Philosophy*, p. 173.
17. Neuhouser, *Foundations of Hegel's Social Philosophy*, p. 173.
18. Hartmann, 'Towards a New Systematic Reading', p. 120.
19. Wood, *Hegel's Ethical Thought*, p. 250.
20. Schlomo Avineri, *Hegel's Theory of the Modern State*, Cambridge, Cambridge University Press, 1980.

readings insist that we ought not lose sight of the fact that Hegel situates his discussion of the problem of poverty and its solutions in the context of seeking to elaborate an *ethical concept*. From this perspective, it has been argued that Hegel's aim is to draw critical attention to the workings of a *free market* economy in order to explain his normative preference for a *regulated* economy.[21]

Stedman Jones and Brod both argue against reading Hegel's account of poverty through normative and sociological categories, whether liberal or Marxist, given that such approaches introduce unnecessary confusions into the Hegel's account of Civil Society.[22] Stedman Jones illustrates this point when he notes that the sociological reading of Hegel's references to poverty renders unintelligible Hegel's peculiar elaboration of the concept of the Corporation, which 'did not even compose an inchoate part of an emerging system of modern social and political forms'.[23] For, if we were to read the references to the creation of a 'rabble of paupers' under the conditions of Civil Society as Hegel's anticipation of the sociological phenomenon of an emergent permanent underclass along the lines of a Marxist reading, we would need to understand his elaboration of the Corporation as attempting to offer a normative solution to this social problem in which the function of the Corporation would be to *prevent* the emergence of a rabble. But on such a reading, one could not then consistently attribute to Hegel a belief in the *inevitability* of the rabble's emergence.[24]

The dominant view amongst Hegel scholars is that Hegel took poverty to be unavoidable in Civil Society. Avineri, Hartmann, Wood, Neuhouser and, more recently, Slavoj Žižek are in agreement that for Hegel Civil Society *necessarily* produces the problem of poverty.[25] As Wood puts it,

21. Walton, 'Economy, Utility and Community in Hegel's Theory of Civil Society'; Plant, *Hegel: An Introduction*, p. 228; and Stephen Houlgate, *Freedom, Truth and History: An Introduction to Hegel's Philosophy*, London and New York, Routledge, 1991, pp. 109-115.

22. Gareth Stedman Jones, 'Hegel and the Economics of Civil Society', p. 125; Brod, *Hegel's Philosophy of Politics*, p. 4.

23. Stedman Jones, 'Hegel and the Economics of Civil Society', p. 125. According to Pinkard, Hegel endorsed 'some of the corporate structures of the ancien régime': Pinkard, *Hegel: A Biography*, p. 484.

24. Stedman Jones, 'Hegel and the Economics of Civil Society', p. 126.

25. Avineri, *Hegel's Theory of the Modern State*; Hartmann, 'Towards a New Systematic Reading', p. 120; Wood, *Hegel's Ethical Thought*, p. 249; Neuhouser, *Foundations of Hegel's Social Philosophy*, pp. 172-174; and Slavoj Žižek, *Less than Nothing: Hegel and the Shadow of Dialectical Materialism*, London & New York, Verso, 2012, p. 433.

poverty in civil society is no accident. It is not a result of contingent imperfections that befall a rational system when it achieves outward existence, or of the arbitrary will of individuals. Part of the evil of poverty is that it subjects people's lives to contingency but poverty is not itself a contingent feature of civil society.[26]

There are exceptions, such as Richard Teichgraeber who objects that Hegel gives 'some account of how poverty comes into being, but he cannot explain why it *has* to be'. Teichgraeber sees this as an intellectual failure on Hegel's part.[27] But other commentators, like Stephen Houlgate and Paul Franco, distinguish between what they see as the *preventability* of the emergence of a rabble of paupers in the sense of a permanent underclass, on the one hand, and Hegel's acknowledgement of the inevitability of poverty, on the other.[28] For Franco, for example, 'Hegel's understanding of what might count as a solution to the problem of poverty is very much determined by his concern to prevent the emergence of a rabble'. This, Franco suggests, is why Hegel rejects solutions such as the provision of welfare payments funded by a direct taxation of the rich or the creation of work for the poor in favour of mutual aid amongst members of the Corporations and the expansion of markets by the Police.[29] Whereas the former solutions reinforce the likelihood of a rabble being formed/perpetuated, the latter reinstate the unemployed poor as *rights bearing members* of Civil Society. Franco suggests that although Hegel himself fails to provide comprehensive solutions in response to the emergence of poverty, this does not pose an insurmountable problem for Civil Society's ethicality since his own suggestions can be supplemented on the basis of the sound criteria he offers for identifying the appropriate solutions to poverty.[30] In a similar vein, more recent discussions argue for the extension and adaptation of Hegel's assertion of rights and duties with respect to so-called 'domestic' poverty to the current reality of decolonization, postcolonial settings and global poverty.[31]

---

26. Wood, *Hegel's Ethical Thought*, p. 249.
27. Richard Teichgraeber, 'Hegel on Property and Poverty', *Journal of the History of Ideas* vol. 38, 1977, pp. 47-64, at p. 58.
28. Houlgate, *Freedom, Truth and History*, p. 114; Franco, *Hegel's Philosophy of Freedom*, pp. 270-271.
29. Franco, *Hegel's Philosophy of Freedom*, pp. 272-273.
30. Franco, *Hegel's Philosophy of Freedom*, p. 275.
31. Lydia L. Moland, 'A Hegelian Approach to Global Poverty', in Andrew Buchwalter (ed.), *Hegel and Global Justice*, New York and London, Springer, 2012, pp. 131-154; Joel Anderson, 'Hegel's Implicit View on how to Solve the Problem of

Another source of disagreement is the question of the status of the rabble in Hegel's theory. Those who discuss Hegel's assignment of a distinctive socio-economic class status to the rabble nevertheless disagree on whether or not he also takes the members of this class to hold a right of rebellion against society.[32]

What should we make of the abovementioned discussions, disagreements and proposals? Is it the case that underpinning Hegel's references to Civil Society's 'physical and ethical degeneration' is the desire to lend support to a regulated market economy? Or does the incorporation of such references in the *Philosophy of Right* signal an entirely different set of concerns? Does Hegel's theory invite acceptance of the existence of a permanent underclass and imperialist colonization as the price of capitalism? Or does the *Logic* provide the basis for a different rationale for his comments as well as of their relevance to the contemporary global reality? From our perspective, Hegel's appeal to the seeming inevitability of certain manifestations of 'ethical degeneration' raises questions on two levels: firstly, concerning the precise sense in which the concept of Civil Society represents a *normative* organizational form; and, secondly, concerning the *relevance* of the concept to today's global reality. In order to appreciate the significance of Hegel's references to the phenomena of poverty or, more precisely, of both 'extravagance and want',[33] of the emergence of a rabble and of colonizing activity, we must firstly understand what precisely it is about Civil Society as a system of interdependence that is *ethical*. Conversely, we should ask how can Civil Society, which admittedly gives rise to poverty, a rabble mentality and colonization, be justifiably presented as a moment of *ethicality* in the order of Ethical Life? Once we appreciate the ethical aspect of this specific organizational form, we will be in a position to consider its implications for the current global system of interdependence.

In this chapter we will begin to address these questions by showing how the logical analysis of the previous chapter provides

---

Poverty: The Responsible Consumer and the Return of the Ethical to Civil Society', in Robert R. Wartenberg (ed.), *Beyond Liberalism and Communitarianism: Studies in Hegel's Philosophy of Right*, Albany, State University of New York Press, 2001, p. 187; Peter G. Stillman, 'Hegel, Civil Society and Globalization', in Andrew Buchwalter (ed.), *Hegel and Global Justice*, New York and London, Springer, pp. 111-130.

32. See Wartenberg, 'Poverty and Class Structure in Hegel's Theory of Civil Society'; Wood, *Hegel's Ethical Thought*, p. 251-252; Franco, *Hegel's Philosophy of Freedom*, p. 272; Žižek, *Less than Nothing*, p. 433.

33. Hegel, PR, §185.

the basis for answers. An appreciation of the ways in which the Hypothetical Syllogism informs the initial appearance of Civil Society as a system of interdependence explains what it is about Civil Society that distinguishes it as a necessary stage in the categorial development of Ethical Life and, as a result, the analysis shows both the precise respect in which Civil Society manifests a certain limited embodiment of freedom and the ways in which the concept figures in an ethical-ontological theory that addresses the inherent diversity currently operating in global civil society. Once we have examined the precise sense in which Civil Society's ethical aspect concerns the development of subjectivity to formal freedom, we will be in a position to see why explanations of Hegel's statements about the potentially devastating effects of life in Civil Society in terms of the desire either to indicate his personal preference for a regulated market economy or to find solutions to the sociological phenomena that were taking shape at the time of writing the *Philosophy of Right* miss the point of the analysis, which is at base to elaborate an aspect of the concrete manifestation of the denied ethical substantiality characterizing modernity in its negative moment. In the light of this understanding, we will proceed to evaluate the commentators' assessments of Hegel's reasons for including a discussion of poverty in the elaboration of Civil Society before going on to explain the relationship of the concept both to the current global reality and to human rights and global citizenship discourses aimed at dealing with problems of poverty, rights and duties on a global scale. This discussion serves as the general theoretical framework within which we will return to the questions of the significance of the emergence of a class of rabble and of Hegel's treatment of institutional responses to poverty, including his references to colonization (in Chapter Seven).

CIVIL SOCIETY'S ETHICAL ASPECT

According to Hegel, with the appearance of Civil Society,
> individuals can attain their ends only in so far as they themselves determine their knowing, willing and acting in a universal way and make themselves links in this chain of social connexions. In these circumstances the interest of the Idea— an interest of which these members of Civil society are as such unconscious—lies in the process whereby their singularity and their natural condition are raised, as a result of the necessities imposed by nature as well as of arbitrary needs, to

> formal freedom and formal universality of knowing and willing—the process whereby their particularity is educated up to subjectivity.[34]

Hegel further describes the process of development of the consciousness of Particularity through its relation to formal Universality in terms of

> the absolute transition from an Ethical substantiality which is immediate and natural to the one which is intellectual and so both infinitely subjective and lofty enough to have attained universality of form [...]
>
> Moreover, this form of universality—the Understanding, to which particularity has worked its way and developed, brings it about at the same time that particularity becomes individuality genuinely existent in its own eyes.[35]

From our earlier analysis of the Hypothetical Syllogism we note that the mediation of Particularity and Universality must show them to be contradicting their substantive identity. Here mediation—the Universal 'gathered into individuality' by Particularity—exhibits the self-determination of the notion's unity in so far as it contradicts the ethical substantiality, the identical content characterizing the totality of the conditions. This aspect of the categorial interrelation manifests in the *process of development* of subjectivity to formal freedom already described.

In so far as there is indeed a mediation of Particularity and Universality, in so far as the concrete person 'thinks, wills and acts universally' in satisfying his or her needs, this structure of relations also exhibits the *necessity* of the relation between the categorial moments. According to Hegel,

> in developing itself independently to totality, the principle of particularity passes over into universality, and only there does it attain its truth and the right to which its positive actuality is entitled. This unity is not the identity which the Ethical order requires, because at this level, that of division, both principles are self-subsistent. It follows that this unity is present here not as freedom but as necessity, since it is by compulsion that the particular rises to the form of universality and seeks and gains its stability in that form.[36]

The totality into which the principle of Particularity develops does not exhibit a realized *positive* unity of the principles of Particularity

---

34. Hegel, *PR*, §187.
35. Hegel, *PR*, §187 Remark.
36. Hegel, *PR*, §186.

and Universality. The unity that characterizes this totality is a negative one in that it is no longer an immediate unity and not yet incorporated in the person's awareness—the person achieves only *subjective* freedom even though this achievement is socially mediated. Recall from the Hypothetical Syllogism that the unity of the notion is a unity of an indifferent abstract Universality and a Particularity which, though the actuality of the Universal, is equally indifferent to it. As a negative unity the relation of Universality and Particularity exhibits necessity rather than freedom. In our analysis of the Syllogism we saw that mediation exhibits the 'simple immediacy' of the objective being of the categories and that this being is necessity. Precisely because the principles retain their self-subsistent appearance in this negative relation, the outcome of the relation is to *posit the implicitness* of the principle of self-determination.

The above elaboration of Civil Society's two principles draws our attention to the features of each from the standpoint of their *apparent* self-subsistence, a standpoint that exhibits their contradictory form as mediating and mediated immediacies. In manifesting a unity that has 'fallen apart', on its own each of these standpoints is limited. Neither the reasoning of Particularity as the singular person's employment of self-interested instrumental rationality nor that of the formal Universal can adequately express the nature of their relation given that, contrary to the standpoint of each, neither principle shapes this interaction exclusively. The Universal is shown to mediate the need satisfaction arising as a result of the person's own willing but not in fact secured by the instrumental rationality that Particularity employs. At the same time, even though it is the Universal that secures satisfaction the Universal cannot also guarantee the activity of persons required to affirm its being as self-subsistent. Persons themselves must postpone the satisfaction of their needs since only the satisfaction of a need that is capable of postponement connects them to the Universal in the appropriate way.

It is this contradictory interrelation of Universality and Particularity that gives rise to the 'process whereby particularity is educated up to subjectivity', that is, to the conditions that enable the emergence of the socially instituted formal embodiment of freedom as a result of the existence of individuals who have achieved consciousness of themselves as free.[37] This then is what

---

37. Hegel, *PR*, §187.

Hegel takes to be the 'rational' ground for presenting Civil Society as no less a moment of Ethical Life even though it is the sphere in which the activity of concrete persons exhibits the phenomena of infinite desire and limited satisfaction, phenomena that result in 'ethical' as well as 'physical degeneration'.

THE LOGICAL SIGNIFICANCE OF EXTRAVAGANCE AND WANT

The process we have been analyzing along with its underlying categorial interplay are crucial for persons' development toward the complete socially instituted and culturally embedded freedom that Hegel associates with life in the ethical State. But, as we noted at the outset, Hegel associates Civil Society with a less than appealing reality:

> Civil society affords a spectacle of extravagance and want as well as of physical and Ethical degeneration common to them both.[38]

He also suggests that, left unchecked, the activity of the Particular results in the destruction of 'itself and its substantive concept in the process of gratification'.[39] How should we make sense of these claims? On our analysis, the process of 'gratification' that arises from the failure to postpone need satisfaction is (self)destructive in so far as it *affirms the immediacy* of Particularity, rather than overcoming it. As such, even though the extravagance that Civil Society makes possible does not contribute to the liberation of the concrete person from his or her immediacy, it still belongs to the contradictory logic at play in Civil Society. First and foremost, Hegel's references to the extravagance and want characterizing Civil Society speak to the *unavoidably contradictory* reality of the mediating and mediated immediacy defining the terms of a relationship that accords with the structure of the Hypothetical Syllogism. From this perspective, when we ask why and in what sense must it be the case that Civil Society manifests the conditions of excessive poverty and the creation of a rabble of paupers, we are calling for a consideration of the role they play in the elaboration of this logic. From the standpoint of the *Logic* then, the extremes of poverty and wealth are on a par. This is why the rabble mentality can just as easily accompany both of them. As Hegel allows,

> the rabble disposition arises also with the rich. The rich man thinks that everything can be bought because he knows

---

38. Hegel, PR, §185.
39. Hegel, PR, §185.

himself as the might of the particularity of self-consciousness. Hence wealth can lead to the same mockery and shamelessness that we find among the rabble.[40]

So what precisely is the logical connection between the presence of extravagance and want, on the one hand, and the attainment of subjective freedom, on the other? As we have seen, in so far as it is produced, the freedom of the self-interested individual is a product of *necessity*. But this is nevertheless still *only a possibility* for anyone in particular. As Hegel puts it, the attainment of formal freedom and Universality 'is the rationality of which [... reason's] external condition is *capable*'.[41] This is why, along with the fact that the two principles of Civil Society exhibit a contradictory form, Civil Society must manifest a certain degree of ethical and not just physical degeneration that manifests with the presence of want and extravagance. Since the development toward (formally) free subjectivity must be an achievement of Particularity and not the *mere* necessary outcome of a structure of relations, this structure of relations also exhibits the reality of Particularity in so far as it *falls short of this achievement*. The 'physical and ethical degeneration' characterizing the extremes of 'extravagance and want' reflects precisely this possibility.

Here it is also worth repeating that Civil Society is defined by the contradictory relation of that which mediates—the formal Universal—to the ethical substantiality that underpins this mediation. This means that, despite the fact that the principle to which Civil Society gives effect in relation to the subjective particular demands, as Hegel clarifies in relation to 'Abstract Right', that one 'be a person and respect others as persons',[42] it must inevitably undermine this very form of mediation by denying the ethical substantiality as that which provides the proper context of operation of the principle. Once we have elaborated the logic of the Disjunctive Syllogism that gives the precise formulation of this contradictory relationship, we will see in Chapter Seven that this logic explains why Hegel introduces a range of otherwise very different phenomena. These phenomena include the rabble's existence, both as the class of the unemployed poor and as that of the rich and its relationship to Civil Society's transformative potential; the existence of dispossessed colonized peoples; and even the existence of organized criminals.

---

40. Hegel lectures cited in Wood, *Hegel's Ethical Thought*, p. 253.
41. Hegel, *PR*, §187 Remark, our emphasis.
42. Hegel, *PR*, §36.

With the above logical analysis we have an explanation for *why* Hegel should have included reference to phenomena such as Civil Society's creation of poverty in this moment of Ethical Life. When we explain Hegel's discussion of poverty by reference to the abovementioned contradictory logic of Civil Society we establish the link between the phenomena in question and their place in the unfolding of the concept just as Hartmann suggests. But the logical analysis also shows why Hartmann's conclusion—that poverty points to the need for a movement to the higher order of the State—appeals prematurely to the concept's transitional logic. The logical analysis supports a rejection, of Hartmann's interpretation to this extent.[43] But it also establishes that Wood's approach, which focuses on giving a causal account of Hegel's claims, will not suffice. Neither will explanations that are based on speculation regarding Hegel's preference for a regulated economy. As Brod maintains, 'Hegel is concerned with the effect of poverty on the degree of social integration rather than with poverty as an issue of economic injustice'.[44]

Indeed Brod objects to both liberal and Marxist readings of Hegel's discussion of poverty, which typically superimpose their own non-Hegelian categories to explain Hegel's ideas arguing that

> without the background of Hegel's conception of what the appropriate questions for political philosophy are and with a contemporary concept of "poverty" one can only be baffled by the inadequacy of Hegel's proposed solutions to the problem.[45]

Moreover, 'if one remains solely within the framework of "the problem of poverty" as defined by liberal or Marxist notions of the economic responsibilities of the state' then one fails to see that for Hegel the issue here is that 'by the standards of self-worth generated by civil society, one group is denied access to a conception of human selfhood and independence deemed necessary by that society'.[46] Our analysis of Hegel's references to poverty in terms of the manifestation of the contradictory logic of mediating/mediated immediacies supports this conclusion. It also points to the inadequacy of the Marxist inspired critique of Hegel which, having linked his discussion of poverty to the phenomenon of economic class divisions, then objects that Hegel fails to follow through the implications of recognizing these phenomena. Wartenberg's

---

43. See also Wood, *Hegel's Ethical Thought*, pp. 248-249.
44. Brod, *Hegel's Philosophy of Politics*, p. 107.
45. Brod, *Hegel's Philosophy of Politics*, p. 4.
46. Brod, *Hegel's Philosophy of Politics*, p. 4.

critique of Hegel's account of poverty and class divisions is a case in point to which we will return when we examine Hegel's account of class and Estate relations in Chapter Seven.[47]

If the strict organization thesis is sound, then the *Logic* supplies a very precise rationale for distinguishing aspects of the account of Civil Society that, on the one hand, reflect modernity's achievement from an ethical standpoint—the recognition of socially instituted formally free subjectivity—and, on the other, clarify the concept's ethical significance as an abstract moment, that is, as the elaboration of modernity in its moment of self-denial and, hence, as necessitating the existential manifestations of the incompleteness of its fundamentals. Next we want to elaborate the claim that it is the concept *in its abstraction* that manifests the current global reality in the sense of the single world phenomenon produced by the globalization processes we discussed in Chapter One.

CIVIL SOCIETY AND THE GLOBAL REALITY

We have already commented that unlike CSI and CSII, the models that commentators typically attribute to Hegel, Hegel's concept of Civil Society envisages one all-inclusive space within which diverse social, political and economic processes and activities are differentiated (Chapter Three). So, unlike Keane's account of global civil society (Chapter One), sovereign states, governmental agencies and their interrelations with governmental and non-governmental actors all fall *within* the domain of the abstract concept, which is temporally distinguishable from that of the Hegelian State. What does this mean for the concept's connection to the current global reality? Onuf maintains that although the Hegelian concept of Civil Society first manifests regionally in late modern Europe, in the current reality 'there are many europes already'.[48] Moreover,

> taken together these many europes constitute [...] a variable segment of an even more inclusive structure. At global and regional levels, institutions that have [territorial] states as members—commonly known as international regimes—link public offices in administering the global system of needs.
> [...] Forming institutions into ascending levels and side-by-side

---

47. Wartenberg, 'Poverty and Class Structure in Hegel's Theory of Civil Society'. See also Joachim Ritter, *Hegel and the French Revolution*, trans. Richard Dien Winfield, Boston, Mass., MIT Press, 1984, p. 71.
48. Onuf, 'Late Modern Civil Society', p. 53.

functional sectors, however misshapen, this structure gives the late modern world a Hegelian character.[49]

When locating this *Hegelian character* in what is now referred to as 'global civil society' we may typically have in mind global civil society as the product of autonomous global processes of production, exchange and technological development that we mentioned in Chapter One and, as we will see below, we can understand these processes by reference to the logic characterizing the Hegelian System of Needs. But, first we should consider a possible objection. As already noted, global civil society is also taken to be the arena in which [the members of] global social movements define themselves *against* territorial states and act in response to them. This raises the question of whether the Hegelian concept provides the conceptual resources to account for the activities of fluid social movements that now constitute a significant form of oppositional agency in the world produced by globalization. Indeed, one may think that there is an obvious lack of fit between the current global reality and the Hegelian concept given that the former includes a variety of fluid social movements, such as the women's, environmental, peace and global justice movements that are explicitly oriented toward universal ends in opposition to the professed universal ends of particular territorial states and whose activities cannot be understood in terms of their conformity with self-interested particularistic goals.

One way to respond to the above objection would be to treat the human beings qua individual participants of fluid social movements as the proper bearers of agency. In other words, we might represent today's global social movement participants simply as global citizens who choose to act on their *individual ethic* in Dower's first sense of global citizenship that we noted in Chapter One. Hegel's system treats this sort of activity as an aspect of the moral agency elaborated in 'Morality', an earlier moment within the *Philosophy of Right*, whose logic, we maintain, is strictly organized in accordance with the Syllogism of Reflection. Although it may well be the case that the thinking and acting of a proportion of social movement participants is an existential manifestation of the abovementioned form of thought, nevertheless, it would be inappropriately reductive to treat the activities of fluid social movements *as such* in these individualist terms. Many of the movements in question may define themselves by reference to the

---

49. Onuf, 'Late Modern Civil Society', pp. 53-54.

collective goals of countering the unjust effects of economic globalization and of creating conditions of justice on a global scale. We will say more about the specifics of these associational forms later but for the purposes of determining the relevance of the Hegelian concept to the current conditions, note that the fact of the complexity of global civil society does not render the dominant organizational forms, the relationship of the Universal and the Particular that we have analyzed thus far, irrelevant, especially if, as we will show in the next chapter, this relationship entails the co-presence of a number of alternative associational forms.

Without appealing to the *Logic*, Onuf draws attention to three modes of structuration that together position agents within the all-inclusive structure of Civil Society. He suggests that 'agents locate themselves in these crisscrossing arrangements [those 'formed from ascending levels of association and side-by-side functional sectors of activity'] by reference to the rules constituting them as agents' that in turn follow certain 'additional processes that actualize agency and ensure continuity.[50]

The terms participation, representation and recognition broadly describe the three ways that agency instantiates in particular human beings, institutions come to life, at least metaphorically, and society constitutes a structured totality of relations.[51] Onuf's discussion of these processes remains rather general but once we have acknowledged the connection between the Hegelian concept of Civil Society and the global reality of the twenty-first century, it becomes possible to explain precisely how the concept incorporates processes of recognition, participation and representation, in strict and very precise accordance with the concept's logical underpinnings. Here one must bear in mind the claim of the strict organization thesis that whereas the logic of the Hypothetical Syllogism informs the concept of Civil Society in its initial appearance as a system of *interdependence*, its system *differentiation*, which forms part of the account of the possibilities for agency within the global reality, follows a different logical form, that of the Disjunctive Syllogism. So, both these aspects of the *Logic* as well as the movement from one to the other must form our analysis of the forms and possibilities for agency within the global reality that existentially manifests the concept of Civil Society.

Returning to the analysis so far drawn from the logic of the Hypothetical Syllogism, two observations are in order. Firstly,

---

50. Onuf, 'Late Modern Civil Society', p. 55.
51. Onuf, 'Late Modern Civil Society', p. 55.

if the principle of inherent diversity in the generation of needs and the means of their satisfaction informs the concept of Civil Society, as we argued in Chapter Four, and this diversity manifests through the operation of global markets, then the abstract concept—Civil Society as the negative moment of modernity—at least partly manifests the current global reality in respect of the operations of global capitalism. Lydia L. Moland maintains that the dissimilarities between Hegel's account of 'domestic civil society' and the global economy are such that the latter cannot be thought of as an extension of the former.[52] She points to factors such as the scale of interaction, the operation of different regulatory laws and representational institutions, most notably, at the domestic level labour organizations may or may represent the interests of participants whereas at the global level it is typically nation-states that represent the interests of global participants. What Moland fails to realize is that once we appreciate that the concept of Civil Society is manifested by the global economic reality and not just 'domestic civil society'—the bounded space within the confines of any particular nation-sate that is designated as the civic sphere—such differences reflect the differences between the concept as such and the reality of a given moment.

From the standpoint of the concept that manifests the existential reality of a global economy (social agents' responses to the effects of) global markets no longer appear to fall beyond the scope of the concept and so it becomes possible to make sense of a greater range of activities by reference to the Hegelian system. These latter are precisely the sorts of activities linked to social phenomena that have arisen in direct response to the processes of economic globalization in a world of capitalist accumulation that cannot be fully appreciated within a traditional reading of Hegel's Civil Society as the nation-state's civic sphere. To give just one example, we are now able to position, and hence appreciate the shared logic underpinning the alternative solidarity activities of otherwise dissimilar economic actors, like the Latin American *nation-states* operating within MERCOSUR and the transnational anti-globalization movement *networks*, such as worker-owned cooperatives and micro-lending loan funds. As we will see in a later chapter, despite their vast differences at the *institutional* level of acting as nation-states, NGOs or cooperatives, what the activities of such economic actors share is the fact of being implicated and ultimately linked

---

52. Moland, 'A Hegelian Approach to Global Poverty', p. 145.

through the constraints imposed by the categorical differentiated unity defining the System of Needs. To illustrate this point we will need to elaborate the logical forms that define Civil Society as a complex comprehensive categorical differentiated unity, a matter to which we will turn in the next chapters. For now the point is that the globally extended principle of inherent diversity in the generation of needs and means of their satisfaction manifests as the activity of global market relations with certain clear implications for our appreciation of the workings of otherwise diverse institutions as ethically oriented economic agents.

Such lines of continuity are lost from view if we follow Keane in defining global civil society as an ideal type that excludes from its domain member-state organizations with global economic reach such as MERCOSUR or the European Union. Insisting on the novelty of the current emerging *world polity* Keane prefers to analyze governmental agencies and their interrelations with non-governmental actors in terms of the operations of what he calls a 'cosmocracy'. This is a three-tiered

> system of world-wide webs of interdependence—of actions and reactions at a distance, a complex mélange of networks of legal, governmental, police and military interdependence at world-wide distances [with] interlocking and overlapping sub-state, state and suprastate institutions and multi-dimensional processes that interact, and have political and social effects on a global scale.[53]

Keane claims that 'cosmocracy stands on the spectrum between the so-called 'Westphalian' model of competing sovereign states and a single unitary system of world government'.[54] While useful on some level, the problem with an approach such as this is that in offering a taxonomy of models of government from an external reflective standpoint it misses the opportunity to differentiate and explain global transitional processes as such. This said, there are some interesting points of comparison to be made with the Hegelian account of the transition to the ethical State, which we discuss in the next volume in this series.[55]

The second observation relates to the fact that as an indirect effect of the abovementioned activity of global capitalism, commitment to the principle of formal freedom has also been extended

---

53. Keane, *Global Civil Society?*, pp. 97-98.
54. Keane, *Global Civil Society?*, p. 98.
55. We elaborate this in the next volume in this series, which is devoted to the analysis of Hegel's ethical State.

globally. Some liberal theorists take this to signal the timely globalization of liberal values, like the right to make choices from amongst a plurality of available options within the societal culture, even going so far as to advocate 'exporting liberalism' to non-Western countries.[56] Advocates of inclusive democracy link it to the emergence on a global scale of individuals' engagement in morally motivated activist politics that appeal to an ideal of universal inclusiveness.[57] But what precisely is the relevance to non-western cultural contexts of a globally extended notion of formally free subjectivity? On our Hegelian analysis, consciousness of oneself as formally free does not entail consciousness of one's formal freedom in conformity with a commitment to certain universalist values. Indeed, within a non-western non-liberal social-cultural setting the principle of formal freedom only entails self-awareness that accords with the exercise of *subjective willing*. This is entirely consistent with individuals' willing identification with a diversity of non-liberal cultural or religious norms as well as with the absence of any commitment to universal values of inclusiveness. So, for example, it is compatible with the concept of the individual that accords with the Islamic ideal of the *umma*. According to Hanafi this ideal holds that

> the individual is one, which means that his powers and energies are one. His thoughts should express what he feels, and what he feels can be rationally demonstrated. [...]
>
> Man's external powers of action are also one. His words should also be related to his acts; what he says he should do and what he does he should say. [...] The unity between the inside world—feeling and thinking—and the external world—saying and doing—makes the human personality one, free of fear, double-talk, double-face; it creates a free individual. To believe is to attest. To declare is to testify. This is the meaning and the significance of *shahada*, the first pillar of Islam, the

---

56. See for example the editors' introduction in Will Kymlicka and Magdalena Opalski (eds.), *Can Liberal Pluralism Be Exported? Western Political Theory and Ethnic Relations in Eastern Europe*, New York, Oxford University Press, 2001. But see Toula Nicolacopoulos, 'What's Wrong with "Exporting Liberal Pluralism"?: On the Radical Self-denial of Contemporary Liberal Philosophy', *Philosophical Inquiry*, no. 1-2, 2007, pp. 89-111.

57. See, for example, Iris Marion Young's position cited in Carol C. Gould, 'Varieties of Global Responsibility: Social Connection, Human Rights and Transnational Solidarity', in Ann Ferguson and Mechthild Nagel (eds.), *Dancing with Iris: The Philosophy of Iris Marion Young*, Oxford, Oxford University Press, 2009, pp. 199-211.

solemn declaration that there are no other gods except the only God [...]

All human beings are equal before this Universal Principal, equal in birth and death, equal in life and worth. [...] All human beings are the sons and daughters of Adam and Eve. Every human being has a body and a soul, a reason to distinguish good from evil, and a free will to choose the good, not the evil. They are all created from one soul.

Society is a unity of equal individuals.[58]

A similar point can be made about the Jewish tradition. According to Suzanne Last Stone,

> Such a system [the Judaic system of social solidarity] may, and does, respect individual rights of personhood and property, but it cannot confer on its members the kind of freedom or autonomy presupposed by [the Western idea of] civil society. In the Jewish conception the individual is neither sovereign over his or her own life and experience nor a fully independent source of moral values. Freedom is not defined in terms of subjective rights or the choice of one's aims and desires. Freedom means individual accountability, the free will to obey or disobey the law.[59]

Here Last Stone is comparing the Jewish and liberal conceptions of civil society. But in doing so she draws attention to the significance of *individual willing* for the Jewish subject, for whom the covenantal community plays the critical role in defining individual identity. This is the very aspect of subjective freedom that the Hegelian concept of Civil Society recognizes as ethical.[60] The same can be said for the well-cultivated Confucian. Reflecting upon what he sees as the more liberal strands within the Confucian tradition, Madsen suggests that for the neo-Confucian perspective freedom

> consists in creatively constextualizing those commitments which fate has assigned. Freedom involves more deeply understanding the meaning of one's roles as parent/child, ruler/minister, husband/wife, older sibling/younger sibling and friend—so that one can flexibly, even playfully, reconcile these with each other and with all the other confusing roles that one must play in an evolving modern world. This task can provide wide latitude for action and immense challenges for personal

---

58. Hanafi, 'Alternative Conceptions of Civil Society', p. 176.
59. Last Stone, 'The Jewish tradition and Civil Society', p. 153.
60. Last Stone, 'The Jewish tradition and Civil Society', p. 160.

creativity, and it can lead to a plethora of individualized responses to particular situations.[61]

So the endorsement of a globally extended Hegelian principle of formal freedom is entirely compatible with a range of cultural and religious traditions. Such endorsement does not entail the justifiability of the extension to non-Western countries or religious communities of the *liberal values* of freedom of speech, movement, choice, association or property ownership that are typically recognized as aspects of liberal ideals of citizenship. Nor does it entail the normativity of global citizenship in either the community participation sense or the aspirational sense of engaging in visionary politics (Chapter One). Instead to recognize that the structure of Civil Society is existentially manifested on the global scale is to view the consequent extension of property-owning subjectivity and its characteristic subjective particularity as a matter of recognizing the plurality of ways in which this conception of subjectivity may be culturally embodied. The important point from the perspective of our analysis is that, irrespective of its cultural articulations, Hegel's Civil Society provides the conceptual resources to explain the trans-cultural appeal of the abstract idea of formally free subjectivity in the abovementioned sense. With these fundamental clarifications in mind regarding the global impact of market relations on the constitution of subjectivity, let us now turn to the issue of human rights advocacy versus global citizenship discourses.

GLOBAL CITIZENSHIP AND / OR HUMAN RIGHTS

Although the concept of Civil Society does not necessitate the normativity of a commitment to either certain universal values or indeed the concept of global citizenship, as we will see in more detail in later chapters, it nevertheless supplies the logic underpinning certain forms of global citizenship practice. It also supplies an ethical-ontological justification for the global expansion of human rights discourse as well as a rationale for the assignment of responsibility for the global effects of actions.

As we indicated in Chapter One, the global expansion of human rights discourse has been accompanied by debates, not only surrounding the justifiability of the recognition of human rights, but also of the comparative usefulness or otherwise of appeals to the notion of global citizenship. Critics of 'global citizenship'

---

61. Madsen, 'Confucian conceptions of Civil Society', pp. 202-203.

models who raise doubts about the efficacy of this notion in the absence of an established world polity and related coercive authority with global reach typically advocate reliance on a human rights discourse instead. For example, taking into account the historical emergence of modern citizenship, Turner and Khondker argue that the notion of citizenship is rendered meaningless beyond the territorial confines of the nation-state. Unlike human rights which are founded on 'our common vulnerability, citizenship rights must be conferred and regulated by the territorial state.[62]

> 'Global citizenship' may be desirable but not feasible. Discussion of 'global citizenship' and 'flexible citizenship' ignore the fact that citizenship can only function in the context of the nation-state. Modern citizenship evolved with the nation-state, the creation of nationalism, the growth of the passport, the development of national systems of education and the evolution of conscription as a duty of the citizen. [...] The nation-state to which the idea of citizenship is organically linked remains a powerful and meaningful institution in the context of globalization and shows no signs of withering away.[63]

In the light of their observations, Turner and Khondker suggest that a better solution to the problem of providing protection and security to people outside state limits would be 'to make human rights more serviceable'.[64] To this end the enforceability and concrete effectiveness of human rights could be strengthened through the United Nations but it is also necessary 'to give ordinary people a sense of ownership over human rights via the introduction of a global tax on human mobility'.[65] Here, Turner and Khondker implicitly acknowledge an unresolved tension that exists between the assignment of a right in virtue of one's humanity, rather than one's membership in a political community, and the dependence of its enforceability on such membership.

Other skeptics regarding the usefulness of the idea of global citizenship point, on the one hand, to the tendency amongst global citizenship theorists to continue analyzing the notion by analogy with the theorization of membership in civil society within the liberal territorial state. For example, Kimberley Hutchings argues that global citizenship theorists typically conflate elements of the different and incompatible humanist and republican intellectual

---

62. Turner and Khondker, *Globalization: East and West*, p. 174.
63. Turner and Khondker, *Globalization: East and West*, p. 211.
64. Turner and Khondker, *Globalization: East and West*, p. 169.
65. Turner and Khondker, *Globalization: East and West*, pp. 170-171.

traditions that, respectively, take human beings to be equal bearers of universal human values and define membership in terms of participatory actions.[66] Focusing on advocates of global citizenship in the *aspirational* sense (Chapter One), she observes that, despite the fact that 'neither the political nor the moral prerequisites of [global] citizenship appear to be in place', global civil society advocates insist that global citizenship is 'the necessary underpinning to democratic politics' on a global scale at the same time as they look forward to the establishment of a cosmopolitan political authority.[67] Global citizenship advocates rely on a highly moralized notion of global civil society—one that 'operates as the vehicle for individuals' pursuit of the ideals of freedom and justice (pilgrimage) and thereby for the transformation of coercive power into legitimate authority'—whose salience is yet to be determined.[68] Hutchings concludes that this renders the concept of a *universally applicable* global citizenship meaningless and ineffective since very few people are in a position to exercise this form of citizenship under current conditions.[69] Although Hutchings argues convincingly in relation to the aspirational view of global citizenship, her arguments seem less applicable to Dower's *community participation* conception that, on the one hand, detaches participation from paradoxically presupposing formal membership of a currently non-existent world state or cosmopolitan democracy and, on the other, allows for a deliberative contextualization of the universal goals that global citizens might pursue. As we will see later, the logical analysis of Civil Society's differentiated moments will enable us to make sense of both the place and the limits of the idea of global citizenship in its community participation sense. For now, taking for granted the community participation sense of global citizenship, we want to consider the question of its co-existence with human rights discourse from the Hegelian perspective we have elaborated thus far.

Our reading of global civil society in the light of the Hegelian concept enables us to see how it is possible for contemporary advocates of human rights consistently to insist both on the necessity

---

66. Kimberly Hutchings, 'Subjects, Citizens or Pilgrims? Citizenship and Civil Society in a Global Context', in Randall D. Germain and Michael Kenny (eds.), *The Idea of Global Civil Society: Politics and Ethics in a Globalizing Era*, London, Routledge, 2005, pp. 84-99 at p. 93.
67. Hutchings, 'Subjects, Citizens or Pilgrims?', pp. 94-95.
68. Hutchings, 'Subjects, Citizens or Pilgrims?', pp. 85-86.
69. Hutchings, 'Subjects, Citizens or Pilgrims?', p. 97.

of the institutional framing of human rights, which is indispensable for their enforcement, *and* on their universality as non-conventional rights, that is as rights whose ethical source and justifiability cannot be reduced to their endorsement in a codified form, such as the United Nations Declaration of Human Rights. Carol Gould offers a good example of such an attempt. In developing her theory of global democracy and human rights, Gould seeks to ground human rights non-conventionally at the same time as relying on conventional associational links for securing their practical realization.[70] For Gould 'human rights hold in principle as claims of each on all others in virtue of *our interdependence*' even as we acknowledge that 'they can only be realized practically through devising social, economic and political institutions that would serve to fulfill them'.[71] That is, even though human rights claims appeal to our mutual implication in a system of interdependence, social responsibility for their realization depends in part on the willingness of agents to become active in *creating* (not just enforcing) the latter. Gould defends the view that there is 'a set of mutual obligations that arise within co-operative systems and communities that are transnational and transborder'.[72] In contrast to a social connection model of responsibility, such as Iris Marion Young's, which holds individuals equally responsible for the unjust global effects of their actions irrespective of differences in their powers to choose alternative courses of action, for Gould this responsibility does not attach to agents just in virtue of being actors within the global system. In this she differs also from Moland who claims that 'the expanded nature of global interdependence argues for expanded ethical obligations', that is, to the extent that we benefit from unfair trade agreements that deny basic rights to citizens of developing countries 'we have a duty as partially responsible for their impoverishment'.[73] Rather responsibility attaches to particular agents via their *willing identification* in a relevant associational form. In Hegelian terms, whereas each one of us, in our capacity as particular property-owning subjects, is the bearer of what we now refer to as universal 'human rights' in virtue of our unavoidable participation in the system of interdependence and regardless of our particular cultural affiliations, the same cannot be said of the enforceability of such claims

---

70. Gould, 'Varieties of Global Responsibility', pp. 199-211.
71. Gould, 'Varieties of Global Responsibility', p. 208, emphasis added.
72. Gould, 'Varieties of Global Responsibility', p. 204.
73. Moland, 'A Hegelian Approach to Global Poverty', p. 144; pp. 148-149.

against us. For reasons that we will examine in some detail in the next chapter, with the elaboration of the internal differentiation of the system of interdependence, the System of Needs, the system of market relations, is posited as *one* of the forms of the unity of the Universal and the Particular to which the system of interdependence gives rise and in which the subjective Particular is determined as the human being, or 'man' to use Hegel's terminology, as distinct from the citizen, 'the bourgeois'.[74] In taking the place of the citizen within Hegel's System of Needs the category of the human being manifests the *implicitness* of this unity but it remains the case that Civil Society's principle of Particularity becomes the *self-determining* bearer of formal Universality in so far as the particular *willingly* identifies with a universal purpose. Interestingly, Manfred Riedel suggests that with this move in the elaboration of the System of Needs from 'the bourgeois' to 'man' Hegel overcomes the Natural Law opposition between, on the one hand, man as species being and individuality that is subordinated to the laws of universal ethics and, on the other, the citizen, the member of political society who is subject to the rules of politics. According to Riedel, Hegel's 'man', the representative of the species, *is reduced to* natural need and contained within bourgeois citizenship.[75] But, as we will see following the analysis of the Disjunctive Syllogism in the next chapter, on the analysis we are proposing it would be more accurate to say that for Hegel bourgeois citizenship *emerges from* the implicit form of the unity of the Particular and the Universal that the *activity of human beings* generates.

Let us illustrate this fundamental link between the categories of (rights derivable from) human activity and (duties derivable from) participatory citizenship and the way that it underpins the meaningfulness of a globally extended enforceable human rights discourse irrespective of the world's cultural and socio-political diversity. To this end consider Moland's discussion of global poverty. Arguing that 'the global economy' has duties to alleviate the wrong done to its impoverished members analogous to the duties that Hegel assigns to Civil Society organizations in relation to its members who are poor, Moland highlights a number of similarities between the production of poverty at the level of the global economy and Hegel's account of the emergence of poverty. As Moland points out, global civil society

74. Hegel, PR, §190.
75. Riedel, *Between Tradition and Revolution*, p. 140.

is established and sustained solely by human behaviour. Like the members of [Hegel's] civil society, its members are subject to others' unpredictable desires, volatile market fluctuations, and cycles of excess production and unemployment. The global economy is also characterized by entrenched poverty and staggering inequalities. [...]
The global economy also produces the rabble mentality Hegel describes. Those negatively affected sometimes become painfully aware that their destitution is linked to others' extreme wealth and power. Their indignation, like the indignation of the chronically poor in [Hegel's concept of] civil society, is then "necessary"—it is an appropriate response to their unjustly disadvantaged situation. [...] Those of us who are wealthy, by contrast, risk thinking that everything can be bought, and we are unlikely to examine the consequences of our consumption. The threat of new needs generated by others' financial ambitions is acute. [...] We risk denying or ignoring our own implication in the poverty of others and so hindering our own freedom [...] We risk foregoing the mutual recognition that frees us from this cycle of desires and needs.[76]

The so-called 'similarities' that Moland identifies are in substance consistent with our reading of Hegel's concept of Civil Society as being manifested by today's global civil society. Moreover, Moland rightly identifies global poverty as a wrong that emerges from human behaviour in the system of interdependence. But she also seeks to derive what, in the light of our discussion so far, we would refer to as *global citizens'*—in the community participation sense of the term 'global citizenship'—*duties to the global poor* from this same source, human behaviour in the system of interdependence. Here the noteworthy point is that she not only refers interchangeably to 'the global economy' and 'global civil society' as the bearers of duties to the global poor but she also identifies 'those of us who are wealthy' as such bearers. For example, she concludes, 'if the global economy indeed contributes to sustained impoverishment, the global economy has duties also towards its "children" that go unfulfilled'.[77] But she also insists 'if we accept the association of rights with duties, *we* have a duty to alleviate global poverty as well'.[78] In Chapter Nine, we will return to Moland's discussion of the most appropriate institutional forms for *exercising* these duties on behalf of their bearers. But here we

---
76. Moland, 'A Hegelian Approach to Global Poverty', pp. 145-146.
77. Moland, 'A Hegelian Approach to Global Poverty', p. 146.
78. Moland, 'A Hegelian Approach to Global Poverty', p. 143, our emphasis.

want to point out that in taking global citizens, understood as the wealthy participants of global civil society *in general*, to be the bearers of such duties Moland fails to realize that she in fact assigns these duties to the wealthy rabble just as much as to the conscientious wealthy. The problem here is that in characterizing the global wealthy in a way that links them to the rabble mentality of the rich— a mentality according to which, as Moland points out, the wealthy 'develop the belief that they are independent of the whole, or in other words, that they have no responsibility towards their society' — Moland draws our attention to those features of the Hegelian concept that manifest its contradiction of the ethical substantiality and hence its *limitations* with regard to manifesting its own principle concerning the mutual recognition of persons.[79] So it makes little sense, within the Hegelian conceptual framework to which Moland appeals, to insist upon a duty to the global poor on this basis. Indeed, in the present context such insistence takes the form of an empty *ought*, something of which Hegel is of course critical. Instead on our Hegelian analysis the existence of duties to the global poor can only be justifiably derived via persons' *willing membership* not in the global economy or global civil society in the abstract, but *in appropriately differentiated institutional forms*, which, as we will see following the analysis of Civil Society's system differentiation in Chapter Six, take shape along the lines of the Corporation-Police unity.

So far we can conclude that Civil Society, the abstract concept of Ethical Life, is manifested by the current global capitalist order in so far as the latter expresses the instrumental logic we have analyzed in connection with the activities of property-owning subjective particularity. Although we have been discussing these latter in terms of the activities of human agents, the analysis extends to all bodies to whom one can attribute the combined status of concrete persons, whether individual or collective, and property-owning subjectivity, including business organizations or small-scale co-operatives. As we will see in the next chapters, the logic of Civil Society, and the form of the Disjunctive Syllogism in particular, also allows for an appreciation of the activities of a range of institutions and networks operating within global civil society, quite apart from what Hegel himself might have been in a position to anticipate.

---

79. Moland, 'A Hegelian Approach to Global Poverty', p. 139.

6. FROM THE HYPOTHETICAL TO THE DISJUNCTIVE SYLLOGISM AND CIVIL SOCIETY'S SYSTEM DIFFERENTIATION

We have been arguing that the Hegelian concept of Civil Society has the potential to inform our understanding of key issues arising in connection with the reality of a global civil society. We can draw upon Hegel's concept of Civil Society to explain issues, like the rational ground underpinning the global recognition of human rights or the terms in which we might explain the development of a sense of global citizenship, when we appreciate that, in its fundamentals, this reality already accords with the logic of the Hegelian concept. Moreover, the abstract concept of Civil Society elaborates a system of interdependence as a whole, namely the global system of interdependence understood as modernity in its negative moment, the moment of its self-denial. In the previous chapters we also saw that the form of the Hypothetical Syllogism informs the initial appearance of Civil Society as a system of interdependence and that attention to the specific dynamics of this form explains both the precise sense in which Civil Society constitutes an *ethical* moment and the reasons for incorporating its main features. As well as explaining the details of Hegel's characterization of the initial appearance of Civil Society by reference to the complexities of the form of the Hypothetical Syllogism, our analysis thus far has allowed us to see what it is about Civil Society that distinguishes it as a *necessary* stage in the categorial development of Ethical Life and the precise respects in which Civil Society manifests a certain embodiment of freedom.

In the present chapter we will try to show how the movement in the *Science of Logic* from the Hypothetical Syllogism to the Disjunctive Syllogism informs the system *differentiation* of Civil

Society. We will begin by outlining key aspects of the transition from the Hypothetical to the Disjunctive Syllogism. From here the discussion will proceed to advance the interpretive claim concerning the relation between the logic of the Disjunctive Syllogism and the internal differentiation of Civil Society into its distinct moments. We will conclude with a discussion of the variety of associational forms that this structure makes possible.

THE TRANSITION TO THE DISJUNCTIVE SYLLOGISM

The Hypothetical Syllogism interrelates its terms in such a way that it also has the effect of positing the implicitness of the unity of the Particular and the Universal, as we saw in the previous chapters. This Syllogism is part of the process of development of the already justified unconditional middle term that seeks to construct the categorial interrelation from the standpoint of its unconditionality. It is a negative affirmation of the unconditionality of the middle term. The unconditional middle term puts itself forward as the potential to negate its negation when it affirms—as distinct from loses itself in—its negation. The Hypothetical Syllogism makes this explicit in the way that it relates the terms, A and B. Recall that they are mutually indifferent and thus negate their unity. At the same time, the terms' mutual referring is grounded in the fact that the being of each one of them is equally the being of the other. (This claim may appear to be based on a formal logical error on Hegel's part if we think of the relation 'If A then B' as asymmetric but the reciprocal identity of the one substantial being that defines the terms of the Hypothetical Syllogism follows from the fact that A is the abstract totality of which B is the actuality.)

So, A and B are involved in mediation. They are united as differentiated moments of the one actuality and their unity now emerges as that which effects their mediation and grounds their self-subsistent appearance:

> the *form-activity* of translating the conditioning into the conditioned actuality is *in itself* the unity in which the determinatenesses of the opposition, that previously were liberated into an indifferent determinate existence, are *sublated* and the difference of A and B is an empty name. Thus it is a unity reflected into itself—hence an *identical* content; and it is not merely *implicitly* but it is also *posited* as such through this syllogism in that the being of A is also not its own but B's and vice versa.[1]

---

1. Hegel, *SL*, pp. 700-701.

If the analysis so far is correct then the question that the unconditional middle term's development raises at this point is how to achieve the transcendence of its other, which is here immediacy in the presence of mediation that the self-subsistent extremes exhibit. Because the unity in question is 'reflected into itself' or is a 'self-related negativity' it is not absorbed in its implicitness. Reflection on its essential unity has been made possible in so far as it has been *posited* as an implicit unity and thereby has been *shown to be* implicit. From this standpoint the *implicit* actuality of the unity is now open to thematization as being *only one* of the forms of the unity's actuality. In other words, the unity takes its implicit form to be one 'species' of the 'genus' of unity. From the standpoint of the genus, otherness can be transcended insofar as that which otherness expresses—the implicit unity that is due to the presence of immediacy—is shown to be *one instance* of unity as distinct from the affirmation of (negative) unity itself.

If the implicit unity is indeed one of the species and so not the complete expression of the genus, the construction of the whole of the species must be able to be realized immanently to the reality of the implicit unity. Being itself an instance of the unconditional, the implicit unity must point to the differentiated reality—all the species of the genus.

In the first instance this means that mediation—that in which the mediated and the mediating are united—has acquired a being of its own. As a 'self-related negativity' mediation has 'individuality', that is, awareness of its essence as well as awareness that this essence can be asserted only through its immanent self-differentiation. When the positing of the unity's implicitness presents as an *instance* of the unity's determinate being both the need and the capacity for such unconditional differentiation become explicit.

Now the emergence of self-determined mediation is syllogistically formulated by rendering explicit the unconditionality of the middle-term. According to Hegel, this is achieved in the Disjunctive Syllogism:

> The mediation of the syllogism has hereby determined itself as *individuality, immediacy,* and as *self-related negativity,* or as an identity that differentiates itself and gathers itself into itself out of that difference—as absolute form, and for that very reason as objective *universality,* a *content* that is identical with itself. The syllogism in this determination is the *disjunctive syllogism.*[2]

---

2. Hegel, *SL*, p. 701.

The middle term of this Syllogism:
> is the *universality* that is *pregnant with form*; it has determined itself as *totality*, as *developed* objective universality. Consequently the middle term is not only universality but also particularity and individuality. As universality it is first the substantial identity of the genus; but secondly an identity that *embraces within itself particularity*, but a particularity *co-extensive with this identity of the genus*; it is therefore the universal sphere that contains its total particularization—the genus disjoined into its species: A that is B *and* C *and* D.[3]

This Syllogism exhibits internal categorial *unity* as well as *differentiation*, or, what we referred to at the outset as the 'comprehensive categorial differentiated unity' of Universality, Particularity and Individuality. Universality as 'absolute form' and 'identical content' is the totality of the species, the genus that has achieved its objective Universality, the substantive unity of form and content.[4] This Universality is immanent to the species; it is not an external Universality like that characterizing the Syllogism of Allness, a less advanced syllogistic form that gathers the Particulars together into Universality in order to form *a sum* of all the Particulars. Accordingly, each species is not just a Particular but also a Particular from which the genus extends itself to the totality of Particulars. Individuality constitutes this kind of immanent connection between the Particulars, a connection that exhaustively embodies the unity of the genus.

If the standpoint of the genus, the Universal, is locatable in any one of its species, then the unity of the embodied genus must be expressed as *species differentiatedness of the totality from the standpoint of any one of its species*. In this formulation of the unity the standpoint of the Universal is not identifiable independently of that of the Particular; it is always expressed as the view of one of the Particulars—each Particular species is one form of the genus—that asserts its qualitative difference from the rest by excluding them, despite their immanent connectedness. The Particulars are related in a way that affirms their separate identity and this way of relating exhibits their negative unity:

> particularization is differentiation and as such is just as much the *either-or* of *B*, *C* and *D*, the *negative* unity, the *reciprocal* exclusion of the terms. Further, this exclusion is not merely a reciprocal exclusion, or the determination merely a relative one,

---
3. Hegel, *SL*, p. 701.
4. Hegel, *SL*, p. 703.

but it is just as essentially a *self-related* determination, the particular as *individuality* to the exclusion of the *others*.

A is either B or C or D,
But A is B,
Therefore A is neither C nor D.

or again:

A is either B or C or D,
But A is neither C or D,
Therefore A is B.[5]

The middle term of the Syllogism is the Universal, the genus, (A), that in the first premise particularizes itself into its species. The second premise locates its being; it exhibits the determinate genus as one particular species (through either affirmation or denial). Finally, the conclusion posits the genus: it is 'the exclusive, *individual* determinateness', that is, the determinateness that has its Individual being due to the activity of the Particular in its relation to others.[6]

It follows from this formulation of the comprehensive categorial differentiated unity that in their distinction from the Particular both the Universal and the Individual appear as abstract: their determinate being as a comprehensive categorial differentiated unity is exhibited *through Particularity*. According to Hegel, 'the unity of mediating and mediated [the truth of the Hypothetical Syllogism] is thus *posited*':

Hence [in the form of the Disjunctive Syllogism] what appears in general as *mediated* is the *universality* of A with *individuality*. But the *mediating* factor is this A, which is the *universal* sphere of its particularizations and is determined as an *individual*.[7]

Even though the Disjunctive Syllogism comes under the schema of the Third Figure, I-U-P in which the Universal is the mediating factor—the First and Second Figures are I-P-U and P-I-U respectively—it nevertheless *appears* that the *Universal* and the Individual are mediated through the Particular because the conclusion of the Syllogism expresses determinate being as a comprehensive categorial differentiated unity *from the limited standpoint of the Particular*.[8] In their distinctness from Particularity, Universality and Individuality remain abstract in the sense that they do not also exhibit the differentiated unity from their own respective standpoints.

---

5. Hegel, *SL*, pp. 701-702.
6. Hegel, *SL*, p. 702.
7. Hegel, *SL*, p. 702.
8. Hegel, *SL*, p. 701.

THE DIFFERENTIATION OF CIVIL SOCIETY INTO THREE MOMENTS

What does the logic of the Disjunctive Syllogism suggest for our reading of the three moments of Civil Society? If the Disjunctive Syllogism strictly organizes the differentiation of Civil Society into its three moments, then we should expect the establishment of the implicitness of the unity of the two principles of Civil Society, the Particular and Universal that conform to the logic of the Hypothetical Syllogism, to be followed by the activity of differentiation *immanently to this unity*. As we will see below, the differentiation of Civil Society into its three moments is a self-differentiating activity that gives rise to the differentiated forms of the unity of the Universal and the Particular immanently to the unity that defines Civil Society in its initial appearance as a system of interdependence.[9] Accordingly it gives rise to the market, justice and welfare systems or in Hegel's terminology, the System of Needs, the Administration of Justice and the Police-Corporation. Drawing upon the analysis of the Disjunctive Syllogism one can read these three systems in terms of three distinct forms of the unity of the Universal and the Particular that, on the one hand, presuppose these moments' external relatedness, albeit in different ways and, on the other, give rise to an internally related comprehensive categorical differentiated unity. As we will see with the emergence of the third form of the unity that is jointly exhibited by the Police or 'universal authority'[10] and the 'Corporation' or 'labour organization of Civil society',[11] we arrive at a completely actualized differentiated unity in a concrete whole.

FIRST FORM OF THE UNITY OF PARTICULAR AND UNIVERSAL: THE SYSTEM OF NEEDS

The System of Needs expresses the form of the unity of the Universal and the Particular that also defines the initial appearance of Civil Society as a system of interdependence. Although this unity continues to be grounded in the logic of the Hypothetical Syllogism, pursuant to the notion's movement from this form to that of the Disjunctive Syllogism, when the *Philosophy of Right* introduces the System of Needs it reformulates the relation between Civil Society's two principles. At this point, the System of Needs is

---

9. Hegel, *PR*, §188.
10. Hegel, *PR*, §231.
11. Hegel, *PR*, §251.

given a more precise determination specifically in terms of *regulated* satisfaction of subjective need.

The aim here [in the System of Needs] is the satisfaction of subjective particularity, but the universal asserts itself in the bearing which this satisfaction has on the needs of others and their free arbitrary wills.[12]

As Hegel explains, the System of Needs is 'the sphere of particularity' that 'fancies itself the universal [but] is still only relatively identical with the universal'.[13] This reformulation of the relation of Particularity to Universality as the aim of the System of Needs (species) renders explicit that this form of the unity is but *one of the forms* of the unity constituting Civil Society (genus). In other words, the System of Needs is here explicitly differentiated as *only* one of Civil Society's moments. As distinct from having the form of its unity identified with Civil Society *as such*, here, the implicit categorial unity of Civil Society's initial appearance becomes *one* of the forms *explicitly*. As we will see in later chapters, this observation allows us to appreciate Hegel's rationale for including within Civil Society seemingly irreconcilable modes of recognition.

Accordingly, the more precise determination of the System of Needs continues to exhibit the implicitness of the unity of Universality and Particularity:

Particularity is in the first instance characterized in general by its contrast to the universal principle of the will and thus is subjective need [...] This attains its objectivity, i.e. its satisfaction, by means of (a) external things, which at this stage are likewise the property and product of the needs and wills of others, and (b) work and effort.[14]

Now in the sphere of market relations, of commodity production and exchange, *regulated* need satisfaction constitutes the abstract sphere of objective Universality in which Particularity, as subjective need, obtains satisfaction and is thereby united with Universality. Hegel's description of the kind of need that emerges and the satisfaction obtained in this sphere emphasizes the *implicitness* of the unity of Particularity and Universality. As we have already noted, in the System of Needs Particularity takes the more precise determination 'man', the human being as distinct from 'the bourgeois'. This is because needs initially present as natural

---

12. Hegel, *PR*, §189.
13. Hegel, *PR*, §200 and §200 Remark.
14. Hegel, *PR*, §189.

or immediate (unmediated).[15] Indeed, in line with the logic of the Syllogism, needs become 'abstract' and generate abstract reciprocal relations between needy persons, through activity towards their satisfaction and, in particular, through the infinite multiplication and particularization of needs and means to their satisfaction that we examined in the previous chapter.[16] These relations constitute the abstract sphere of Universality, the principle of inter-subjectivity as this is constituted in the System of Needs, a system whose operation renders concrete or 'social' the otherwise abstract needs and means.[17] As we saw when examining the logic of the Hypothetical Syllogism, Universality has its actuality in the, indifferent towards it, being of Particularity. Given their Universal element, social needs—'mental [as distinct from natural] needs'—form the basis of subjective freedom, but this freedom remains abstract or formal 'since the particularity of the ends remains their basic content'.[18]

Similarly, the Particular and Universal elements in Hegel's account of work, the 'means of acquiring and preparing particularized means appropriate to our similarly particularized needs',[19] also reflect the implicit unity that defines the terms of the Hypothetical Syllogism. The objective Universal element of work is the division of labour that produces complete necessary interdependence.[20] The gap between the subjective reasons for work—the attainment of particular satisfaction—and the Universal element of work manifests the relation of *apparently* immediate (self-subsistent) beings that are nevertheless necessarily related. In the System of Needs then the unity of Particularity and Universality remains implicit in the relations that manifest the kind of needs, means and satisfaction to which the activities of human beings give rise.[21]

The analysis of the Disjunctive Syllogism also suggests that the System of Needs is a self-determined totality, that is, as a *comprehensive* categorial differentiated unity. What general features of the System of Needs render it as this kind of totality? Firstly,

---

15. Hegel, *PR*, §190 and §191.
16. Hegel, *PR*, §191.
17. Hegel, *PR*, §192.
18. Hegel, *PR*, §195.
19. Hegel, *PR*, §196.
20. Hegel, *PR*, §198.
21. For an extensive discussion of Hegel's concept of labour see Paul Ashton, 'Hegel and Labour', Legacy of Hegel Seminar, University of Melbourne, February 5, 1999, http://www.marxists.org/reference/archive/hegel/txt/ashton.htm

as a comprehensive categorial unity that manifests the power of self-differentiation, the System of Needs does not merely manifest an implicit unity of the Universal and the Particular but posits *the very implicitness of this unity*. According to Hegel, the necessity characterizing the system of interdependence

> now presents itself to each as the universal permanent capital [...] which gives each the opportunity [...] to draw a share from it and so be assured of his livelihood, while what he thus earns by means of his work maintains and increases the general capital.[22]

Here, the unity of Universality and Particularity is no longer absorbed in its implicitness but is posited *as such* as a result of the activity of subjective Particularity in pursuing the means of its satisfaction. The 'universal permanent capital' is the developed objective Universality of the principle of inter-subjective recognition and this is the determinate form into which the abstract Universality of Civil Society first particularizes itself in accordance with the movement of the Disjunctive Syllogism.

Second, as one of the species of the genus, Civil Society, the System of Needs expresses the negative unity of the whole of the species by *excluding* the others (the other two moments of Civil Society). This is achieved through its determination as a totality. Although the System of Needs is structured in accordance with the explicit aim of securing particular satisfaction, it does not self-reflectively stand for the economic sphere of a larger social whole but instead *represents the whole as a system of particular needs, means and satisfactions*. This is why Hegel's presentation of the System of Needs does not include reflective interaction between the various moments of Civil Society. Incidentally, failure to appreciate this subtle distinction between how the System of Needs represents itself to itself—as the whole of the system—and what the System of Needs manifests—one aspect of the whole system—is perhaps the reason why a number of Hegel commentators conflate the concept of Civil Society and the System of Needs, as we have already seen. This conflation in turn leads to the reduction of the concept of Civil Society to the form of inter-subjective recognition that operates specifically within the System of Needs. For example, Axel Honneth's explanation for why Civil Society represents a higher normative sphere of Ethical Life by comparison with the Family presupposes just this sort of conflation and reduction.[23]

22. Hegel, *PR*, §199.
23. Honneth, *The Pathologies of Individual Freedom: Hegel's Social Theory*, pp.

Thirdly, being *one* of the species, its determination is not just exclusive but also *relative* to the other species as well. Market relations are accordingly presented as relations that (a) give rise to the demand for formal equality of satisfaction, thereby manifesting an element of justice and (b) require regulation for the purposes of securing such equality.[24] Jay Drydyk has argued that Hegel's analysis of the System of Needs provides two key principles that take economic theory 'beyond free market and non-market systems', namely 'the right to participation in the community of taste by which needs are multiplied' and 'the right to dignity and self-reliance as a producer, entailing capitalization and self-management'.[25] In this context, he makes the point that because Civil Society is based on a morality of the pursuit of self-interest, in the sense of 'acting on one's own behalf', it cannot institutionalize the right to non-exclusion.[26] After all, the latter involves an effective right to capital and this cannot be secured by reference to the self-interested framework of Civil Society.[27] On our analysis this inability of the System of Needs to institutionalize particular subjects' right to non-exclusion follows from the logical structure that the System of Needs manifests, rather than from the presumption of the operation of a morality of self-interest. Locating this limitation of the System of Needs within the specific logical structure is important because it is this logical structure and *not the market's presumption of a morality of self-interest* that must be transcended with the transition to the ethical State. Elsewhere, we develop the argument that the market's presumption that individuals act on the basis of self-interest continues to serve an important role within the ethical context of the State, which, we maintain, secures an effective right to non-exclusion via the reconstitution of market relations through the transcendence of capitalist accumulation, as distinct from the right to property.[28]

In modernity's negative moment, however, individual rights, though visible, remain limited. The structure of the System of Needs as a whole recognizes individuals in their capacity as private

---

61-62.

24. Hegel, PR, §193.

25. Jay Drydyk 'Capitalism, Socialism and Civil Society', *The Monist*, 1991, pp. 457-477.

26. Jay Drydyk 'Capitalism, Socialism and Civil Society', p. 458.

27. Jay Drydyk 'Capitalism, Socialism and Civil Society', pp. 461-464.

28. We elaborate this claim in a book devoted to Hegel's concept of the ethical State, in progress.

persons whose right to satisfaction is formally rather than substantively recognized.

As the private particularity of knowing and willing, the principle of this system of needs contains absolute universality, the universality of freedom, only abstractly and therefore as the right of property. [29]

Social interaction for the purposes of satisfying particular needs is grounded in personality, which is abstract. Indeed in *The Philosophy of Right* section on 'Abstract Right' Hegel shows why taking possession of external things is an activity of the abstractly related person whose self-relation is objectified in property ownership (commodity ownership including ownership of one's labour power and its products) and recognized in the exchange of property between property owners.[30] Because the System of Needs recognizes the Universal element in the activities of men and women *only abstractly* or *formally* it manifests *recognition* of their being as the bearers of the right to property. But this form of the unity does not supply a ground for others to recognize concrete persons' desires for the satisfaction of their needs as a demand *on them*.

Instead, the interaction that the System of Needs implicitly recognizes as belonging to *property owning subjects* gives rise to the explicit recognition of the latter as such through the Administration of Justice, the system in which the right of property 'is no longer merely implicit but has attained its recognized actuality as the protection of property'.[31]

Before turning to this second form of unity within Civil Society, we should note finally that if, as we have been arguing, the System of Needs is strictly organized as a self-determined totality then the comprehensiveness of its categorial differentiated unity must also be manifested in the nature of the specific systems into which it differentiates itself. According to Hegel,

> the entire complex [of market relations] is built up into particular systems of needs, means and types of work relative to these needs, modes of satisfaction and of [...] education.[32]

Hegel insists that this complex includes a rationally grounded division of the Estates system into the *'substantial'*, the *'formal'* and the *'universal'* Estates.[33] We will examine the specifics of this

---

29. Hegel, PR, §208.
30. We discuss this further in the next volume of the series.
31. Hegel, PR, §208.
32. Hegel, PR, §201.
33. Hegel, PR, §202.

system differentiation along with the question of its relevance for the twenty-first century in the next chapter.

SECOND FORM OF THE UNITY OF PARTICULAR AND UNIVERSAL: THE ADMINISTRATION OF JUSTICE

The justice system is 'the sphere of relatedness'.[34] It expresses another form of the unity of the Particular and the Universal, one in which their unity is *explicit yet limited*. That is, the Universal is explicitly known and willed as such. It therefore takes the form of positive law.[35] But since it does not embrace the whole of the concrete person but only his or her abstract being, the being of property-owning subjectivity, the relation between the two takes the form of an *'external obligation* to obey' the laws.[36] The unity is accordingly limited to this extent.[37]

Once again, one can locate the rational ground for this claim in one of the features of the form of the unity of the Particular and the Universal that the System of Needs manifests. We have already suggested that in the System of Needs reflective awareness (the moment of Individuality) is confined to the person (Particularity) and is expressed in terms of an instrumental rationality in which the Universal is taken to be a means toward the satisfaction of particular needs. Even though it is the Universal that secures satisfaction, this is not incorporated into the person's identity; the Universal as such is not an end for the human being. Accordingly, the attainment of satisfaction marked by contingency or arbitrariness results in the failure of the System of Needs fully to secure that which the Universal is taken to secure, namely the livelihood or welfare of each person:

> In the system of needs, the livelihood and welfare of every single person is a possibility whose actual attainment is just as much conditioned by his caprices and particular endowment as by the objective system of needs [...] the right actually present in the particular requires, first, that accidental hindrances to one aim or another be removed, and undisturbed safety of person and property be attained; and secondly, that the securing of every single person's livelihood and welfare be treated and actualized as a right, i.e. that particular welfare as such be so treated.[38]

---

34. Hegel, *PR*, §209.
35. Hegel, *PR*, §210 and §211.
36. G.W.F. Hegel, *Hegel's Philosophy of Mind: Being Part Three of the Encyclopaedia of the Philosophical Sciences*, §530.
37. Hegel, *PR*, §229.
38. Hegel, *PR*, §230.

The 'right actually present in the particular' gives rise to what contemporary rights language distinguishes as welfare rights or rights of recipience as well as negative rights to welfare. Such rights are not merely positive in the sense of 'entitlement to do certain things' but also generate demands on appropriate others to provide relevant 'services, aids or facilities'.[39] These others must therefore manifest the unity of Universal and Particular in yet another form.

THIRD FORM OF THE UNITY OF PARTICULAR AND UNIVERSAL: THE POLICE - CORPORATION

According to Hegel, due to the limited nature of the unity that defines the Particular and the Universal in the justice system,

> the actualization of this unity through its extension to the whole ambit of particularity is (i) the specific function of the Police [...] [and] (ii) it is the Corporation which actualizes the unity completely.[40]

So the third of these forms of unity is expressed in the combined activity of the Police and the Corporation as the third moment of Civil Society. Following the analysis of the Disjunctive Syllogism one can note that the Police-Corporation emerges out of the inability of the System of Needs fully to define and care for individuals' welfare, an inability that results from the Universal's incapacity for self-thematization in the implicit unity that characterizes the System of Needs.

The Police takes up this role, having as 'its primary purpose [...] to actualize and maintain the universal contained within the particularity of Civil society'.[41] In reflectively seeking its unification with the concrete person (the Particular) the activities of the Police give effect to that which is posited as implicit in the System of Needs, namely the unity of the Universal and the Particular. In other words, when necessary the Police authority regulates the activities associated with need satisfaction given that the exposure of privately acting agents to contingencies beyond their control results in injury to others.[42] In the light of our analysis in the previous chapter it follows that this regulatory power extends to domestic, local and global activities.

The specific purpose of the Police's supervisory and intervening role is to counteract contingency and arbitrariness. Accordingly,

---

39. H.J. McCloskey, 'Rights' *The Philosophical Quarterly*, vol. 15, 1965, pp. 115-127.
40. Hegel, *PR*, §229.
41. Hegel, *PR*, §249.
42. Hegel, *PR*, §232-233.

the forms of intervention vary in accordance with the variety of ways in which activities directed to need satisfaction are subject to contingency, arbitrariness and non-recognition. These include ensuring the security of concrete persons against injury arising from contingency in the form of wrong doing; overseeing the activities of small-scale collectives and 'general utility' organizations, which arise through private activities that become Universal in meeting common interests; making adjustments to produce a balance between competing interests or to take account of factors beyond the control of particular individuals; taking the place of the family to provide for education, to counteract extravagance and provide care for the poverty stricken; and taking measures to expand markets beyond territorial borders in order to provide surplus workers with a means of subsistence.[43]

Pursuant to the logic of the Disjunctive Syllogism, the public authority's control 'takes the form of an external system and organization for the protection and security of particular ends and interests *en masse*'.[44] This control remains 'external' in character in so far as it is directed at the activities of 'private persons' (immediate Particularity) who do not as such recognize the Universal as their own (the Universal is taken to be external to the immediate Particular). As Hegel puts it,

> inasmuch as it is still the particular will which governs the choice of this or that end, the universal authority [...] remains in the first instance, (a) restricted to the sphere of contingencies, and (b) an external organization.[45]

Given that this form of unity is both 'restricted' and 'external' in the ways just indicated, 'the unification [of the Universal and the Particular] which it effects is only relative'.[46] From this it follows that within Civil Society, the universal authority's regulatory practices and intervention in the affairs of (global) civil life are limited to *counteracting the effects of*, as distinct from eliminating, the contingencies and arbitrariness associated with the operations of market relations. This then is the fundamental limit of the public authority, regardless of the field of operation of its powers.

---

43. Hegel, *PR*, §231-§248. In the next volume we discuss the relationship of this account to the current racial neoliberal reality. For an insightful analysis of the latter see David Theo Goldberg, *The Threat of Race*, pp. 327-376.
44. Hegel, *PR*, §249.
45. Hegel, *PR*, §231.
46. Hegel, *PR*, §229.

By way of contrast to the activity of the Police, within the Corporation the concrete person gives effect to the unification of the Particular and the Universal:

> This Universal [that 'contained within the particularity of Civil society'] is immanent in the interests of particularity itself and, in accordance with the Idea, particularity makes it the end and object of its own willing and activity. In this way Ethical principles circle back and appear in Civil society as a factor immanent in it; this constitutes the specific character of the Corporation.[47]

In the Corporation the object of reflection is individuals' welfare interests qua Corporate members or 'the universal immanent in the interests of particularity'. Relations between Corporate members are defined by the principle of mutual aid; the support that each gives to and receives from others reflects their universal interest. This is why the Corporation offers an appropriate way of addressing the problem of poverty amongst members. According to Hegel,

> [w]ithin the Corporation the help which poverty receives loses its accidental character and the humiliation wrongfully associated with it. The wealthy perform their duties to their fellow associates and thus riches cease to inspire either pride or envy. In these conditions rectitude obtains its proper recognition and respect.[48]

Significantly, the Corporation's object of reflection (the Universal) and the reflecting agents for whom the Universal is their own end (the Particular) are *internally* related:

> In the Corporation these moments ['subjective particularity and objective universality [...] sundered in Civil society to begin with'] are united in an inward fashion, so that in this union particular welfare is present as a right and is actualized.[49]

Thus the Corporation manifests the *completely actualized unity* of the Universal and the Particular *in a concrete whole*.[50]

As already suggested, within this associational form, members have the opportunity to detect the significance of the Universal in what interests them directly. Because this opportunity arises in connection with the *specific ways* in which they go about pursuing their own interests, its proper site is the specific

---

47. Hegel, *PR*, §249.
48. Hegel, *PR*, §253 Remark.
49. Hegel, *PR*, §255.
50. Hegel, *PR*, §229.

labour organization that is differentiated by reference to members' particular skills:

> The labour organization of Civil society is split, in accordance with the nature of its particulars, into different branches. The implicit likeness of such particulars to one another becomes really existent in an association, as something common to its members. Hence, a selfish purpose, directed towards its particular self-interest, apprehends and evinces itself at the same time as universal; and a member of Civil society is in virtue of his own particular skill a member of a Corporation, whose universal purpose is thus wholly concrete and no wider in scope than the purpose involved in business, its proper task and interest.[51]

To summarize, for Hegel the Corporation and, specifically, the institutional form of the labour organization, manifest the unity of the Universal and the Particular in the distinct form of an *internally related* unity of a *concrete whole*. Here although subjective particularity assumes a specific Corporate identity pursuant to the particular shared skills that serve to further each subject's particular interests, participation in Corporate relations also cultivates the subject's reflective identification with the Universal that is in turn immanent in these specific interests. This is why, on the one hand, the ethical achievement of this institutional form is the actualization of particular welfare *as a right* and, on the other, the completeness of this actualized right resides in the Corporate body as a concrete whole.

CIVIL SOCIETY'S INTERNALLY DIFFERENTIATED SYSTEMS

In an attempt to explain why Hegel includes the justice system and the Police in his discussion of the concept of Civil Society rather than in that of the State, Brod suggests that Hegel arranges his topics with a view to overcoming the conflation, characteristic of liberal theory, of the *economic regulatory* and *political legislative* functions of governments.[52] But Brod does not explain Hegel's reasons for insisting on such a differentiation. By contrast, our analysis has shown that the inclusion of the justice and welfare systems meets with the logical demand that the three moments of Civil Society manifest the different forms of the unity of the Universal and the Particular. Moreover, the second and third forms of the unity, which define the respective structures of the justice system

---

51. Hegel, *PR*, §251.
52. Brod, *Hegel's Philosophy of Politics*, pp. 92-93.

and the Police, emerge from the first, implicit unity characterizing the System of Needs. Together these forms of unity exhaustively manifest the forms that the unity can take at the 'stage of division', modernity's moment of self-denial.[53] At the same time each one of them also defines the totality, rendering the concept of Civil Society as a comprehensive categorical differentiated unity.

These are the forms of unity available within our current global reality in so far as this reality conforms to the logic of a comprehensive categorical differentiated unity. That is, in so far as the abovementioned set of relations, the relations characterizing global civil society, manifests the Judgement 'A is B and C and D' that is also 'the *either-or* of B, C and D',[54] each of the moments qua one form of the unity manifests the logical form of the Disjunctive Syllogism. First, the moments of Civil Society are defined in terms of the way in which each expresses the principle of inter-subjectivity—their interrelation or the unity of the Universal and the Particular—while retaining its own character as a Particular. That is, the definition of each moment in terms of the unity it effects is also one that *excludes* the reflective standpoint of the other moments or particulars. Second, by determining itself in its interrelation with all the determinate instances of the principle of the unity of the Universal and the Particular, Civil Society reinforces the differentiatedness of each of its moments.

According to Hegel, the abovementioned exclusion also manifests 'the particular as *individuality* to the exclusion of *others*'.[55] If the strict organization thesis is correct, then we should expect to find each and every Particular Individual belonging to the system differentiated Civil Society—the System of Needs, the Administration of Justice and the Police-Corporation—to manifest *a tendency to exclude others*. Here we should pause to consider a possible objection to the reading we are proposing. One might think that the *intervening* activity of the Police presents a counter-case in so far as its activity does not imply such *exclusion*. But this would be to misunderstand the meaning of exclusion in the present context. For even the Police qua distinct moment (albeit together with the Corporation), is itself taken to *give effect to a unity* of the social whole and *the form of this unity* is not reducible to that of the other moments even as it incorporates within its activity the phenomena at the heart of the other moments, namely law and

---

53. Hegel, *PR*, §184.
54. Hegel, *SL*, p. 701.
55. Hegel, *SL*, p. 701.

market relations. It is in this sense of exclusive self-determining activity that the Particular system manifests Individuality to the exclusion of others.

The final point to note in the present context is that by excluding the forms of the unity that the other moments manifest, in its own effecting of the unification, each moment asserts its qualitative difference from the rest suggesting its relative *autonomy*. The Particular qua Individual 'to the exclusion of others' is 'a *self-related* determination' and not 'merely a relative one'.[56] In the next chapters we will turn to consider some of the implications of this analysis of Civil Society's differentiated moments as well as its usefulness for making sense of some salient features of global civil society.

---

56. Hegel, *SL*, p. 701.

7. THE LOGIC OF THE ESTATES AND GLOBAL CIVIL SOCIETY

In the previous chapter we noted that in manifesting the logic of a self-determined totality, the Hegelian System of Needs must internally differentiate itself into the Estates system, which consists of three Estates. One is the 'substantial' Estate, which characteristically organizes agricultural activity. A second, the 'formal' Estate, deals with business or market related activity and is further divided into craftsmanship, manufacturing and trade. Finally, the 'universal' Estate explicitly addresses the Universal interests falling within its scope.[1] Hegel's assignment of a role to the Estates system has divided commentators. Notably, H.S. Harris argues that Hegel's approach consistently proposes a specific economic and political role for each of the Estates in the context of a self-governing social organism.[2] But others have called for a revision or abandonment of Hegel's theory of the Estates on the grounds that his account is internally incoherent and/or unsuited to the demands of the world as we now live it. For example, as we saw in Chapter Five in the context of discussing Hegel's reasons for acknowledging the condition of poverty, Wartenberg maintains that Hegel implicitly relies on a second unacknowledged theory of class structure, which renders the Hegelian concept of the Estates system incompatible with an implied notion of the working class.[3] Reading Hegel's concept of Civil Society as offering an account of the economy understood as a sphere of social justice, Winfield argues that only

---

1. Hegel, *PR*, §202; §204.
2. H. S. Harris, 'The Social Ideal of Hegel's Economic Theory', in L.S. Stepelevich and David Lamb (eds.), *Hegel's Philosophy of Action*, Atlantic Highlands, New Jersey, Humanities Press, 1983, pp. 49-74 at pp. 57-65.
3. Wartenberg, 'Poverty and Class Structure in Hegel's Theory of Civil Society', pp. 169-182.

Hegel's formal Estate can be consistently included in the System and he makes the point that the substantial Estate seems blind to the contemporary reality of a significant degree of social mobility amongst at least part of the world's population.[4] Ludwig Siep also maintains that Hegel's Estates system limits individuals' freedom to choose their occupation at the same time as relying too much on 'stable conditions of socially necessary labour' that are no longer predominant.[5] Franco complains that Hegel's account of the agricultural Estate was already out of step with occupational developments in Hegel's own time.[6] Stedman Jones also argues that Hegel's account of the Estates system is outdated in so far as it presupposes 'a stable social and occupational geography of professional associations and artisanal guilds'.[7] This critique raises the question of whether Hegel's account can accommodate the global mobility of the labour market and the related reality of rapidly changing skills.

In this chapter we want to indicate how reading Hegel's claims concerning the Estates through the categorial interrelations that define the Disjunctive Syllogism enables us: firstly, to resolve the interpretive dispute surrounding Hegel's inclusion of the Estates system in the account of Civil Society; secondly, to evaluate conflicting assessments of the relationship of the Estates system to the notions of the working class and the unemployed poor; and, thirdly, to appreciate how the Estates system addresses some of the complexities of our current global reality. We will begin by considering the question of the internal coherence of Hegel's account of the Estates system firstly in terms of the logic that grounds the system's internal differentiation and then in terms of its relationship to the concepts of the working class and the unemployed poor. From here we will proceed to a discussion of the system's application to contemporary labour relations and, in particular, to the issue of labour market fluidity, whether in terms of social or global population mobility or of the increased reliance on transferable and rapidly changing skills. For the purposes of this discussion we are in agreement with Keane's observation that we have indeed entered the era of 'turbocapitalism', which is marked by 'lighter

---

4. Winfield, 'Hegel's Challenge to the Modern Economy', pp. 239-242.
5. Ludwig Siep, 'The Contemporary Relevance of Hegel's Practical Philosophy', in Katerina Deligiorgi (ed.), *Hegel: New Directions*, London, Acumen, 2006, pp. 143-158 at p. 147.
6. Franco, *Hegel's Philosophy of Freedom*, pp. 259-260.
7. Stedman Jones, 'Hegel and the Economics of Civil Society', pp. 129-130.

regulations of capital flows, the deregulation of labour markets and welfare cutbacks'.[8] It represents the desire for the emancipation of profit-oriented capital from all external restrictions on its free movement, including taxation and other territorial state restrictions, labour conditions secured by trade unions and social custom.[9] With turbocapitalism globalization forces are now the norm. These latter include global commodity chains that produce, assemble and distribute products in different parts of the world, trade investment within firms that facilitates tax avoidance, and the establishment of a global competitive labour pool.[10]

THE SELF-DIFFERENTIATION OF THE SYSTEM OF NEEDS INTO THE ESTATES

What precisely does it mean to claim, as Hegel does, that the internal division of the Estates system, as distinct from particular membership in any particular Estate, is rationally grounded?[11] The previous chapter's analysis of the Disjunctive Syllogism suggests that in order to manifest its Individuality the System of Needs must incorporate into its own identity the unity defining the other moments of Civil Society. The determinateness of the System of Needs exhibits Individuality, the third moment of the comprehensive categorial unity, when the Particularized Universality constitutes itself as a self-related determination. Here we want to suggest that the division of the System of Needs into the Estates manifests precisely this logic. Indeed taken together the descriptions of the three Estates exhibit all the forms of unity that are possible within Civil Society in its negative moment and, by extension, within the reality of global civil society. The substantial Estate manifests the immediate positive unity first encountered in the abstract sphere of the Family as the (implicit) organizing principle of its way of life.[12] The formal Estate manifests the negative unity that Civil Society exhibits in its initial appearance as a system of interdependence while the universal Estate reveals a way of life that is explicitly organized around securing 'universal interests'.[13] Thus the System of Needs expresses the social whole through excluding the other systems of Civil Society—Administration of Justice,

---

8. Keane, *Global Civil Society?*, p. 67.
9. Keane, *Global Civil Society?*, pp. 67-68.
10. Keane, *Global Civil Society?*, pp. 73-74.
11. Hegel, *PR*, §202.
12. Hegel, *PR*, §203.
13. Hegel, *PR*, §204-§205.

Police-Corporations—in a way that establishes its Individuality through its immanent connectedness with the unity defining the other moments. This is what we take Hegel to mean when he claims that the division of the Estates constitutes Estate organization 'as particularity become objective to itself'.[14]

THE INTERNAL COHERENCE OF THE ESTATES SYSTEM

Clearly, the substantial and universal Estates fail to conform to the instrumental logic characterizing Civil Society as a system of interdependence (Chapter Four). As we noted at the outset, Winfield suggests that only the formal Estate, which deals with business relations, ought to have a place in the Hegelian system. His reason is that it alone issues from the structure of commodity exchange relations. On this reasoning, to update Hegel's account of the System of Needs we should eliminate references to both the substantial and universal Estates replacing them with 'a class division wholly endogenous to commodity relations', something like the way in which Hegel himself specifies the division within the business Estate.[15] In contrast Franco suggests that despite occupational developments even in his own time, Hegel includes the agricultural Estate because 'the conservative, trusting, substantial disposition' by which this Estate is characterized 'serves to counteract the instability and uncertainty that flow from the innovative and individualistic spirit of the bourgeoisie'.[16] This said, Franco does not clarify how Hegel might have conceived the presence of one Estate as serving to counteract the effects of another and Franco's reference to the *Logic's* dialectical method offers no assistance in this regard.

Although Winfield is correct to point out that two of the Estates exhibit forms of relations that are *external* to that characterizing the market, our analysis of the Disjunctive Syllogism indicates that this is not an oversight on Hegel's part. What Winfield fails to realize is that the differentiation of the Estates should not be derived pursuant to (the unity exhibited by) market relations but in accordance with the logical requirement that this unity should be posited as *one of the forms* of unity that Civil Society makes possible. This means that the way of life associated with market relations constitutes only *one* of a range of possibilities and this range becomes visible with the presence of productive relations that are not reducible to regulated commodity production and exchange

---

14. Hegel, *PR*, §206.
15. Winfield, 'Hegel's Challenge to the Modern Economy', p. 242.
16. Franco, *Hegel's Philosophy of Freedom*, p. 259.

between formal equals (formal Estate relations). Accordingly in Hegel's scheme both the substantial or agricultural Estate, which expresses the possibility of an immediate (unreflective) substantial unity, and the universal Estate, which is explicitly concerned with the pursuit of the universal interest, serve this role.

Of course, these subtleties are rendered invisible when one treats Hegel's concept of Civil Society as conforming to CSII, the model that conflates civil society with market capitalism (Chapter One). Indeed when one fails to have regard to the details of the analysis that the Disjunctive Syllogism makes possible and one insists, as do Winfield and Franco, on reducing the Hegelian concept to an account of the economy and its regulatory institutions, then one cannot appreciate the rationale for the diversity of productive relations that Hegel's account envisages, when one takes into account a broadly conceived dialectical method that derives from the *Logic*.

THE ESTATES, THE WORKING CLASS AND THE UNEMPLOYED POOR

As we mentioned above, one way in which Hegel's account of the Estates is said to be out of sorts with the demands of the contemporary world concerns its failure explicitly to incorporate a theory of economic class relations. Wartenberg argues that although Hegel's account of Civil Society explicitly invokes one sort of class structure in the Estates, it also implies a second theory of class that recognizes the divisions between rich and poor and the existence of a working class. According to Wartenberg, the implicit theory emerges only in the context of Hegel's discussion of poverty and in particular of the rabble of paupers. Wartenberg claims that the implicit theory is crucial not only for assessing Hegel's discussion of poverty, but for understanding the flaw in Hegel's theory of the ethical State that supposedly stems from the fact that the problems of the working class are never acknowledged, let alone resolved in the State.[17] Wartenberg makes it clear that his criticism is 'theoretical' rather than methodological—and in this respect distinguishes his criticism from that of Marx—meaning that the failure in Hegel's theory 'stems from his failure to grant theoretical status to phenomena that he sees as necessary to that society'.[18]

---

17. For a summary of this argument see Wartenberg, 'Poverty and Class Structure in Hegel's Theory of Civil Society', p. 176. See also Ritter, *Hegel and the French Revolution*, p. 71.

18. Wartenberg, 'Poverty and Class Structure in Hegel's Theory of Civil

How should we understand Wartenberg's reference to 'the failure to grant theoretical status' to the phenomena in question? In the context of his critique it cannot mean merely that Hegel fails to acknowledge the existence of economic class divisions since he must clearly be doing at least this much if he 'sees [such phenomena] as necessary to that society'. Rather in order to have critical force, Wartenberg's point must be that the concept of the working class plays no *special role* in Hegel's account of the categorial development, as it should. In other words, Wartenberg needs to establish that the notion of the working class has an implied ethical or rational significance within the Hegelian system that Hegel has overlooked. Yet Wartenberg does not, and arguably cannot, make out this claim. As we noted in Chapter Five, Hegel's theory does indeed have the conceptual resources to identify the existence of a class of individuals, the unemployed poor, who are excluded from the benefits of the System of Needs. But Wartenberg wants to claim further that Hegel ought to have developed the category of economic class in line with the sociological significance of this feature of capitalist society. This is because he reads Hegel as offering a *sociological* critique.

But what if we read Hegel as proposing a logically informed normative theory in the sense of an ethical-ontological theory, instead of a merely sociological account of the features of 'society's existence', as Wartenberg would have us believe?[19] In this case we should understand the concept of Civil Society as offering an account only of those features of society that are of ethical significance on logical systemic grounds. Accordingly, in order to succeed Wartenberg's objection must presuppose that the ethical significance of (the development of) Civil Society calls for an exposition of the role of workers as an economic class. Here it is worth noting that Wartenberg's discussion conflates the concepts of 'workers' and 'the working class'.[20] Whereas the former is properly part of the subject matter of the concept of Civil Society, the latter and its Marxist association with the logic of class conflict, have no place in the elaboration of the concept of Civil Society unless it can be shown to be an ethically significant (logically informed) phenomenon and not just a sociologically noteworthy one. Let us explain.

Society', p. 181.

19. Wartenberg, 'Poverty and Class Structure in Hegel's Theory of Civil Society', p. 179.

20. Wartenberg, 'Poverty and Class Structure in Hegel's Theory of Civil Society', p. 180.

From the standpoint of the operative logical categorical relations, there are two possible grounds for assigning a place to the concept of the working class and the related concept of class conflict. The first concerns aspects of Civil Society that are ethical in the sense that we have already discussed in relation to the emergence of formally free subjectivity and the Estates system. These are the aspects of Civil Society that are not informed by the transitional logic that gives rise to the movement from Civil Society to the ethical State and they are not part of that which must be overcome. The concept of the working class does not fall into this category. As H.S. Harris maintains when explaining the role of the Estates, in order to meet their political function in the ethical State, the Estates 'must already have resolved economic "class" conflict before the political process can properly begin'.[21] H. S. Harris shows that the Estates can address the question of the political mediation of *different* (competing though not opposed) interests emerging in industrial relations only when economic class based problems have been resolved. Because for Hegel, this resolution presupposes that 'capitalist accumulation must be brought to an end', capitalist accumulation also does not play a role in his account of the modern economic exchange relations within the ethical State.[22]

If this reading is correct then Hegel must and indeed does assign a place to *economic class divisions* in Civil Society, divisions that as Harris argues must be overcome if the Estates are to play their assigned role within the more advanced order of the ethical State by comparison with that of Civil Society. As we will see shortly in relation to the class of the unemployed poor, there are indeed logical categorial grounds for acknowledging class relations defined by economic inequality within Civil Society. Although this is the other possible logical ground for assigning a role to the *working* class, on our analysis, unlike the unemployed poor, the workers of Hegel's Civil Society do not form an economic class *as such*; they do not form a class with interests opposed to capitalist accumulation. Hegel is therefore consistent in not assigning *ethical* significance to the concept of the working class

---

21. Harris, 'The Social Ideal of Hegel's Economic Theory', p. 58. See also Onuf, 'Late Modern Civil Society', p. 52.
22. Harris, 'The Social Ideal of Hegel's Economic Theory', p. 68. Although Harris' discussion draws on Hegel's earlier writings, it forms part of a defence of the view that 'there is one concept of 'political justice' implicit in all of his [Hegel's] social writings': Harris, 'The Social Ideal of Hegel's Economic Theory', p. 51.

and of class conflict within the conceptual framework of the concept of Civil Society.

What of the position and role of the unemployed poor in the Hegelian account? Wood argues that having been deprived of their humanity the members of the rabble have neither rights nor duties toward society. He notes that the presence of the rabble threatens the very principles of Civil Society in so far as the poor who are denied their existence as free persons come to deny the like existence of others. Since this is a systematic wrong against the individuals who belong to the class of the unemployed poor, it constitutes a violation of their right as persons and this in turn gives rise to a criminality that Hegel defines in terms of the rejection of the Universal.[23] Despite this rebelliousness amongst the members of the rabble, Wood suggests further that Hegel nevertheless sees the rabble 'not as the creator of a new order, but only as the corruptor of the old' given that it is constituted by no more than 'an alienated mentality of envy and hatred [...] a contemptuous refusal to recognize anyone's rights'.[24]

Žižek's analysis agrees with that of Wood in relation to the lack of mutual recognition. According to his reading of Hegel,

> Poverty is not only a material condition, but also the subjective position of being deprived of social recognition, which is why it is not enough to provide for the poor [...] they are still deprived of the satisfaction of autonomously taking care of their own lives.[25]

He also agrees with the claim that for Hegel the members of the rabble have no duties:

> Those who do not find this recognition [those who cannot actualize their freedom in "the rationality of the universal ethical order", which provides subjects with their "substantial content and recognition"] have also the right to rebel: if a class of people is systematically deprived of their rights, of their very dignity as persons, they are *eo ipso* also released from their duties towards the social order, because this order is no longer their ethical substance [...] the "rabble" is a class of people to whom systematically, not just in a contingent way, recognition by the ethical substance is denied, so that they do not owe anything to society, and are dispensed of any duties towards it.[26]

---

23. Wood, *Hegel's Ethical Thought*, pp. 253-254.
24. Wood, *Hegel's Ethical Thought*, p. 255.
25. Žižek, *Less than Nothing*, p. 433.
26. Žižek, *Less than Nothing*, p. 433.

The Logic of the Estates and Global Civil Society 157

But unlike Wood who does not see any positive implications flowing from this position, Žižek emphasises the supposed implications of the *non-place* of the class of rabble in favour of the existence of a right to rebel: as 'the non-recognized element of the existing order' the rabble is 'inherent to it, but with no place within the order'. Moreover, Žižek claims, 'as excluded, lacking recognition of its particular position, the rabble is the universal as such'.[27] What does Žižek mean by this? On his interpretation of the operative Hegelian concept of the concrete universal, in the present context,

> universality [is the genus] which includes itself among its species, in the guise of a singular moment lacking particular content—in short it is precisely those who are without their proper place within the social whole (like the rabble) who stand for the universal dimension of the society which generates them. This is why the rabble cannot be abolished without radically transforming the entire social edifice—and Hegel is fully aware of this.[28]

Franco opposes the suggestion that Hegel assigns to the unemployed poor a right of rebellion against the social order on the basis of the observation that there is little textual support for it. He maintains that, instead of Hegel supporting the overthrow of the structure of civil society as a whole, he offers a revisionist vision of bourgeois society.[29] But it is worth noting here that Žižek claims that on this question Hegel actually fails to follow through the implications of his own analysis.

We want to suggest that in fact in order to assign to Hegel's class of rabble the potential to take part in radical social transformation Žižek introduces into Hegel's analysis an inappropriate conception of universality. To explain we must recall the analysis of the Disjunctive Syllogism, which provides the conceptual resources for explaining why Civil Society necessarily gives rise to the rabble. It also allows us to comment on the connection of the rabble's relationship to Civil Society's transformative potential. Within the logical categorical development, the Disjunctive Syllogism manifests the completed Syllogism. Recall from Chapter Two that the completed Syllogism gives rise to a comprehensive categorical differentiated unity. In other words, we have here a mutually informing unity of the Universal, Particular and Individual.

---

27. Žižek, *Less than Nothing*, p. 433.
28. Žižek, *Less than Nothing*, p. 432.
29. Franco, *Hegel's Philosophy of Freedom*, p. 272.

However, within the confines of the concept of Civil Society in its abstractness, this concrete Universality does not characterize Civil Society as a whole but is instead restricted in its existential manifestation to the Corporation-Police unity. So the ethical substantiality plays *an explicit role* in giving effect to the unity of the categories only via the mediation of the Particularized Individual but otherwise finds itself in a contradictory relationship to the mediation characterizing Civil Society. This contradictory relationship arises given that in its completed form the single Syllogism does not yet give adequate expression to the comprehensive categorical differentiated unity. As we explained in Chapter Six, the conclusion of the Syllogism expresses determinate being only from the limited standpoint of the Particular and so in their distinctness from Particularity, Universality and Individuality remain abstract in so far as they do not also supply the reflective standpoint from which to express their unity. For this to be achieved the logical categorial development must proceed to the concept of Objectivity at which point the structure of logical categorial relations acquires the complexity of a differentiated unity of three Syllogisms, each from the reflective standpoint of one of the moments of Universality, Particularity and Individuality. Accordingly although the Disjunctive Syllogism is the *completed form* of the single Syllogism, this form itself is still incomplete relative to the subsequent categorial development, which gives rise to the concrete Universality of the ethical substantiality that takes the form of a unity of three Syllogisms.

Here we have the full logical structure that exhibits the moment of denial of the ethical as self-denial, which characterizes Civil Society. Accordingly, since the unity of the Police-Corporation manifests the Disjunctive Syllogism, it also serves as the existential manifestation of the completed Syllogism and, hence, also contains the aspect of incompleteness in the sense explained above. Within the structure of the single Syllogism this element of perpetual incompleteness—incompleteness that is not preventable—is manifested by the existence of the unemployed poor, but also of the class of wealthy who no less manifest the mentality of the rabble. This same logic also permits us to explain Hegel's implied acknowledgement that the logic of Civil Society leads to the dispossession of Indigenous peoples as a result of colonization. Although Hegel does not mention it, this logic also underpins the notion of organized criminal activity. For different reasons, each of these groups is denied the potential to take part in Civil Society's ethical aspect that, as we have seen, consists in the subjective particular being educated towards the universal interest. Each of these otherwise very different phenomena serves as a case of an existential manifestation of the radical incompleteness of the unity of Civil Society's two principles since, in one way or another, the subjective particular denies its unity with the Universal and in doing so manifests the denied ethical substantiality that characterizes modernity's self-denial.

It follows from the above, that contra Žižek, it is not the ethical substantiality that denies to the rabble recognition. Rather it is the class of rabble, whether as the poor unemployed or the indignant wealthy, the class of criminals and the objects of criminal dispossession, whose presence renders visible Civil Society's very denial of its underlying ethical substantiality. Although Žižek is right to suggest that Civil Society denies a proper place to the rabble, far from thereby linking the rabble to Civil Society's potential for radical social transformation towards an ethical order that renders rights effective, the non-place of the rabble merely gives rise to the demand for a place for its members as individuals within the existing order or, in other words, for individuals' access to the enabling conditions of membership in an Estates system and the benefits of Civil Society. Let us turn next to the question of what the concept of Civil Society envisages for individual membership of the Estates and whether the theory can accommodate the reality of social mobility that we mentioned above.

INDIVIDUAL PARTICIPATION IN THE ESTATES SYSTEM AND SOCIAL MOBILITY

So far we have argued that the organization of society into the Estates is necessitated by the structure of the Disjunctive Syllogism. How does this affect individuals' choice of membership in a particular Estate? As well as Winfield's objection that social mobility is denied to members of the agricultural Estate, Siep argues that individuals' occupational freedom is unavoidably restricted due to the fact that membership is tied to faculties and education.[30] But Hegel also makes the point that even though a number of factors influence the question of the particular Estate to which any particular individual is to belong, 'the essential and determining factors are subjective opinion and the individual's arbitrary will'.[31] The reason is that although the Disjunctive Syllogism necessitates

---
30. Siep, 'The Contemporary Relevance of Hegel's Practical Philosophy', p. 147.
31. Hegel, PR, §206

the internal differentiation of the Estates, this does not change the fact that it is the individual qua *subjective particular* whose agency and participation are at issue.

Individual persons' assignment of membership in a particular Estate is not determined systemically, for this would be to suppress the full range of the diverse forms of relatedness available to the subjective particular. Instead, the structure of the Disjunctive Syllogism renders these diverse forms fully visible. Because the idea of social mobility is usually associated with the way of life of the formal or business Estate, on the face of it the notion of socially mobile individuals seems incompatible with the way of life characterizing the substantial or agricultural Estate. But this need not, and for Hegel should not, be the case. As Pinkard points out, the possibility of mobility is a distinctively modern aspect of Hegel's account of the Estates system. This means that one's birth and family cannot *determine* one's Estate even in the case of someone who chooses the Estate into which he or she was born.[32] Due to the existence of the formal Estate *alongside* the other Estates, it is always possible for someone (in their capacity as a subjective particular) to resist encouragement toward or renounce participation of one of the other Estates.

Hegel's system can and does accommodate social mobility that contributes to the development of formally free subjectivity even though the Estates differentiation supplies a necessary structure of relations. Winfield and Siep fail to appreciate this point because in focusing on the logic governing the Estates system's self-differentiation, they misunderstand the character of individual participation in the system. By comparison, Stedman Jones' critique concentrates on the way the Estates system functions in combination with the account of individuals' membership in Corporations:

> It is clear from his apparent exclusion of mere day labourers from corporations that the institutions which Hegel devised to mediate the otherwise depersonalized relationship between the individual and the state still presupposed a stable social and occupational geography of professional associations and artisanal guilds connected to the state through a renovated system of estates'.[33]

Stedman Jones concludes that, in so far as it relies on a concept of the Corporation that is functionally tied to an outdated Estates

---

32. Pinkard, *Hegel: A Biography*, p. 485.
33. Stedman Jones, 'Hegel and the Economics of Civil Society', pp. 129-130.

system, Hegel's concept of Civil Society ultimately fails to speak to the current demands of modernity.³⁴

But here it is important to bear in mind the role that the Estates play in contributing to the shaping of individuals' outlook. As Pinkard points out,

> Without the estates, individuals would have only the "moral" standpoint to guide them, only a very general sense that they satisfy their "universal" obligations: with the estates, individuals have a much more concrete sense of how to orient themselves in life. [...] the peasant estate, because of its ties to the land, finds what is good and best for itself has to do with tradition and trust in nature [...]. The "reflective" or business estate finds that what is good and best for it is the rational, "reflective" calculation of what is most efficient for producing and exchanging goods. The "universal" estate of civil servants has as its good the overall flourishing and proper functioning of civil society as a whole, and it thus reasons out its life projects in terms of the virtues involved in a career in public service.³⁵

Stedman Jones' critique fails to take into account the differences in potential outlook between those who do and those who do not have the opportunity to share membership in one of the Estates. It is no accident that Hegel describes 'the Ethical frame of mind' of those who take part in the Estates system, even those who belong to the agricultural Estate, as one of:

> rectitude and *esprit de corps*, that is, the disposition to make oneself a member of one of the moments of civil society by one's own act, through one's energy, industry and skill, to maintain oneself in this position, and to fend for oneself only through this process of mediating oneself with the universal, while in this way gaining recognition in one's own eyes and in the eyes of others.³⁶

For membership gives to individuals their substantive being. This means that in the absence of on-going participation in one of the Estates individuals function as private persons who cannot fully realize their Universal essence.³⁷ This is the unavoidable situation of day labourers or seasonal workers whose relationship to other workers and to the skills they exercise remains limited in this way.

---

34. Stedman Jones, 'Hegel and the Economics of Civil Society', pp. 129-130.
35. Pinkard, *Hegel: A Biography*, p. 484-485.
36. Hegel, PR, §207.
37. Hegel, PR, §207 and §207R.

It follows from the above analysis that one may experience the inability fully to realize one's universal essence as a result of functioning as a private person irrespective of whether one's employment is taken up within the confines of a particular territorial state or whether, as in the case of economic migrants, it is pursued on a global scale. We should add that the same holds for a proportion of today's professionals who, in the interests of remaining globally competitive in their service delivery, concentrate on developing their so-called transferable skills at the expense of developing and enjoying any deep connections with the particular products of their labour. This brings us to the question of the relevance of the Estates system to the current global labour market.

THE GLOBAL LABOUR MARKET

As we indicated at the outset, Siep and Stedman Jones' critique also draws our attention to the issue of whether Hegel's account of the Estates, which serves to embed the concept of the labour organization within a particular structure of labour relations, does not after all underestimate the effects of the global fluidity of the labour market and consequently overlook the related reality of the dependence of workers on rapidly changing skill sets. Franco anticipates this sort of concern when he objects that by including the agricultural Estate Hegel invokes 'a social condition that has almost completely disappeared from the modern world'. In fact Franco reads Hegel's insistence that the agricultural Estate's substantial disposition will continue despite his having observed that the agricultural economy of his own time was being run in accordance with the reflective disposition characterizing the formal Estate, as evidence that 'Hegel obviously lets the desirabilities of his political philosophy overwhelm his otherwise acute observation of emergent social realities'.[38]

Regardless of what Hegel himself was in a position to observe, by focusing on the *different forms of unity* that the logically derived differentiated Estates system makes possible, whether between substantially united beings or between *merely* formal equals, or between formal equals whose activities implicitly or explicitly orient them toward shared universal ends, at the very least we are in a position to recognize a much more complex set of relations than might initially seem to be the case in the current global reality. Siep's objection to Hegel relies on the following observation.

---

38. Franco, *Hegel's Philosophy of Freedom*, pp. 259-260.

> In a technological society where immediate human labour [such as that defining the agricultural Estate] is becoming increasingly redundant and the domain of the leisure and entertainment industry is becoming increasingly important, we cannot deny that socially necessary occupations and professions are also becoming rarer. [...] The production of goods and the supply of services, and the way in which they are distributed through the operation of the market, is effectively turning into a relationship between "private" individuals. In this respect "recognition" now consists almost entirely in relevant financial rewards and other forms of personal "gratification".[39]

There is no doubt that within the current reality mutual recognition is significantly shaped by what Hegel refers to as the mediation of the thing.[40] Nevertheless, as Keane observes, even though we have entered the era of turbocapitalism and are experiencing the effects of its globalizing forces,
> this has not yet resulted in a fully *globalized* world economy in which the lives and livelihoods of every person and patch of the earth are bound to and integrated with all others. Turbocapitalism does not lead to a 'global marketplace', let alone a 'global village'. It has a variety of different effects, ranging from very weak or non-existent forms of integration to very strong or full integration.[41]

At one extreme, whole peoples and regions of the world, as, for example, in sub-Saharan Africa, are left out of the system whereas at the other, twenty-four-hour money markets implicate the whole earth in the effects of their buying and selling activities. Various degrees of market integration are located between these two extremes, depending on the workings of global commodity chains.[42] Accordingly, through the logic informing the substantial Estate one can acknowledge activity that envisages the continued operation of subsistence economies, however small when measured on the global scale.

Similarly, through the co-presence of the formal and the universal Estates one is in a position to recognize the different logics

39. Ludwig Siep, 'The Contemporary Relevance of Hegel's Practical Philosophy', p. 147.
40. See Toula Nicolacopoulos and George Vassilacopoulos, 'Racism, Foreigner Communities and the Onto-pathology of White Australian Subjectivity', in *Whitening Race: Essays in Social and Cultural Criticism*, Aileen Moreton-Robinson (ed.), Canberra, ACT, Aboriginal Studies Press, 2004, pp. 32-47.
41. Keane, *Global Civil Society?*, p. 71.
42. Keane, *Global Civil Society?*, pp. 71-71.

informing the distinctive activities of those working within contemporary NGOs, that is, according to whether their activities are oriented toward attending to the universal interests underpinning their reason d'être or whether they are focused on income generation via activities that model business corporations operating within the confines of market capitalism.

When one looks carefully at the current reality one ought to be able to make sense of the *co-presence* of increasingly fluid market and labour market relations *alongside* more stable modes of productive activity that have not ceased to exist despite the increased global population mobility and, relatedly, alongside non-governmental market interventions that are guided by substantial ethical principles. The approach of some fair trade organizations illustrates this point. For example, Café Direct is a successful global distributor of small growers' coffee, tea and coco. When the supply base for which it was established became unreliable due to the effects of climate change, consistently with a business point of view, and in accordance with the logic that underpins formal Estate relations within the Hegelian system, this distributor could have chosen to look elsewhere for product suppliers. Instead, Café Direct decided to meet the challenge of responding to the unreliability of its supply base by collaborating with its existing suppliers to develop a climate adaptation program. In doing so it sought self-reflectively to implement an ethical business approach by acting on principles of harmony and fairness to the supplier base for whose interests the organization had been established.[43] For present purposes, the important thing to note is that this Café Direct response is not just *atypical* in refusing on this occasion to implement a business model point of view that would have seen it loosen or cut ties with its existing supplier base. The point is rather that one cannot fully explain the activities of this fair trade organization taken as a whole solely by reference to a business model or, in other words, in terms of the fundamentals that define formal or business Estate relations. Even though the activities in question are for the most part compatible with the model that derives from the business Estate, the full picture only comes to view when one takes into account the logic defining the substantial Estate.

The above examples show that rather than failing to appreciate the global labour market in the current reality, Hegel's account offers a way of making sense of its subtleties and complexities.

---

43. See Café Direct, 'Adaptation for Smallholders to Climate Change', http://www.adapcc.org/

From the standpoint of the *Logic* the significant point is that membership of the Estates exhibits the social integration of individuals who identify with one of the ways of life that the Estates system makes available. Because, as already indicated, the Estates do not simply express the form of unity that characterizes market relations their differentiation is not merely aimed at allowing mobility through the reflective identification with the formal Estate that manifests this unity. Since mobility is not the only concern, individuals' identification may also be immediate (non-reflective) or explicitly directed toward the universal interest. This identification, and the associated possibility of realizing one's universal essence, continues to take forms that depend on stable occupational groups and locations as the Estates presuppose. Rather than providing evidence of being outdated in the light of the current dominant modes of labour activity on today's global scale, Hegel's Estates system accommodates the operation of groups, such as the world's fair trade guilds and occupational networks, within the global network of commodity production and circulation. Understood in this way the phenomenon of rapidly changing skills merely adds a further dimension to the global reality of production and exchange processes and relations. Let us turn next to examine the relationship of the logic of the Corporation to the current global reality.

8. THE CORPORATION AS AN ASPECT OF ETHICAL LIFE IN THE GLOBAL ORDER

In Chapter Six we saw how in providing welfare functions, the Police-Corporation unity establishes a third form of the unity between the Universal and the Particular. Here the Universal relates *reflectively* to the Particular (through the Police) and is unified with *the whole* of the Particular (in the Corporation). We also observed that the Corporation provides a certain kind of recognition of individual rights to welfare. But beyond this, Hegel's account raises some interesting questions. One is whether the inclusion of the Corporation in the account of Civil Society threatens the coherence of this account. For example, Honneth has recently argued that the concept of the Corporation cannot be consistently retained within the Hegelian account of Civil Society.[1] As we will see, this critique is related to the further interpretive problem of the significance of Hegel's elaboration of Corporate activity for his wider account of the system of Ethical Life. Another is the question of the relevance and usefulness of the concept of the Corporation for making sense of the global reality of the twenty-first century. Here one should bear in mind both how the logic of Corporate activity might inform the current reality and how widely this logic might extend to the global reality. We will consider these issues in turn.

THE CORPORATION AS AN ASPECT OF CIVIL SOCIETY

The inclusion of the Corporation within the account of Civil Society has puzzled Hegel commentators who ask why Hegel should have insisted on including the concept given the competing conceptions of individual freedom and forms of inter-subjective recognition that the Corporation and the market relations of the System

---

1. Honneth, *The Pathologies of Individual Freedom*.

of Needs respectively embody. As Honneth notes, 'with the arrival of the "corporation" the interactive relation of the market has been joined by an entirely different sphere of communication whose norms of recognition are of a totally independent kind'.[2]

Honneth goes on to suggest that had Hegel, somewhat less awkwardly, placed Corporate activity within his account of the ethical State the fit would still not have been a perfect one, given that corporations function within civil life rather than engaging concrete persons' citizenship capacities. Nevertheless Hegel

> would at least have been spared the embarrassment of having to accommodate in the same sphere two completely different forms of recognition, the first linked to transactions mediated by the market and the second to value oriented interactions. [...] Hegel himself cannot see through the awkwardness of such an overloading of civil society.[3]

Here Honneth overlooks the implications of the fact that Hegel does indeed incorporate civil life into his account of the ethical State. This suggests that he does not want to insist on a strict separation of spheres that respectively engage persons' corporate and citizen capacities. It therefore indicates the unlikelihood of an oversight on Hegel's part of the sort Honneth relies upon and points us in the direction of a positive explanation for the Corporation's inclusion in the account of Civil Society.

Can we find the explanation in the *Logic*? When we think of the logical underpinnings of the concept of Civil Society merely in the general terms of a 'stage of difference', it is no less difficult to explain the place of the Corporation, and indeed of the Police, in terms of the demands of the *Logic*. Precisely for this reason Garbis Kortian maintains that Hegel's account of the Police-Corporation unity appears *contrary* to the demands of the *Logic* giving rise to Civil Society.[4] Suggesting that Hegel succumbs to awareness of 'the empirical facts of history [that] belie the contemplative view which attempts to resolve contradictions and work an unreal reconciliation', Kortian claims further that in the face of empirical reality Hegel is 'forced to evoke powers which are not ideal agents of reconciliation, but mere empirical forces'.[5] But, as we noted in

---

2. Honneth, *The Pathologies of Individual Freedom*, p. 76.
3. Honneth, *The Pathologies of Individual Freedom*, p. 77.
4. Garbis Kortian 'Subjectivity and Civil Society', in Z.A Pelczynski (ed.), *The State and Civil Society: Studies in Hegel's Political Philosophy*, Cambridge, Cambridge University Press, 1984, pp. 197-220.
5. Kortian 'Subjectivity and Civil Society', p. 205.

a different context, Stedman Jones makes the point that in fact Hegel's account of the Corporations renders them 'out of step with [Hegel's] contemporary historical reality'.[6]

A very different picture emerges with the aid of the strict organization thesis and the logical analysis that it makes possible. Having established the logical grounding of the Police-Corporation, one can appreciate why Hegel's precise way of including these institutional forms in the elaboration of Ethical Life, neither sought to introduce some 'ideal agents of reconciliation' nor was it a mere reaction to the circumstances of his times. Here, one must bear in mind that at this point in the logical progression, the demand is for the comprehensive categorial differentiated unity of Universality and Particularity to render itself *explicit*. That is, in so far as Civil Society conforms to the logic of the Disjunctive Syllogism, and the latter manifests a unifying activity that constitutes a comprehensive categorial differentiated unity, together the Police and the Corporation serve to give effect to this unity in different but complementary ways. As explained in Chapter Six, Corporate activity results in the actualization of the unity of the Universal and Particular in the being of the concrete whole. Of course in the absence of an appreciation of this logical demand the inclusion of this institutional form in Hegel's account of Civil Society would continue to appear puzzling, if not confused. This problem of interpretation can only be resolved with the aid of a non-reductive analysis in the light of the differentiated forms of unity that are supplied by the logic of the Disjunctive Syllogism. With this observation in mind we will now turn to the question of the role of the Corporation within the system of Ethical Life.[7]

THE CORPORATION AS AN ASPECT OF ETHICAL LIFE

What then is the significance of the Corporation for the order of Ethical Life? Consider first the reasons—other than being necessitated by the *Logic*—that commentators have offered in response to this question. Honneth attributes Hegel's treatment of Corporate activity to a misguided attempt to combine two separate tasks: 'to carry out a normative structural analysis of modern societies [...] at the same time as trying to legitimize certain organizations that

---

6. Stedman Jones, 'Hegel and the Economics of Civil Society', p. 125.

7. Here we leave to one side the question of the role of the Corporation in Hegel's account of the transition from Civil Society to the State, a matter that we will discuss in the next volume of this series.

have arisen organically and are anchored in the legal system by subjecting them to institutional analysis'. In short, for Honneth, Hegel sacrifices his 'formal intention' of developing a normative ethical theory 'because his eye is too firmly fixed on concrete institutional constructs'.[8] But as we noted in the previous section, Hegel's concept of the Corporation has little to do with an empirical phenomenon that was emerging or had emerged in his time.

More generally, the Corporation is typically seen as attempting to fill a gap in the elaboration of Hegel's ethical ideal by creating a non-atomistic inter-subjective space. Characteristically, Stedman Jones suggests that in introducing the concept of the Corporation (alongside the Police), Hegel was taking a 'quasi-familial approach' to Civil Society that sought to reconnect the pursuit of individual ends with supra-individual values. For Stedman Jones, with the inclusion of the Corporation as an associational form, Hegel's concept of Civil Society creates 'a new space of subjective freedom' that is 'not as atomistic as first seems' and together the Police and the Corporation function 'as a new universal family' in place of the former household organization of welfare antiquity'.[9] In Hegel's system the Corporations 'were to be *both* the surrogate in the modern economic and social domain for the functions once played by the family *and* the means by which members of civil society would be politically represented'.[10]

Like Stedman Jones, Bernhard Schlink maintains that 'the corporations, as they appear in the *Philosophy of Right*, are something that Hegel simply constructs'.[11] But Schlink thinks that Hegel is unsuccessful in appealing to the unifying power of the Corporation because

> it is hard to see how the corporations could possibly hold together the civil society that Hegel has shown as being so conflict ridden, centrifugal, explosive.[12]

Schlink concludes that Hegel is unconvincing on the role he attributes to the Corporations 'because he leaves the track of portraying and comprehending the historical development of the modern

---

8. Honneth, *The Pathologies of Individual Freedom*, p. 77.
9. Stedman Jones, 'Hegel and the Economics of Civil Society', pp. 122-123.
10. Stedman Jones, 'Hegel and the Economics of Civil Society', p. 129.
11. Bernhard Schlink, 'The Inherent Rationality of the State in Hegel's *Philosophy of Right*' in Drucilla Cornell, Michel Rosenfeld and David Carlson (eds.), *Hegel and Legal Theory*, New York and London, Routledge, 1991, pp. 347-354 at p. 350.
12. Schlink, 'The Inherent Rationality of the State in Hegel's *Philosophy of Right*', p. 350.

state'.[13] So a number of interpretive possibilities arise when one is prepared to invoke some externally derived hypothesis to determine what Hegel's claims amount to but these typically render other aspects of the theory unintelligible.

By contrast, when one has recourse to the strict organization thesis, quite specific aspects of the system come into play and explain the significance of the Corporation for the system of Ethical Life. One can see from the categorial analysis based on the Disjunctive Syllogism that Hegel does not include the Corporation in his account of Civil Society with the misguided aim of supplying a unifying power in Schlink's sense. Nor is the point of the *Philosophy of Right* to describe and explain the empirical development of civil institutions as part of the historical emergence of the modern state or, more specifically, to offer an empirical/sociological or normative explanation of the ways in which labour organizations (ought to) fit into, or give shape to, the social whole. Instead, as Honneth acknowledges, the historical development of labour organizations, like the history of other institutions of Western modernity, points to a distinctive organizational principle, namely the actualized internal unification of the Universal with the Particular as a whole. This is what the concept of the Corporation expresses. It is this principle of associational life, with its insistence on the achieved willingness of subjective particularity to identify with an immanent Universal purpose that the concept makes manifest in the development of Ethical Life.

THE CORPORATION AND THE REALITY OF GLOBAL CIVIL SOCIETY

This brings us to the third question noted above, namely what, if anything, is the relevance and usefulness of Hegel's concept of the Corporation to the global reality of the twenty-first century? Of course in giving a teleological account of the transition to the ethical State, the Hegelian system assigns a historical role to the Corporation as existentially manifested by the labour organization but we will return to the meaning and significance of this in the next volume. In the remainder of this chapter we want to indicate firstly how one can make sense of the dynamics and internal workings of a variety of associational forms currently operating in global civil society in so far as they *resemble* the logic of the Hegelian Corporation, without also implying that they hold

---

13. Schlink, 'The Inherent Rationality of the State in Hegel's *Philosophy of Right*', p. 350.

the ethical significance that the Hegelian system assigns to the Corporation. So for the purposes of the discussion that follows we must keep in mind the distinction, on the one hand, between the Corporation taken abstractly as an associational form, as a form of recognition, and, on the other, the Corporation's manifestation as a certain institution, namely the labour organization. Leaving aside the Hegelian system's assignment of ethical-ontological significance to the labour organization as existentially manifesting the logic of the Corporation, and focusing our discussion on the Corporation as a form of recognition we will be able to see how this logical form manifests in a variety of global contexts beginning with the advocacy of participatory citizenship in non-Western contexts..

THE CORPORATION AS A MODEL FOR CIVIL SOCIETY ASSOCIATIONS IN NON-WESTERN CONTEXTS

Kaviraj reflects on the uses of western conceptions of civil society in relation to Third World societies, in which marginal and dispossessed groups are viewed as struggling to establish democratic processes and limits to the coercive power of the territorial state in the interests of allowing individual autonomy to flourish. In the context evaluating 'anti-state arguments' in relation to Third World societies he draws attention to a conceptual difficulty surrounding the internal differentiation of civil society's associations. In particular, Kaviraj points out that 'writers who call for a re-assertion of "civil society" in the South' are typically calling on people to gather up *all resources of sociability* to form their own collective projects against the state.[14] Yet, the conceptual difficulty with such 'anti-state arguments' is that the appeal to civil society's associations may well involve, not just modern *Gesellschaft* associational forms but also *Gemeinschaft* ones, in Tonnies' sense of this distinction between voluntary and non-voluntary ties.

> Individual autonomy is smothered as much by a state with totalitarian pretensions as by religious groups or community identities which require total commitment and provide injunctions for all of life's activities, not just some of them. In fact the major problem lies in the fact that if *Gemeinschaft* identities are used to fight against the state successfully, the political order these are likely to produce after their victory would be similarly opposed to autonomy and principles of choice.[15]

---

14. Kaviraj, 'In Search of Civil Society', p. 391.
15. Kaviraj, 'In Search of Civil Society', pp. 320-321.

Kaviraj thus highlights the risks associated with analyzing the Third World by reference to conceptual dichotomies—such as that between voluntary/non-voluntary associational forms—that theorists originally introduced to illuminate aspects of the development of *Western European* modernity. He also suggests that much more sophisticated conceptual resources are required for any appreciation of the radical diversity of Third World communities and he does not accept the grafting of Western socio-political concepts onto Third World realities as an inevitable consequence of the transition to a globalized world. Instead he takes the view that the question of whether traditional practices 'can generate indigenous traditions of "civility" if not "civil society" must depend significantly on [...] the internal structure of existing practices of community'.[16] For the same sorts of reasons Mikael Karlstrom challenges the relevance to postcolonial Africa of European derived concepts defined primarily in terms of the operations of voluntary associations, which mediate between society and state. Karlstrom argues that the formation of voluntary associations may be *one* societal response to the emergence of the postcolonial African state but the African response to the modern state is more diverse as ethnographic and historical studies show. He illustrates this point by reference to Uganda's 1990s revival of kinship and the establishment of the Local Council system, both of which modes of association fall beyond the scope of civil-society institutions understood in terms of the state-independent voluntary associations that Western liberal discourses of civil society envisage.[17]

These comments raise the question of how to conceptualize the various internal structures of such diverse practices within non-modern and non-Western communities as well as the interrelations between such communities and between them and modern Western communities.

To be sure, Kaviraj's and Karlstrom's discussions are directed to social theorists' efforts to understand social change within the Third World, rather than to something like our narrower focus on the onto(logical) grounds underpinning Ethical Life, in the Hegelian sense, in the context of a global order. Even so, their observations are useful for reflecting upon the current relevance and

---

16. Kaviraj, 'In Search of Civil Society', pp. 321-322.
17. Mikael Karlstrom, 'Civil Society and its Presuppositions: Lessons from Uganda', in John L. Comaroff and Jean Comaroff (eds.), *Civil Society and the Political Imagination in Africa: Critical Perspectives*, Chicago, University of Chicago Press, 1999, pp. 104-123.

potential uses of Hegel's concept of Civil Society and that of the Corporation in particular in non-Western contexts. With Kaviraj and Karlstrom's concerns in mind, we can make two observations in connection with the global significance of our analysis of the logic of the Corporation.

To begin with, let us clarify the nature of the application of the Corporation as an associational form to circumstances such as those Kaviraj and Karlstrom describe. Unlike binary concepts, such as the Gemeinschaft / Geselleschaft binary, the Corporation manifests a categorial inter-relation with a degree of externality as well as the internally related unity of Universality and Particularity that we have already noted. Accordingly, the features of this associational form not only cut across a Gemeinschaft / Geselleschaft type binary, which distinguishes voluntary and ascriptive ties, but they are not fully pre-determined. The Corporation's internal differentiation is grounded in an objectively ascribed *shared specificity* characterizing the participants and not just their willingness to be members. Hence it is a combination of some specificity—in the labour organization of Hegel's ethical order this is the members' particular skills—alongside subjects' willingness to be members in the association that brings them into a Corporate unity. This in turn allows for the possibility of a diversity in the range of substantial ties that bind the members of particular associations.

It follows that associations that otherwise conform to the fundamental logic of the Corporation may differ radically in the specific substantive item—such as a kinship based or religiously derived ascriptive bond—that draws members together as well as in the further details of their specific organizational structures. Because the isomorphism characterizing the Corporation's associational form operates at a sufficiently abstract level, it does not preclude the incorporation of some further form-differentiation in the reality of Corporate living. Accordingly, the substantive values and further details characterizing particular associations can be drawn from a variety of traditions, including egalitarian and hierarchical ones, like those that Kaviraj and Kalstrom have in mind. Here we may also include various forms of sociality, which culturally and religiously diverse groups envisage in aspiring to realize their substantive universalist ideals. As we outlined in Chapter One, such groups might define themselves in any number of ways: as members of the covenantal community bound together by the law of the Torah who seek to love their neighbours as themselves and hate evil doers; or as the Christian members of the imperfect earthly city who are dedicated to fellowship in the love of God; or as the Confucian community whose members' proper performance of their inter-dependent roles depends upon extensive self-cultivation; or as the *umma*, the community of Muslim believers who attest to the one and only God.[18] We can also acknowledge the diversification of voices within such conceptions of order across and within regions. For example, Adeline Masquelier maintains that when the anti-Sufi movement, Izala, spread across southern Niger in the 1990s, it not only 'sparked intense struggles over the meaning of Islam' in the light of its advocacy of individualist values.[19] It also encouraged the emergence of a civil society that 'is not simply about the power of the Muslim collectivity against the state, it also means the co-existence of multiple and competing Muslim voices that struggle to be heard in the cacophony'.[20]

In each of these cases, despite the fact that a range of hierarchical relations may define and order the community in question, in today's global reality, participation in such communities may well manifest the form of unity characterizing the Disjunctive Syllogism in so far as members *willingly affirm* their participation in an association that is in turn bound together by the *specific ascribed terms* to which the group is dedicated. To this extent it becomes possible to make sense of the dynamics, internal workings and limits of such associational forms in so far as they resemble the logic of the Hegelian Corporation, even though the former do not share the specificity and ethical significance that the Hegelian system assigns to the Corporation as manifested by the labour organization.

Kaviraj also makes the point that on a global scale people refuse simply to choose either consistently modern or consistently traditional associational forms. In colonial Calcutta, for example, there was room for the operation of what he describes as:

> extremely powerful associations which were based on ascriptive loyalties of either caste or homeland or language. These associations aspired to a certain kind of universal membership

---

18. In addition to the sources discussed in Chapter One, see Michael Banner, 'Christianity and Civil Society', in Simone Chambers and Will Kymlicka, (eds.), *Alternative Conceptions of Civil Society*, Princeton, Princeton University Press, 2002, pp. 113-130.

19. Adeline Masquelier, 'Debating Muslims, Disputed Practices: Struggles for the Realization of an Alternative Moral Order in Niger', in John L. Comaroff and Jean Comaroff (eds.), *Civil Society and the Political Imagination in Africa: Critical Perspectives*, Chicago, University of Chicago Press, 1999, pp. 219-250 at p.219.

20. Masquelier, 'Debating Muslims, Disputed Practices', p. 228.

[consisting of everyone in the relevant ascriptive category but exclusively so ...] they were associations artificially created [voluntarily joined] to petition and pressure the colonial state [...] yet they were based on entirely ascriptive, *gemeinschaftlich* criteria. Or, from a somewhat different angle, they used a strange complex of the opposite principles of universality of access and particularity of membership.[21]

Similarly, in her analysis of the struggles of the Otovala Indigenous communities of northern Ecuador, Tanya Korovkin argues that, in contrast to the campaigns of the 1970s, the cultural experiments of the 1990s gave rise to certain implicitly "statist elements'. These consisted of building infrastructure, monitoring bilingual education and punishing thieves in accordance with the traditional justice system of the Indigenous people. Although universalist on one level, these governance activities, were also informed by the Indigenous peoples' 'ability to blend the old with the new' in ways that reoriented their governance practices to the particularities of communal membership.[22]

Read through the Disjunctive Syllogism, the logic of the Corporation expresses an explicit comprehensive categorial differentiated unity that accommodates just the sort of unity of Universal and Particular aspects that both Korovkin and Kaviraj describe. In doing so it has the potential to demystify what would otherwise appear as a 'strange complex' from the standpoint of principles that a modern Western conceptual framework can acknowledge. This is particularly useful since, arguably, as experience of life in the globalized mediated society and its expanded communication networks spreads ever more widely, the very distinction between 'modern' and 'traditional' associational forms collapses to the extent that this distinction is understood in terms of *alternative* substantive ideals rather than in terms of the fundamental difference between, on the one hand, substantive ideals whose Universality and Particularity are immediately related and, on the other, the formal universality of particularity that, as we indicated in Chapter Two, is the defining feature of modernity in its negative moment.

This brings us to the second observation one can make about the relevance of Hegel's concept of the Corporation to the current global order of civil/communal life broadly conceived. The unity

---

21. Kaviraj, 'In Search of Civil Society', p. 311.
22. Tanya Korovkin, 'Reinventing the Communal Tradition: Indigenous Peoples, Civil Society and Democratization in Andean Ecuador', p. 59.

of Universal and Particular that defines the associational form giving rise to Corporate activity also has the potential to (re-)orient the organizational practices of specific (otherwise traditional) communities towards a type of activity that seeks *reflectively* to combine substantive universal and particular elements. Here is where the opportunity arises for people to choose to distinguish and reject aspects of their community commitments that smother individual autonomy, as Kaviraj worries. That is, once the means of *internally* differentiating become clear—means that binary differentiations like the Gemeinschaft / Gesellschaft distinction do not make available in the appropriate way—it becomes possible to identify the enactment of the sort of global citizenship ideal that Dower advocates, namely global citizenship in the community participation sense. Recall from Chapter One that, having disconnected this sense of citizenship from the requirement of membership in a territorial state, Dower advocates an ideal of citizenship that invokes mindful engagement within a variously delineated community. From this perspective, the members of the sorts of religious communities that Kaviraj discusses are also positioned as having the capacity to deliberate upon and recognize a selective range of their cooperative activities as activities that also bind them to a global community defined by respect for human rights. The logic of the Corporation enables recognition of this potential to (re-)orient the organizational practices of otherwise traditional communities towards a type of activity that seeks *reflectively* to combine substantive universal and particular elements. Of course this does not mean that in practice successful civil society opponents to totalitarian territorial states, who nevertheless refuse to adopt the deliberative standpoint of participatory global citizens, will not in all likelihood favour the establishment of a political order that is no less 'opposed to autonomy and principles of choice' as Kaviraj maintains. But, as the application of the logic of the Corporation shows, the rejection of this likely scenario need not be linked to the adoption of a Western conception of civil society that presupposes the abandonment, as distinct from adaptation, of non-Western conceptions of the political bonds of communities.

Despite their obvious differences, at the abstract level of their conformity with the logic of the Corporation the activities of the religious communities we have been discussing are similarly structured. The same holds for the Corporate activity of organizational networks, such as MERCOSUR or the micro-lending loan funds, we mentioned in Chapter Five. Taking the example of MERCOSUR one can say that here the members of the group atypically consist of territorial states rather than small-scale organizations. Nevertheless, each of these units of agency willingly participates in activities that further the shared goal of distributing goods and services within the Latin American community. In this way one can appreciate both the nature and limits of this sort of associational form, rather than analyzing its workings through the lens of relations between territorial states as would normally be the case. Before discussing the limits of the associational form, however, we will turn to one more possible application of the concept of the Corporation to global civil society.

THE CORPORATION AS A MODEL OF GLOBAL CIVIL SOCIETY AND THE LIMITS OF SOLIDARITY

The model of the Corporation might also be applied generally to the civil sphere. In this case membership would be defined by reference to a substantive universal, which each particular participant would need to adopt willingly. The resulting unity would be restricted to this extent. That is, other relations governed by other substantive ties would fall beyond its scope and this external relation would, accordingly, give rise to tensions and pressures hindering the actualization of the substantive universal.

This is precisely the form of unity to be found in the model of civil society that Alexander advocates in developing CSIII. Recall from Chapter One, firstly, that Alexander's preferred model defines civil society as a civil sphere that consists of values and institutions that are grounded in the universality of social solidarity and bounded by non-civil institutions, like the communal, the religious and the familial. Secondly, Alexander's civil sphere functions as a fragile project, which repeatedly fails as a result of coming into conflict with the non-civil and this gives rise to social participants' efforts at civil repair. In appealing to the bounded universality of social solidarity this model implicitly invokes a form of substantive universality that is compatible with that defining the logic of the Corporation. Let us turn now to examine the model's limits.

According to Hegel, the Corporation's end is 'restricted and finite'.[23] Moreover, the Corporation as a whole is itself 'restricted' in that it is an ethical unity to which *Particularity* gives effect.[24] Though it expresses the explicit comprehensive categorial

---

23. Hegel, PR, §256.
24. Hegel, PR, §229.

differentiated unity, this is achieved from the standpoint of the Particular and so does not exhibit the comprehensive unity of the categories from the standpoint of the truth of the whole. If our analysis has merit and Alexander's conception of the civil sphere mirrors the logic of the Corporation then it, along with the other types of association we discussed above, must be similarly restricted. The organization of the social whole from the standpoint of social solidarity does not manifest as an internally differentiated unity but rather as a unity that, although attending to the activities of the whole, such as justice issues falling within the spheres of the family or the economy, does so only from the standpoint of *one particular sphere*. Despite enacting the bonds of social solidarity and despite engaging the whole of the being of particular subjects to this extent, the model of solidarity is nevertheless restricted in that it manifests its unity only from the limited standpoint of the Particularized Individual and not from the standpoint of the social whole itself.

Participation in Alexander's civil society, that of a solidary community, is not incompatible with global citizenship understood in any of the three senses we identified in Chapter One. But, in relying upon feelings of respect for unknown others as a matter of principle, it coincides more closely with global citizenship understood as the commitment to community participation than with global citizenship understood more broadly as an individual ethic. This said, it also shares with *aspirational* citizenship some reliance upon *an unactualized vision*. Just as aspirational citizenship presupposes ties with a non-existent global political order, Alexander's civil society insists that a solidary community does not exist *as such*. Recall from Chapter One that it can only be sustained to a degree given that it is always subject to dynamic interpenetrating boundary relations, which give rise to repeated struggles over civil repair. On our reading of Hegel's teleological account, this reflects the presence of distinctively transitional elements within global civil society, which we examine further in the next volume. Next we will turn to the relationship between the logic of the Police and the current global reality.

9. THE POLICE, THE WELFARE STATE AND GLOBAL GOVERNANCE

We have been arguing that the analysis of the logic of Civil Society's internally differentiated moments provides the basis for a rather sophisticated reading of the role and limits of institutions operating in the current global reality. In this chapter we want to lend further support to this claim by considering the implications of our account for organizations with global governance responsibilities. More specifically, we maintain that the logic characterizing the concept of the Police or public authority has certain implications for the way we understand and explain key aspects of the role and workings of institutions like the territorial state, but also of international and supranational organizations that have a role in global governance such as the United Nations ('UN'), the World Trade Organization ('WTO') and the European Union. Despite significant differences in the historical development of such institutions, like their relationship to and level of dependence on territorial states, and the impact of their peculiar history on that organization's effective powers, on the basis of the shared logic that underpins them we can identify certain dimensions and inescapable limits to their powers and their domains of operation. (This is not to suggest, however, that the logic of the Syllogism informs the existential relations that are governed by international law. Given that the treatment of international law follows the transition to the ethical State we will return to this issue in the next volume.)

The starting point for an examination of the question of how the public authority's logic informs the current global reality is the central idea that, whatever its further details, as one of the units of the externally combined system constituting Civil Society, the Police functions as an *external authority*. When we take the logic of the Police to be straightforwardly manifested by the regulatory activities of territorial states with respect to individuals' welfare interests (hereafter 'the domestic welfare state') this means, of course, that we must take the domestic welfare state to stand over and above the units of agency whose welfare interests it addresses in order to intervene in their affairs. But in Chapter Six we also saw that the unity of the Police is also *external* in the sense that is directed to persons or agents who stand before it in their capacity as 'private' units of agency. Because the relationship of the Police to private agents does not engage private agents' concrete being as a whole but only those aspects of their being that manifest their formal rights bearing capacities, the question arises how to determine the scope and extent of the public authority's powers. In elaborating the Hegelian response, we will illustrate how the externality Hegel refers to when elaborating Civil Society's associational forms characterizes all the units of agency operating within the current global reality on some level, regardless of whether they are individuals, family units, small-scale associations or global governance bodies, public agencies and governments. We will also indicate the potential usefulness of this conceptual framework for making sense of the relationship between welfare states and civil life in some non-Western cultural and intellectual contexts in the light of their operative concepts of publicness and privateness.

The second idea we must recall for the purposes of the present analysis concerns the relative authority of the Police. As we noted in Chapter Six, due to their inevitable exposure to contingencies beyond their control, privately acting agents cause injury or wrong others and in doing so their actions ground the right of the Police to intervene. Even so, the unity of the Police is only *relative* in that it is unavoidably restricted to the sphere of contingencies. That is, on Hegel's account of the Police, although the public authority's powers are directed to meeting welfare interests, these powers are necessarily restricted to *counteracting the effects* (as distinct from addressing the causes) of the contingencies and arbitrariness that are largely associated with the activities and interactions of private units of agency in market relations and civil life more generally. We have already seen (Chapter Five) how the problem of responding to global poverty is subject to such limitations. When we take certain international and supranational organizations to manifest the Hegelian concept of the Police operating at the global level of addressing welfare interests (hereafter 'global public authority') we can make sense of the unavoidable limits to their powers.

After illustrating this point in connection with institutions conforming to the logic of a global public authority in the Hegelian sense, we will move on to consider the related question of whether or not there is still a place for the domestic welfare state to operate directly in relation to global issues. We will illustrate how the logic of the Police can productively inform our understanding of phenomena that otherwise seem to point us in different directions regarding the question of the continued relevance of territorial states acting as welfare states in the global arena. In the final section of this chapter we will suggest that our Hegelian analysis of the global public authority can also be extended to non-western organizational ideals. If our analysis is sound it shows: that certain lines of continuity are worth bearing in mind when attempting to understand the role and limits of the domestic welfare state and the global public authority in the current global reality; that these lines of continuity extend to non-Western cultural and intellectual contexts; and that we can make sense of them by reference to the Hegelian concept of the Police.

THE PROBLEM OF DETERMINING THE EXTENT OF REGULATORY MEASURES

Let us turn firstly to the problem of determining which (aspects) of the activities of private agents within global civil society are publicly accessible and hence capable of falling within the regulatory control of the public authority. If the reality of global civil society is one in which, irrespective of cultural and intellectual contexts, at least at some level, all units of agency function as *external existents* in Hegel's sense, then should an adequate account provide some principled way of determining the scope of their relative autonomy and conversely, of governmental interventions? For some intellectual traditions the very fluidity of the concepts of publicness and privateness inhibits any rigid designations of the sort that might specify the domain of a public authority. For example, in Chapter One we noted that in the ideal Jewish social order, it is the particularistic solidary covenantal community that serves as the primary social unit from which individual members derive their rights and obligations in relation to one another. Accordingly, the various realms of experience, such as the household, the economic and political domains are not conceived as independent, sharply distinguished public or private spheres. Still it is worth noting that the covenantal community nevertheless functions as an externally related unit of agency relative to a non-Jewish welfare state.

Similarly, Confucian thought 'is unable to make fixed distinctions between public and private, voluntary and involuntary forms of association' precisely because it conceives of society along the lines of the rings of successive ripples like those one creates by throwing a stone in surrounding water.[1] '*Gong* [public] and *si* [private] are relative terms; anything in the circle in which one is standing can be called gong.'[2] So, for example, depending on the context, acting in the interests of one's family may be conceived as a matter of public rather than private interest and membership in this social unit might extend beyond one's kinship group through voluntary affiliation.[3] Madsen claims that in so far as civil society envisions 'a social framework that can gather together certain individual parts while excluding others'—in so far as the various units of agency are externally related to one another—the question of what civil society includes is incomprehensible within the tradition of Confucian thought given that it 'does not conceive the world in terms of delimited parts' akin to a bundle of rice stalks.[4] For the same reason, this perspective renders problematic the related question of how far public authority extends in today's global civil society. When it comes to resolving potential conflicts within and between society's small-scale associations, Confucian thought relies on the ability of an appropriately cultivated self to resolve apparent conflicts that may arise in relation to one's roles and attendant responsibilities, but this ideal seems insufficient in the circumstances. On the one hand, the Confucian configuration of society as analogous to rippling waves implies that the conception of civil society, in the sense of *minjian shuhui* (people-based society), lacks the conceptual resources with which to proclaim the relative autonomy of various small-scale associations but, on the other, the current practice of religious, ethnic, environmental or feminist groups is effectively to act independently of the territorial states that govern them. In Taiwan, for example, the practice has been for such groups to register with a government authority against the background knowledge that the 'government supervision' that is supposed to follow will not be forthcoming.[5] Thus the relation of the public authority to the units of agency in question remains external in practice. Regardless of their cultural

---

1. Madsen, 'Confucian conceptions of Civil Society', p. 192.
2. Fei Xiaotong in Madsen, 'Confucian conceptions of Civil Society', p. 192.
3. Madsen, 'Confucian conceptions of Civil Society', p. 192.
4. Madsen, 'Confucian conceptions of Civil Society', p. 191.
5. Madsen, 'Confucian conceptions of Civil Society', pp. 193-194.

and intellectual context then both individuals and social groupings functioning in the current global reality would appear to be externally related to others units of agency on some level of their interactions. To this extent they conform to the Hegelian picture.

Nevertheless, granted the reality of global civil society is one in which, irrespective of cultural and intellectual contexts all units of agency function as *external existents* on some level, there does not seem to be some principled way of determining the scope of governmental interventions within the abovementioned traditions. By contrast a liberal theoretical perspective looks for principles that set the limits to government power over private agents because it presumes a *prima facie* right to non-interference in relation to whatever is designated as private. However, as Toula Nicolacopoulos argues, the failure of liberal theory to produce such principles is due to the fact that it presupposes but does not appropriately acknowledge the dichotomous organization of publicness and privateness, not just in the division of social life, but also in the conceptual organization of its deep structure.[6]

Where does Hegel stand in relation to the abovementioned question? On the face of it he appears to be in conflict with a liberal theoretical approach given his claim that 'no inherent line of distinction can be drawn' between what does and what does not properly fall within the control of the Police. His reason is that 'the relations between external existents fall into the Infinite of the Understanding', which Hegel characterizes as 'the false Infinite'.[7] But commentators see Hegel's relationship to the liberal tradition as complicated by the fact that, as Brod explains, 'Hegel violates the traditional individualist logic [with the political mediation he attributes to the ethical State], but he does so in the name of many of the pluralist freedoms liberalism has been concerned with defending'.[8] The analysis based on the *Logic* suggests that, like liberalism, Hegel does indeed allow for the organization of civil life in terms of a public-private dichotomy but in doing so his theory acknowledges the implications of modernity's organization in its negative moment, rather than as an aspect of its self-affirmation. So Hegel's position incorporates, without being reducible to, an element of modernity to which liberal theory gives expression but treats problematically. In other words, for Hegel, the various units of agency operating within global civil society in their

---

6. Nicolacopoulos, *The Radical Critique of Liberalism*, pp. 49-59.
7. Hegel, *PR*, §234.
8. Brod, *Hegel's Philosophy of Politics*, p. 98.

capacity as private agents are subject to the sorts of dichotomous relations that liberalism presupposes precisely because this structure of relations is a feature of modernity in its negative moment.

If we read Hegel correctly, then the question of distinguishing between public and private matters—between what should and should not be subject to the intervention of the public authority—is not merely unresolved *as a matter of practice*, or subject to ongoing assessment due to changing social conditions, such as technological development, or changes in moral attitudes, as Franco suggests.[9] Rather, given the presupposition of a dichotomous relation between the public (Universal) and private (Particular) dimensions of social life both within and between 'external existents', *the determination of criteria* for drawing the line between public and private must inevitably be subject to contingency and arbitrariness, rendering such criteria *in principle* incapable of satisfactory resolution within the terms of a liberal theoretical framework and relatedly, within the lived terms of modernity's moment of self-denial. For Hegel, this is a fundamental point of difference in the organization of civil life within the ethical State, which follows from the transcendence of modernity's negative moment. In the latter context of modernity's self-affirmation, rather than operating as external existents, the units of social agency are variously internally related. As we saw in Chapter Six, the distinctive feature of the public authority is to actualize and maintain the Universal that belongs to the Particular and this takes effect through the protection of private agents' welfare interests. The public authority thus stands above private interests and seeks to foster ways and means to protect and support the welfare interests of individuals and communities. It follows that, in the absence of a transition to a global ethical State, a public authority must act to secure welfare interests in global civil society without relying on any principled way of determining what does and does not properly fall within its regulatory control. Let us turn next to the question of which organizations might take on the role of the public authority in global civil society.

GLOBAL PUBLIC AUTHORITY IN THE CURRENT GLOBAL REALITY

Exploring the signs of development of a global public authority Butler notes that 'the World Bank and the IMF form the beginnings of a global welfare state paralleling the domestic welfare

---

9. Franco, *Hegel's Philosophy of Freedom*, pp. 266-267.

state [the Police] of which Hegel was the first major theoretician.[10] But, he argues, since these organizations are in practice 'under the control of the US, the chief source of funding', the WTO, which is not controlled by a single or a small group of nations, comes closer to manifesting 'the idea of a global welfare state (world governance, but not world government)'.[11] By comparison Moland draws on a 'Hegelian insight from civil society' and comments that the 'geographical representation [supplied by nation states on the global scene] is problematic in so far as it cannot guarantee different economic levels in society will be represented'.[12] She therefore argues in favour of challenging the 'national partiality' that characterizes organizations like the WTO.

The international global economy is indeed very nation-centred. WTO and IMF members are almost exclusively nation states. Individuals represented in the corresponding negotiations, then, are represented as members of their nation states but not necessarily members of the global economy.[13]

Moland proposes instead the further development of existing signs of non-geographical representation, an idea that she extrapolates from Hegel's elaboration of the ethical State.

The United Nations already includes what it calls "Civil Society Organizations" that represent everything from indigenous peoples to women's issues to economic and social groups. Giving these organizations adequate voice in international affairs would help ensure that geographical representation does not further entrench inequalities.[14]

In addition, both Moland and Butler endorse the establishment of new global welfare oriented institutions whose structures do not favour the representation of geographical interests, like Thomas Pogge's proposal for establishing a global fund to encourage pharmaceutical companies to distribute medicines to the poor globally.[15] Such proposals for establishing public agencies to address specific ends like the provision of global health care are consistent with our Hegelian account of the nature and role of a global public authority. In this their approach is similar to Turner and

10. Butler, 'The Coming World Welfare State which Hegel Could Not See', pp. 168-9.
11. Butler, 'The Coming World Welfare State which Hegel Could Not See', p. 173.
12. Moland, 'A Hegelian Approach to Global Poverty', p. 149.
13. Moland, 'A Hegelian Approach to Global Poverty', p. 149.
14. Moland, 'A Hegelian Approach to Global Poverty', p. 152.
15. Moland, 'A Hegelian Approach to Global Poverty', p. 152; Butler, 'The Coming World Welfare State which Hegel Could Not See', p. 173.

Khondker's proposal, which, as we have already mentioned, is to address the UN's lack of efficacy by introducing a global tax on human mobility (Chapter Five). Their claim here is that in managing a global tax on human mobility the UN would be cultivating a currently non-existent, or at least insufficient, sense of ownership over human rights amongst individuals at the level of global action and this would result in an increase in the effectiveness of the UN as a global authority.[16] Turner and Khondker's observations are also compatible with our Hegelian account.

Although we are in agreement with the abovementioned authors' analyses in so far as they attempt to establish the link between Hegel's account of the Police and the institutions currently operating on the global scene, nevertheless in different ways the authors underplay the significance of the limitations of the institutions they discuss in part because their strategy is to argue by analogy rather than to follow through the onto(logical) implications of making sense of the potential of organizations like the WTO, the IMF or the UN in terms of the Hegelian concept of the Police. To the extent that the logic of the Police informs the operation of these global governance bodies we can anticipate the limitedness of their effectiveness. This is so we suggest regardless of their specific mandate. Let us take the largely ineffective powers of the UN to protect human rights as an example.[17] The Hegelian analysis we have elaborated would suggest that UN operations are *inherently* limited. Recall from Chapter Six that the power of the Police to intervene in the affairs of civil life is limited given that its activities are restricted to the sphere of contingencies. This restriction applies to the potential impact of its regulatory practices. Given the form that its unity takes, the universal authority essentially lacks any power to *eliminate* the contingencies and arbitrariness that pervade this sphere or, in other words, to restructure so as to prevent their emergence. Extending this analysis to the UN, which offers a general supervision and control in accordance with the notion of a global public authority we find that, strategies

---

16. Turner and Khondker, *Globalization: East and West*, pp. 169-171.

17. The failure of European Union governance serves as another example. Gunter Frankenberg attributes the failures to structural problems, such as the tendency of the European Commission to exclude civil associations from its consultative processes as an effect of the stratification of the organized European civil society. However, on our analysis the stratification Frankenberg describes is a symptom of the deeper structure of relations within an 'external state' in the Hegelian sense discussed above: Gunter Frankenberg, 'National, Supranational, and Global Ambivalence in the Practice of Global Civil Society', pp. 284-289.

from improving UN operations cannot develop any potential to provide solutions to the problems of providing protection and security, global poverty and so on. It follows from the above that in so far as it conforms to the logic underpinning the concept of the Police, and hence to the limits of this form of universal authority, an organization such as the UN cannot be made to work effectively to resolve the global problems to which it directs its efforts. If this is correct then we should expect strategies aimed at groups, such as the global poor or the so-called illegal economic migrants who make up a significant proportion of those in need of protection, to at best only *alleviate* some of the pressures they face.

One might object that to analyze the UN in terms of the logic of the Police is to see the UN along the lines of 'the old inherited forms of state constitution' and hence to misrepresent the nature of the new global power.[18] Hardt and Negri would argue that this is to misunderstand that the imperial sovereignty actually marks a paradigm shift. Indeed they claim that historically it is the ambiguous experiences of the United Nations that gave shape to the new global power, which conforms to the juridical concept of Empire. They maintain that the United Nations 'functions as a hinge in the genealogy from international to global juridical structures'. In other words, in recognizing the states' sovereignty at the same time as transferring power to a supranational body—although this transfer was never materialized as a result of political compromises—the very existence of the UN reveals the limitations of the notion of *international* order and points beyond it to the notion of *global* order.[19] But notice that an organizational set-up such as the European Union involves a similar sort of recognition and transfer of power and yet it does not imply an inevitable shift away from international order as such.[20] When one draws ap-

18. Hardt and Negri, *Empire*, pp. 7-8.
19. Hardt and Negri, *Empire*, p. 4.
20. Our observation about the European Union might appear to be contradicted by Paul Cobben's argument that a suitably revised Hegelian concept of the state can be used to analyze the European Union, not in terms of a federation of states 'with treaties that could be a model for international law', but in terms of a 'supra-state into which the individual nation-states are integrated': Paul Cobben, 'The Citizen of the European Union from a Hegelian Perspective', in Andrew Buchwalter (ed.), *Hegel and Global Justice*, New York and London, Springer, 2012, p. 177-192 at p. 189. Although compatible with the view that the current global order is thus distinguishable from the conception of international order that Hardt and Negri examine, Cobben's discussion does not rely upon Hegel's treatment of the Police but instead draws upon a reading of the concept of the State, which on our analysis commits his account to an inappropriate application to the current

propriate parallels between the UN and the European Union, the Hardt and Negri reading of the ontological significance of the UN seems less convincing. In any case, in assessing our claims concerning the application of our Hegelian approach to the case of the United Nations one must bear in mind that it is only the latter's capacity to exercise its powers effectively that is at issue and not the organization's role in the transitional process with which Hardt and Negri are concerned.

From our analysis above it follows that global organizations that do not represent geographical interests and territorial states acting directly or indirectly through supranational organizations may be involved in activities that define them as a global public authority. As such, and irrespective of their internal organizational differences, their role, in their capacity as *welfare states* in the Hegelian sense of this term, is unavoidably limited in its effectiveness. This is why there is no useful answer to questions of the form 'which of these organizations can best provide solutions to the problems of global poverty and economic migration?' Once we have regard to the logic governing the powers and precise limits of the institutional form of the public authority under the conditions of modernity in its negative moment, that is, under *current* conditions, we can appreciate why global organizations that do not represent geographical interests, territorial states and supranational organizations, all of which share this form, do not compete when it comes to addressing the systemic causes of such social problems. It also becomes possible for us to make sense of sociological phenomena that point in seemingly conflicting directions. The impact of globalization on the future of the territorial state form is one such phenomenon. We turn next to the question of the viability of territorial states in the global reality.

THE QUESTION OF THE DEMISE OF TERRITORIAL STATES IN THE GLOBAL ERA

Although it is not our purpose to analyze the empirical evidence concerning the question of the demise of the territorial state in the global era, we will discuss one example to indicate how social theorists who have been grappling with the question of the effects of globalization on this institutional form might benefit from the Hegelian analytic framework. Turner and Khondker argue against sociologists' claims that the territorial state is 'either in retreat or

---

global reality of developments that take us beyond modernity's negative moment of self-denial.

losing its efficacy in the face of globalization'. They try to make sense of relevant empirical evidence by arguing that:

> The state is a functional requirement for steering the processes of globalization. In metaphorical terms states are the navigational systems of the ship that is globalization. You can put the ship on autopilot for a while, but prudence would suggest that a human captain rather than an intelligent system is actually put in charge. How should, and to what extent would, the state act independently or at the behest of the management? These issues have now returned to theories of the state in the context of globalization. The key issue is the autonomy of the state'.[21]

Here, the 'autonomy of the state' refers to whether a territorial state is free and able to make decisions to promote or advance the specific interests it represents.[22] The authors point to the US government's bailout of the big business corporations in response to the 2008 financial crisis as a case that confirms that 'the link between corporate [in the sense of business] class interests and the state remains as fruitful as it is relevant today'.[23] Moreover, economic globalization 'requires an autonomous state' because 'the logic of the market will not be the ultimate solution for differences and the arbiter of disagreements'. So the metaphor of the territorial state as a human navigational system frames Turner and Khonder's response to events that seem to counter earlier theorizations of the demise of the state that emerged in response to 'the euphoria of globalization and borderlessness'.[24]

Drawing from our analysis of the logic of the Police let us consider what we might say in response to Turner and Khondker. Here we must take into account the relatively autonomous self-determining activity characterizing the concept of the Police understood as a Particularized Individual. To begin with note that the abovementioned metaphor of the state understood as the navigation system of the ship that is globalization invokes something of the relationship of the institutional form of the Police to global civil society in so far as it implies that the former responds to the contingencies emerging from the latter in an effort to regulate activity associated with need satisfaction. At the same time, however, from the perspective of our Hegelian analysis, the usefulness of

---

21. Turner and Khondker, *Globalization: East and West*, p. 62.
22. Turner and Khondker, *Globalization: East and West*, p. 59.
23. Turner and Khondker, *Globalization: East and West*, p. 64.
24. Turner and Khondker, *Globalization: East and West*, p. 62.

this metaphor appears rather limited. For it also implies the existence of a *context of movement*, the sea or ocean in which the navigated ship moves. However, the conceptual resources for making sense of the features or influences of this context of movement are absent. By way of contrast, as we have argued, the Hegelian concept of Civil Society gives comprehensive expression to the global understood as consciousness of the world as a single world—Civil Society as a system of interdependence—that is nonetheless internally differentiated by a multiplicity of specific processes, global networks and social flows, as well as the structural and institutional aspects of a world social system—the differentiation of Civil Society into its distinct moments, a differentiation that is at once internal and yet retains a degree of externality. Returning to Turner and Khondher's metaphor, we might say that what is envisaged here is not like the relationship of a human navigational system to a ship. Rather in order to appreciate the impact of globalization on the territorial state as an institution one would need to focus on a more complicated phenomenon, something analogous to a *sea-faring* ship. In line with our Hegelian analysis, this latter metaphor for globalization would better capture both the sense in which the territorial state exercises its power to act in the universal interest, thereby counteracting the arbitrariness inherent in global civil society with a view to regulating need satisfaction, *and* the degree to which the exercise of this power is restricted as a result of its relative autonomy, due to its operation as an externally related unit of agency under the current conditions of modernity, modernity's negative moment.

In suggesting that we must recognize the sea-faring status of Turner and Khondker's metaphorical ship if the issues they mention are to arise at all, we are deferring to an unavoidably teleological appreciation of the sea that is the metaphorical ship's context of movement, but in doing so we must also acknowledge the operation of a significant degree of openness and contingency in relation to its (future) motion. By explicitly acknowledging the metaphorical sea one can acknowledge and address both these dimensions—teleological determination and relative openness—not only as the ship's context of movement but also in determining the role and function of the navigational system.

In the absence of such an analysis the territorial state is simply represented as attempting to balance competing needs and interests, for example, of a *global* economy, on the one hand, and a *local* political community, on the other, as well as of both these against the state's own interests. We can illustrate this point by reference to Turner and Khondker's discussion of the role of the territorial state in managing the movement of people on a global scale. After exploring the variety of forms of migration in the current global setting, their reasons and the social problems to which they give rise, problems ranging from human trafficking to the creation of transnational countries with their associated racial and ethnic tensions, the authors conclude that

> [...] the economy and the state are driven by very different interests and logics. Modern economies require a flexible labour market in which workers can move rapidly and easily between different work sites depending on the local demand for labour inputs. [...] However, large scale migration can often create racial conflicts. [...] More recently, attacks on the Twin Towers, the Madrid railway and London's underground have led to Islamophobia [...] In this context of the demand for greater political security the state becomes involved in more stringent control over borders. These controls inevitably involve the greater management of migration and the result is the interruption of labour mobility. The state's need for sovereignty and security outweighs the economic needs of labour mobility.[25]

To be sure there are competing logics at stake. On the one hand there is the logic underpinning global civil society as an economic organization and this includes the implementation of measures to secure ways and means of satisfaction, which as Hegel indicates, has historically included the possibility of colonial expansion. As we have suggested, this is the logic that conforms to the fundamentals defining Hegel's System of Needs. Such logic does indeed produce tensions for a territorial state charged with the responsibility of population management in the light of the interests of the global economy given the needs of maintaining a flexible labour market and culturally accommodating populations.

But the logic underpinning the territorial state that accords with the concept of the Police in the Hegelian sense, does not involve the management of the tensions created by these logics in terms analogous to the differences between a ship's automatic pilot, which might service the interests of the global economy in maintaining a flexible labour market, and its captain, who might intervene and impose restrictions on such a process in the interests of maintaining the security and control of the ship. Such a

---

25. Turner and Khondker, *Globalization: East and West*, pp. 117-118.

representation misunderstands the *relativity* of the autonomy of an autonomous territorial state under the current conditions of modernity. Turner and Khondker acknowledge that the degree to which any particular territorial state can be effective in exercising its autonomy depends upon its position of power in the interstate system.[26] But the issue here is not whether the sovereignty and security of *particular* states outweighs the interests of the *global* economy but rather that particular states' sovereignty is manifested only in so far as they in turn recognize economic interests that are tied to the security and welfare interests of the concrete persons, communities or groups which they serve but which may in turn not recognize the universal interest as their own. In other words, the gap creating the tensions between the particularity of territorial states and the globality of the economy does not stem from the fact that territorial states must now contend with competing local and global demands. The historical shift from local economies to a global economic system requiring a globally mobile population more fully manifests the territorial state's *externality*, the restriction of its relationship to the units of agency it serves—concrete persons, communities, interest groups—as private agents. As such it manifests the relativity of the territorial state's autonomy or, in other words, the fact that the territorial state that conforms to the logic of the Police does not manifest the absolutely self-determining power of the ethical State. This is what gives rise to a system of international relations in which particular states, which formally recognize each other as sovereign, engage in agreements with one another that are at best only provisional.[27] It is from this perspective that the territorial state is still charged with the responsibility of addressing issues like global poverty *alongside* global organizations that do not represent geographical interests.

THE HEGELIAN CONCEPT OF THE POLICE AND NON-WESTERN IDEALS

We have been arguing that Hegel's concept of the Police has the potential to inform accounts of the role of territorial states operating as (global) welfare states. But if such states are to be understood as manifesting the logic underpinning the powers of a certain type of external authority in relation to other external existents within the current global reality, what should we make of

---

26. Turner and Khondker, *Globalization: East and West*, p. 66.
27. Hegel, PR, §330.

idea(l)s of the state drawn from alternative cultural and intellectual traditions? In this final section we would like to lend support to the claim that our Hegelian account has the potential to inform such accounts in illuminating ways. To this end we will draw once again on Hanafi's reformist modernist reading of the role of the ideal Islamic state, which we outlined in Chapter One. This account serves as a difficult test case for two reasons. Firstly, on the face of it, its ideal does not obviously mirror the Hegelian concept; and, secondly, in invoking an ideal *world order*, the idea of a global civil society being governed by the universal ideal of the *umma* clearly falls outside the scope of the concept of the Police. With these points in mind, recall from Chapter One that within the global society governed by the universal ideal of the *umma*—the Islamic community of believers, which takes moral primacy over other social groupings—the ideal political system forms an internally related, integrated whole by incorporating a variety of religious, social and geographical groupings that make up the community of believers. The various groups constituting the social whole are *relatively autonomous* in the sense that they are free to conduct their affairs with the support of a range of relatively autonomous institutions—recall the work of the *ulama*, the *hisba* performed by *muhtasib* and the *awqaf*—within the parameters of the law of Islam, for which the state is the recognized regulatory authority. In constituting the social whole as a fully integrated system of relatively autonomous units, Hanafi's ideal partly resembles the Hegelian State, a fundamental difference being that in the case of the Islamic ideal of the *umma* this is specifically grounded in the unity of God.

In envisaging that the various units of (individual and group) agency are *internally related* to the Islamic state, taken as this sort of regulatory authority, the units of agency in question contradict any assumption that they relate to the Islamic state as 'external existents'. However, the same cannot be said for the way in which this ideal envisages the relations of non-Muslim communities to the Islamic state. Recall from Chapter One that the freedom from government intervention, which flows from the relative autonomy of the Muslim groups constituting the social whole, also extends to non-Muslim communities via the principles of non-belligerence and mutual respect, which require from the latter that they acknowledge the sovereignty of the Islamic state as well as the cross-community regulatory authority of Islamic law. So in this case, the *externality* that the Hegelian account attributes to all the units of agency operating in the current conditions of modernity—modernity's negative moment—appears at the level of the relationship between the ideal Islamic state and the variety of non-Muslim linguistic, cultural and religious groups that are subject to this state's authority. This said, the Muslim units of agency that are taken as internally relating to the Islamic state do not altogether escape their Hegelian characterization as external existents. Rather, through their identification with the state, they can be said to thereby implicate themselves in the displacement of this attribute onto another level of interrelations, namely those between an externally related Islamic state, which they constitute internally as an integrated whole, and the non-Muslim groups that can be characterized as external existents within this state. Recall from Chapter Three that according to the claim that Civil Society constitutes an external state the various units of agency operating within Civil Society are taken to relate to others as external existents, *on some level of their interactions*, that is, irrespective of the ways in which on other levels they might also identify with others as integral to their own identity.

One might object that in characterizing Hanafi's ideal Islamic state as both an 'external existent' and as partly resembling the Hegelian State, we risk contradiction given the vastly different organizational logics we have attributed to these. (We have supposed that Civil Society, the external state, is governed by the logic of the single Syllogism in its Hypothetical and Disjunctive forms whereas the State is governed by the logic of Objectivity.) In response it is important to note that despite the resemblance to the Hegelian ethical State, which we cannot examine in any detail here, and regardless of its global aspirations, Hanafi's ideal conforms to the logic of the Paricularized Individual that we analyzed in relation the combined unity of the Police-Corporation in Chapter Six. Recall that a characteristic feature of the unity in question is that in incorporating the social whole via its internally related terms, it nevertheless does so from the reflective standpoint of the Particular. What are the signs of the operation of this logical form in Hanafi's account? In grounding the Islamic ideal of the *umma* in God, this account effectively invokes the mediating unity of a substantive particular, which is reflectively positioned as a universal category. As such, it mirrors the mediation of the Universal by the Particularized Individual, which is precisely the form of mediation that characterizes the Disjunctive Syllogism and manifests as the unity of the Police-Corporation. Interestingly it is the abovementioned reflective positioning of the Universal that distinguishes Hanafi's ideal from otherwise pre-modern conceptualizations which, in *conflating*—immediately identifying—the Universal with substantive particulars, would fall outside the scope of the logic of modernity and, hence, also beyond any discussion of their potential to be informed by the Hegelian concept of Civil Society.[28]

Let us now return to the observation that in invoking an ideal *world order*, the idea of a global civil society being governed by the universal ideal of the *umma* clearly falls outside the scope of the logic that informs the concept of the Police. The task of assessing this idea by comparison with the Hegelian state belongs to the next volume of this series, which is devoted to Hegel's account of the ethical State. For present purposes, however, it is important to note that one can draw from Hanafi's account of *the ideal* Islamic state with effective global reach a conception of this ideal *in the making* so to speak. This would be a *territorial* Islamic state—a territorially bounded state with the sorts of internal features already discussed—operating under the current conditions of modernity, albeit with global aspirations. Such a territorial state does indeed have the potential to be informed by the logic of the Police.

If the above analysis is sound, then it supports the conclusion that the logic of the Police is manifested by the welfare regulatory activities, not only of supranational organizations and global organizations that do not represent geographical interests but also of territorial states that in principle operate within culturally diverse intellectual traditions.

---

28. For a discussion of the differences between modern and pre-modern ways of conceptualizing the universal see Nicolacopoulos and Vassilacopoulos, *Hegel and the Logical Structure of Love*, pp. 11-17.

CONCLUSION

THE TRANSITION TO OBJECTIVITY AND HEGEL'S ETHICAL STATE

We have argued that Hegel's Civil Society does not represent one sphere, or even one dimension, of social life. Instead, like the State, it manifests the logic of a social system *as a whole*, but whereas the State existentially manifests the unity of three Syllogisms, in the case of Civil Society its different dimensions are to be understood as manifesting the (differentiated) logic of the single Syllogism. The respective terms of the Hypothetical and the Disjunctive Syllogisms inform the organization of the concept of Civil Society, first in its initial appearance as a system of interdependence and then in its internal systemic differentiation as the market, the administration of justice and governance and productive activity. The analysis of Civil Society's moments in accordance with the claims of the strict organization thesis has enabled us to address a number of puzzling or seemingly contradictory claims that Hegel makes about issues such as the creation of poverty within Civil Society, the role of the Estates and the place of the Corporations. We have seen that Civil Society's ethical significance concerns its role in establishing the notion of the formally free subject whose participation in the collective of the Corporation enables the further cultivation of this form of inter-subjectivity in a variety of (non-Western) cultural contexts. In the light of our analysis we can also conclude that just as the *Logic* provides a solution to the question of what precisely renders Civil Society as a moment of Ethical Life, so too the limits of the abstract moment of Ethical Life are to be found in the way it manifests the logic of the single Syllogism. Although the notion's categorical development in the form of the Disjunctive Syllogism underpins and establishes the necessarily inter-subjective nature of subjective freedom and this form of subjective freedom is achieved through the establishment of a structure of relations—a number of forms of the comprehensive categorial differentiated unity—that together exhaust their genus, as we elaborate in detail in the next volume, these relations are nonetheless associated with certain unresolved contradictions. While Civil Society generates forms of unity that explicitly exhibit the notion's comprehensive categorial differentiated unity, because this is achieved in a limited way, it results in the sublation of the principle of inter-subjectivity itself. This is why it is not possible to secure *effective* (socially mediated) freedom within this structure of relations.

As we noted in Chapter Two, another unresolved interpretive dispute concerning the transition from the second to the third stage of Ethical Life focuses on the nature and rationale for an immanent transition to the ethical State. In line with the strict organization thesis, we should understand the transition from Civil Society to the State in terms of the notion's movement, following the completion of its development through the Syllogism, to that which takes shape in the *Science of Logic* as the process of the notion's objectification. In the next volume we elaborate in detail the meaning and significance of this objectification but it is already evident from the analysis thus far that to render explicit the abstractness of Civil Society is to anticipate a new global order, one generated by principles that accord with the Idea of the ethical State. For as well as supplying a clear response to issues that have been at the heart of unresolved interpretive disputes about the differences and possible lines of continuity evident in the movement from Civil Society to the State, making sense of Civil Society by reference to the logic of the Hypothetical and the Disjunctive Syllogisms has enabled us to see that the question of the Civil Society-State relationship cannot be properly posed as a question concerning co-existents. This means that the Hegelian State does not represent a normative ideal in the sense of an account of the values that ought to define the current global order.

Instead, as we have seen, it is Civil Society that provides an account of the ethical-ontological conditions that inform the current global reality and, in particular, the emergence of global civil society as a system of interdependence, albeit with all the institutional and cultural diversity we have explored. We have seen some of the ways in which the Hegelian concept can inform our understandings of the nature and significance of global phenomena and processes within the parameters of this organizational whole, ranging from questions of the implications of a globally extended notion of formally free subjectivity, the meaning of global citizenship and the expansion of human rights discourse to the manifestation of global capitalism, the global organization of labour and the nature and limits of cooperative associational forms and global governance strategies. Although an appreciation of the processes of making economic globalization fair and socially just does not fall within the parameters of the Hegelian concept of Civil Society in the light of the abstractness of this moment, our analysis suggests that for this we must look forward to the incorporation of civil society into the ethical State that is determined in accordance with the logic of Objectivity.

Finally, in the process of comparing contemporary accounts of the globalization phenomenon we have seen how our Hegelian approach can provide a critical vantage point from which to appreciate the limitations of alternative ways of making sense of the current global reality. While the discussion in this volume has focused mainly on rival conceptions of the idea(l) of global civil society, most notably those by Alexander and Keane, it also signals the potential fruitfulness of extending this approach to more far reaching theories, which speak to *the radical transformative potential* of the current global reality. Hardt and Negri's elaboration of the emergence of the radical transformative power of the multitude in response to the emergence of Empire is a case in point.[1] Hardt and Negri seek to locate the inherent possibilities for resistance and social transformation in the phenomena of globalization they critique. For example, when identifying a tendency toward unification of the world market they suggest that at the same time as constructing a globally mobile labour market Empire also 'constructs the desire to escape the disciplinary regime'.[2] Talk of such transformative possibilities as inherent in the constructive powers of Empire alludes to the limits of global civil society but Hardt and Negri do not realize the degree of conformity of their

---

[1]. Hardt and Negri, *Empire*; Hardt and Negri, *Multitude: War and Democracy in the Age of Empire*.
[2]. Hardt and Negri, *Empire*, pp. 251-253.

fundamental concepts, of Empire and of the multitude, to the logic of the Disjunctive Syllogism, particularly its transitional features. After examining in some detail the precise nature of the transitional logic from the Syllogism to Objectivity, in the next volume we will be in a position to make out the claim that in its fundamentals Hardt and Negri's concepts of Empire and the multitude remain fundamentally tied to the limits of the logic of the Disjunctive Syllogism. Hardt and Negri read Hegel's concept of the State as having achieved a problematic synthesis of the form and content of modern European sovereignty, which they equate with capitalist sovereignty. They take capitalism to be *the content* given to modern sovereignty, which takes *the form* of a single transcendent power whose task it is to re-impose order on an immanent constituent power of the multitude to which modernity has also given rise. Moreover, they argue that this synthesis facilitates the transformation of sovereignty into 'a political machine that rules across the entire society' in order to transform the multitude into an orderly totality.[3] On our reading, their theory belongs to a tradition that fails to appreciate the visionary, anticipatory dimension of the Hegelian Civil Society-State relationship. This is the subject matter of the next volume.

---

3. Hardt and Negri, *Empire*, pp. 69-87.

REFERENCES

Alexander, Jeffrey C., *The Civil Sphere*, Oxford, Oxford University Press, 2006.

Anderson, Joel, 'Hegel's Implicit View on how to Solve the Problem of Poverty: The Responsible Consumer and the Return of the Ethical to Civil Society', in Robert R. Williams (ed.), *Beyond Liberalism and Communitarianism: Studies in Hegel's Philosophy of Right*, Albany, State University of New York Press, 2001.

Arthur, Christopher J., 'Hegel on Political Economy', in David Lamb (ed.), *Hegel and Modern Philosophy*, New York, Croom Helm, 1987, pp. 102-118.

Ashton, Paul, 'Hegel and Labour', Legacy of Hegel Seminar, University of Melbourne, February 5, 1999, http://www.marxists.org/reference/archive/hegel/txt/ashton.htm

Avineri, Schlomo, *Hegel's Theory of the Modern State*, Cambridge, Cambridge University Press, 1980.

Baker, Gideon, 'Civil Society and Democracy: The Gap Between Theory and Possibility', *Politics*, vol.18, no.2, 1998, *pp.* 81-87.

Banner, Michael, 'Christianity and Civil Society', in Simone Chambers and Will Kymlicka, (eds.), Alternative Conceptions of Civil Society, Princeton, Princeton University Press, 2002, pp. 113-130.

Bayeh, Mohammed A., *The Ends of Globalization*, Minnesota, University of Minnesota Press, 2000.

Bernasconi, Robert, 'Hegel at the Court of the Ashanti', in Stuart Barnett (ed.), *Hegel after Derrida*, London, Routledge, 1988, pp. 41-63.

Bobbio, Noberto, 'Gramsci and the Concept of Civil Society', in John Keane (ed.), *Civil Society and the State*, London, Verso, 1988, pp. 73-100.

Brod, Harry, *Hegel's Philosophy of Politics: Idealism, Identity and Modernity*, San Francisco and Boulder, Westview Press, 1992.
Brooks, Thom, 'Between Statism and Cosmopolitanism: Hegel and the Possibility of Global Justice', in Andrew Buchwalter (ed.), *Hegel and Global Justice*, New York and London, Springer, 2012, pp. 65-84.
Brooks, Thom, (ed.), *Hegel's Philosophy of Right*, Oxford, Blackwell, 2012.
Brooks, Thom, *Hegel's Political Philosophy: A Systematic Reading of the Philosophy of Right*, Edinburgh, Edinburgh University Press, 2007.
Buchwalter, Andrew, 'Hegel and Global Justice: An Introduction', in Andrew Buchwalter (ed.), *Hegel and Global Justice*, New York and London, Springer, 2012, pp. 1-20.
Buchwalter, Andrew, 'Hegel, Global Justice and Mutual Recognition', in Andrew Buchwalter (ed.), *Hegel and Global Justice*, New York and London, Springer, 2012 pp. 211-232.
Buchwalter, Andrew, (ed.), *Hegel and Global Justice*, New York and London, Springer, 2012.
Butler, Clark, 'The Coming World Welfare State which Hegel Could Not See', in Andrew Buchwalter (ed.), *Hegel and Global Justice*, New York and London, Springer, 2012, pp. 155-176.
Café Direct, 'Adaptation for Smallholders to Climate Change', http://www.adapcc.org/
Carpinschi, Anton and Tonyeme, Bilakani, 'Cultural minorities and Intercultural Dialogue in the Dynamics of Globalization: African Participation', *Cultura: International Journal of Philosophy of Culture and Axiology*, vol.8, no.1, 2011, pp. 7-26.
Chambers, Simone and Kymlicka, Will, 'Alternative Conceptions of Civil Society', in Simone Chambers and Will Kymlicka (eds.), *Alternative Conceptions of Civil Society*, Princeton, Princeton University Press, 2002, pp. 1-12.
Chambers, Simone and Kymlicka, Will, (eds.), *Alternative Conceptions of Civil Society*, Princeton, Princeton University Press, 2002.
Chanter, Tina, 'Antigone's Liminality: Hegel's Racial Purification of Tragedy and the Naturalization of Slavery', in Kimberly Hutchings and and Tuija Pulkkinen (eds.), *Hegel's Philosophy and Feminist Thought: Beyond Antigone?*, Basingstoke, Palgrave MacMillan, 2010, pp. 61-85.
Church, Jeffrey, 'The Freedom of Desire: Hegel's Response to

Rousseau on the Problem of Civil Society', *American Journal of Political Science*, vol.54, no.1, 2012, pp. 125-139.

Cobben, Paul, 'The Citizen of the European Union from a Hegelian Perspective', in Andrew Buchwalter (ed.), *Hegel and Global Justice*, New York and London, Springer, 2012, p. 177-192.

Comaroff, John L. and Comaroff, Jean, 'Introduction', in John L. Comaroff and Jean Comaroff (eds.), *Civil Society and the Political Imagination in Africa: Critical Perspectives*, Chicago, University of Chicago Press, 1999, pp. 1-43.

Comaroff, John L. and Comaroff, Jean, (eds.), *Civil Society and the Political Imagination in Africa: Critical Perspectives*, Chicago, University of Chicago Press, 1999.

Cullen, Bernard, 'The Mediating Role of Estates and Corporations in Hegel's Theory of Political Representation', in Bernard Cullen (ed.), *Hegel Today*, Aldershot, Gower Publishing Company, 1988, pp. 22-41.

Dallmayr, Fred, *G.W.F. Hegel: Modernity and Politics*, London, Sage, 1993.

Deligiorgi, Katerina, (ed.), *Hegel: New Directions*, London, Acumen, 2006.

Dower, Nigel, 'Situating Global Citizenship', in Randall D. Germain and Michael Kenny (eds.), *The Idea of Global Civil Society: Politics and Ethics in a Globalizing Era*, London, Routledge, 2005, pp. 100-118.

Drydyk, Jay, 'Capitalism, Socialism and Civil Society', *The Monist*, 1991, pp. 457-477.

Dudley, Will, 'A Case of Bad Judgment: The Logical Failure of the Moral Will', *The Review of Metaphysics*, vol. 51, no. 2, 1997, pp. 379-405.

Fischer, Edward F., *Cultural Logics and Global Economies: Maya Identity in Thought and Practice*, Austin, University of Texas Press, 2001.

Franco, Paul, *Hegel's Philosophy of Freedom*, New Haven, Yale University Press, 1999.

Frankenberg, Gunter, 'National, Supranational, and Global Ambivalence in the Practice of Global Civil Society', *Law Critique*, vol.19, 2008, pp. 275-296.

Fritzman, J. M., 'Return to Hegel', *Continental Philosophy Review*, vol.34, 2001, pp. 287-320.

Gamble, Andrew and Kenny, Michael, 'Ideological Contestation, Transnational Civil Society and Global politics' in Randall D. Germain and Michael Kenny (eds.), *The Idea of Global*

Civil Society: Politics and Ethics in a Globalizing Era, London, Routledge, 2005, pp. 20-21.

Garland, Elizabeth, 'Developing Bushmen: Building Civil(ized) Society in the Kalahari and Beyond, in John L. Comaroff and Jean Comaroff (eds.), Civil Society and the Political Imagination in Africa: Critical Perspectives, Chicago, University of Chicago Press, 1999, pp. 72-103.

Germain, Randall D. and Kenny, Michael, (eds.), The Idea of Global Civil Society: Politics and Ethics in a Globalizing Era, London, Routledge, 2005.

Goldberg, David Theo, The Threat of Race: Reflections on Racial Neoliberalism, Madden MA, Wiley-Blackwell, 2009.

Goldstein, Joshua D., Hegel's Idea of the Good Life: From Virtue to Freedom, Early Writings and Mature Political Philosophy, Netherlands, Springer, 2006.

Gould, Carol C., 'Varieties of Global Responsibility: Social Connection, Human Rights and Transnational Solidarity', in Ann Ferguson and Mechthild Nagel (eds.), Dancing with Iris: The Philosophy of Iris Marion Young, Oxford, Oxford University Press, 2009, pp. 199-211.

Habermas, Jürgen, Philosophical Discourse of Modernity, Oxford and Cambridge, Polity Press, 1992.

Hanafi, Hasan, 'Alternative Conceptions of Civil Society: A Reflective Islamic Approach', in Simone Chambers and Will Kymlicka (eds.), Alternative Conceptions of Civil Society, Princeton, Princeton University Press, pp. 171-189.

Hardimon, Michael O., Hegel's Social Philosophy: The Project of Reconciliation, Cambridge, Cambridge University Press, 1994.

Hardt, Michael and Negri, Antonio, Empire, Cambridge, Harvard University Press, 2001.

Hardt, Michael and Negri, Antonio, Multitude: War and Democracy in the Age of Empire, London, Hamish Hamilton, 2005.

Harris, H. S., 'The Social Ideal of Hegel's Economic Theory', in L.S. Stepelevich and David Lamb (eds.), Hegel's Philosophy of Action, Atlantic Highlands, New Jersey, Humanities Press, 1983, pp. 49-74.

Hart, Victor G., Lester J. Thompson and Terry Stedman, 'The Indigenous Experience of Australian Civil Society: Making Sense of Historic and Contemporary Institutions', Social Alternatives, vol.27, no.1, 2008, pp. 52-57.

Hartmann, Klaus, 'Towards a New Systematic Reading', in Z.A Pelczynski (ed.), The State and Civil Society: Studies in Hegel's

Political Philosophy, Cambridge, Cambridge University Press, 1984, pp. 114-136.
Hegel, G.W.F., *Hegel's Logic: Being Part One of the Encyclopaedia of the Philosophical Sciences*, trans. William Wallace, Oxford, Oxford University Press, 1975.
Hegel, G.W.F., *Hegel's Philosophy of Mind: Being Part Three of the Encyclopaedia of the Philosophical Sciences*, trans. William Wallace, Oxford, Oxford University Press.
Hegel, G.W.F., *Hegel's Science of Logic*, trans. A.V. Miller, New York, Humanity Books, 1989.
Hegel, G.W.F., *Philosophy of Right*, trans. T.M. Knox, Oxford, Oxford University Press, 1967.
Hegel, G.W.F., *The Phenomenology of Spirit*, Oxford, Oxford University Press, 1970.
Hicks, Steven V., 'Hegel on Cosmopolitanism, International Relations and the Challenges of Globalization', in Andrew Buchwalter (ed.), *Hegel and Global Justice*, New York and London, Springer, 2012, pp. 21-48.
Hoffheimer, Michael H., 'Hegel, Race, Genocide', *The Southern Journal of Philosophy*, vol.39, no.3, 2001, pp. 35-62.
Honneth, Axel, *The Pathologies of Individual Freedom: Hegel's Social Theory*, New Jersey, Princeton University Press, 2010.
Horstmann, Rolf-Peter, 'Substance, Subject and Infinity: A Case Study of the Role of Logic in Hegel's System', in Katerina Deligiorgi (ed.), *Hegel: New Directions*, London, Acumen, 2006, pp. 69-84.
Horstmann, Rolf-Peter, 'The Role of Civil Society in Hegel's Political Philosophy', in Robert B. Pippin and Otfried Hoffe (eds.), *Hegel on Ethics and Politics*, Cambridge, Cambridge University Press, 2007, pp. 208-240.
Houlgate, Stephen, *Freedom, Truth and History: An Introduction to Hegel's Philosophy*, London and New York, Routledge, 1991.
Hutchings, Kimberly, 'Hard Work: Hegel and the Meaning of the State in his *Philosophy of Right*', in Thom Brooks (ed.), *Hegel's Philosophy of Right*, Blackwell, 2012, pp. 125-141.
Hutchings, Kimberly, 'Subjects, Citizens or Pilgrims? Citizenship and Civil Society in a Global Context', in Randall D. Germain and Michael Kenny (eds.), *The Idea of Global Civil Society: Politics and Ethics in a Globalizing Era*, London, Routledge, 2005, pp. 84-99.
Ilting, K-H., 'The Dialectic of Civil Society', in Z.A Pelczynski (ed.), *The State and Civil Society: Studies in Hegel's Political*

Philosophy, Cambridge, Cambridge University Press, 1984, pp. 90-110.
James, David, *Hegel's Philosophy of Right: Subjectivity and Ethical Life*, London, Continuum, 2007.
Kaehler, Klaus E., 'The Right of the Particular and the Power of the Universal', *The Southern Journal of Philosophy*, vol.39, no.3, 2001, pp. 147-162.
Karlstrom, Mikael, 'Civil Society and its Presuppositions: Lessons from Uganda', in John L. Comaroff and Jean Comaroff (eds.), *Civil Society and the Political Imagination in Africa: Critical Perspectives*, Chicago, University of Chicago Press, 1999, pp. 104-123.
Kaviraj, Sudipta and Khilnani, Sunil, (eds.), *Civil Society: History and Possibilities*, Cambridge, Cambridge University Press, 2001.
Kaviraj, Sudipta, 'In Search of Civil Society', in Sudipta Kaviraj and Sunil Khilnani (eds.), *Civil Society: History and Possibilities*, Cambridge, Cambridge University Press, 2001, pp. 287-321.
Keane, John, *Democracy and Civil Society*, London, Verso, 1988.
Keane, John, *Global Civil Society?*, Cambridge, Cambridge University Press, 2003.
Kenny, Michael and Germain, Randall, 'The Idea(l) of Global Civil Society' in Randall D. Germain and Michael Kenny (eds.), *The Idea of Global Civil Society: Politics and Ethics in a Globalizing Era*, London, Routledge, 2005, pp. 192-199.
Kierens, K., 'The Concept of Ethical Life in Hegel's *Philosophy of Right*', *History of Political Thought*, vol.13, no.3, 1992, pp. 417-435.
Kolb, David, *The Critique of Pure Modernity: Hegel Heidegger and After*, Chicago, The University of Chicago Press, 1988.
Korovkin, Tanya, 'Reinventing the Communal Tradition: Indigenous Peoples, Civil Society and Democratization in Andean Ecuador', *Latin American Research Review*, vol.36, no.3, 2001, pp. 37-67.
Kortian, Garbis, 'Subjectivity and Civil Society', in Z.A Pelczynski (ed.), *The State and Civil Society: Studies in Hegel's Political Philosophy*, Cambridge, Cambridge University Press, 1984, pp. 197-220.
Kymlicka, Will and Opalski, Magdalena, (eds.), *Can Liberal Pluralism Be Exported? Western Political Theory and Ethnic Relations in Eastern Europe*, New York, Oxford University Press, 2001.

Last Stone, Suzanne, 'The Jewish Tradition and Civil Society', in Simone Chambers and Will Kymlicka (eds.), *Alternative Conceptions of Civil Society*, Princeton, Princeton University Press, 2002, pp. 151-170 at 151-153.

Luhmann, Niklas, *The Differentiation of Society*, trans. Stephen Holmes and Charles Larmore, New York, Columbia University Press, 1982.

Lumsden, Simon, 'Beyond and Ontological Foundation for the Philosophy of Right', *The Southern Journal of Philosophy*, vol.39, no.3, 2001, pp. 139-145.

MacGregor, David, *The Communist Ideal in Hegel and Marx*, Toronto, University of Toronto Press, 1984.

Madsen, Richard, 'Confucian Conceptions of Civil Society', in Simone Chambers and Will Kymlicka (eds.), *Alternative Conceptions of Civil Society*, Princeton, Princeton University Press, 2002, pp. 190-206.

Masquelier, Adeline, 'Debating Muslims, Disputed Practices: Struggles for the Realization of an Alternative Moral Order in Niger', in John L. Comaroff and Jean Comaroff (eds.), *Civil Society and the Political Imagination in Africa: Critical Perspectives*, Chicago, University of Chicago Press, 1999, pp. 219-250.

McCloskey, H. J., 'Rights', *The Philosophical Quarterly*, vol. 15, 1965, pp.115-127.

Mercer, Claire, 'NGOs, Civil Society and Democratization: A Critical Review of the Literature', *Progress in Developmental Studies*, vol.2, no.1, 2001, pp. 5-22.

Moland, Lydia L., 'A Hegelian Approach to Global Poverty', in Andrew Buchwalter (ed.), *Hegel and Global Justice*, New York and London, Springer, pp. 131-154.

Nathan, Dev, Kelkar, Govind and Walter, Pierre, (eds.), *Globalization and Indigenous peoples in Asia: Changing the Local-global Interface*, London, Sage, 2004.

Neuhouser, Frederick, *Foundations of Hegel's Social Philosophy: Actualizing Freedom*, London, Harvard University Press, 2000.

Nicolacopoulos, Toula and Vassilacopoulos, George, 'Racism, Foreigner Communities and the Onto-pathology of White Australian Subjectivity', in *Whitening Race: Essays in Social and Cultural Criticism*, Aileen Moreton-Robinson (ed.), Canberra, ACT, Aboriginal Studies Press, 2004, pp. 32-47.

Nicolacopoulos, Toula and Vassilacopoulos, George, 'Rethinking the Radical Potential of the Concept of Multiculturalism', in Tseen Khoo (ed.), *The Body Politic: Racialised Political Cultures in Australia*, University of Queensland, University of Queensland's Australian Studies Centre, 2005, pp. 1-13.

Nicolacopoulos, Toula and Vassilacopoulos, George, 'The Ego as World: Speculative Justification and the Role of the Thinker in Hegel's Philosophy', in Paul Ashton, Toula Nicolacopoulos and George Vassilacopoulos (eds.), *The Spirit of the Age: Hegel and the Fate of Thinking*, Melbourne, re.press, 2008, pp. 259-291.

Nicolacopoulos, Toula and Vassilacopoulos, George, *Hegel and the Logical Structure of Love: An Essay of Sexualities, Family and the Law*, Melbourne, re.press, 2010.

Nicolacopoulos, Toula, 'What's Wrong with "Exporting Liberal Pluralism"?: On the Radical Self-denial of Contemporary Liberal Philosophy', *Philosophical Inquiry*, no.1-2, 2007, pp. 89-111.

Nicolacopoulos, Toula, *The Radical Critique of Liberalism*, Melbourne, re.press, 2008.

Nussbaum, Martha C., 'Iris Young's Last Thoughts on Responsibility for Global Justice', in Ann Ferguson and Mechthild Nagel (eds.), *Dancing with Iris: The Philosophy of Iris Marion Young*, Oxford, Oxford University Press, 2009, pp. 133-145.

Nuzzo, Angelica, 'Dialectic as Logic of Transformative Processes' in Katerina Deligiorgi (ed.), *Hegel: New Directions*, London, Acumen, 2006, pp. 85-103.

Nuzzo, Angelica, 'The End of Hegel's Logic: Absolute Idea and Absolute Method', in David Gray Carlson (ed.), *Hegel's Theory of the Subject*, New York, Palgrave Macmillan, 2005, pp. 187-205.

Nuzzo, Angelica, 'Which Particulars Can Have a Right? Which Universal Can Exercise Power?' *The Southern Journal of Philosophy*, vol.39, no.3, 2001, pp. 163-169.

Onuf, Nicholas, 'Late Modern Civil Society', in Randall D. Germain and Michael Kenny (eds.), *The Idea of Global Civil Society: Politics and Ethics in a Globalizing Era*, London, Routledge, 2005, pp. 47-64.

Osterhammel, Jürgen and Peterson, Niels P., *Globalization: A Short History*, trans. Dona Geyer, Princeton, Princeton University Press, 2005.

Peddle, David, 'Hegel's Political Ideal: Civil Society, History and *Sittlichkeit*', *Animus*, vol. 5, 2000, pp. 113-143.
Pelczynski, Z.A., (ed.), *The State and Civil Society: Studies in Hegel's Political Philosophy*, Cambridge, Cambridge University Press, 1984
Pelczynski, Z.A., 'The Hegelian Conception of the State', in Z.A. Pelczynski (ed.), *Hegel's Political Philosophy Problems and Perspectives*, Cambridge, Cambridge University Press, 1971, pp. 1-29.
Pinkard, Terry, *Hegel: A Biography*, Cambridge, Cambridge University Press, 2000.
Plant, Raymond, 'Economic and Social Integration in Hegel's Political Philosophy', in Donald Phillip Verene (ed.), *Hegel's Social and Political Thought: The Philosophy of Objective Spirit*, New Jersey, Humanities Press, 1980, pp. 59-90.
Plant, Raymond, 'Hegel on Identity and Legitimation' in Z.A Pelczynski (ed.), *The State and Civil Society: Studies in Hegel's Political Philosophy*, Cambridge, Cambridge University Press, 1984, pp. 227-243.
Plant, Raymond, *Hegel: An Introduction*, Oxford, Basil Blackwell, 1983.
Quante, Michael, '"Organic Unity": Its Loose and Analogical and its Strict and Systematic Sense in Hegel's Philosophy', *The Southern Journal of Philosophy*, vol.39, no.3, 2001, pp. 189-195.
Richardson, Henry S., 'The Logical Structure in Sittlichkeit: A Reading of Hegel's *Philosophy of Right*', *Idealistic Studies*, vol.19, 1989, pp. 62-78.
Riedel, Manfred, *Between Tradition and Revolution: The Hegelian Transformation of Political Philosophy*, Cambridge, Cambridge University Press, 1984.
Ritter, Joachim, *Hegel and the French Revolution*, trans. Richard Dien Winfield, Boston, Mass., MIT Press, 1984.
Robertson, Roland, *Globalization: Social Theory and Global Culture*, London, Sage, 1992.
Ross, Nathan, *On Mechanism in Hegel's Social and Political Philosophy*, London, Routledge, 2008.
Schlink, Bernhard, 'The Inherent Rationality of the State in Hegel's *Philosophy of Right*' in Drucilla Cornell, Michel Rosenfeld and David Carlson (eds.), *Hegel and Legal Theory*, New York and London, Routledge, 1991, pp. 347-354.
Sedgwick, Sally, 'The State as Organism: The Metaphysical Basis of Hegel's *Philosophy of Right*', *The Southern Journal of Philosophy*, vol.39, no.3, 2001, pp. 171-188.

Seligman, Adam B., 'Civil Society as Idea and Ideal' in Simone Chambers and Will Kymlicka (eds.), *Alternative Conceptions of Civil Society*, Princeton, Princeton University Press, 2002, pp. 13-33.

Ludwig Siep, 'The Contemporary Relevance of Hegel's Practical Philosophy', in Katerina Deligiorgi (ed.), *Hegel: New Directions*, London, Acumen, 2006, pp. 143-158 at p. 147.

Smismans, Stijn, 'European Civil Society: Shaped by Discourses and Institutional Interests', *European Law Journal*, vol.9, no.4, 2003, pp. 473-495.

Smith, Steven B., *Hegel's Critique of Liberalism: Rights in Context*, Chicago, The University of Chicago Press, 1989.

Stedman Jones, Gareth, 'Hegel and the Economics of Civil Society', in Sudipta Kaviraj and Sunil Khilnani (eds.), *Civil Society: History and Possibilities*, Cambridge, Cambridge University Press, 2001, pp. 105-130.

Steinberger, Peter J., *Logic and Politics: Hegel's Philosophy of Right*, New Haven, Yale University Press, 1988.

Stillman, Peter G., 'Hegel, Civil Society and Globalization', in Andrew Buchwalter (ed.), *Hegel and Global Justice*, New York and London, Springer, pp. 111-130.

Teichgraeber, Richard, 'Hegel on Property and Poverty', *Journal of the History of Ideas* vol.38, 1977, pp. 47-64.

Thompson, Kevin, 'Reason and Objective Spirit: Method and Ontology in Hegel's Philosophy of Right', *The Southern Journal of Philosophy*, vol.39, no.3, 2001, pp. 111-137.

Turner, Brian S. and Khondker, Habibul H., *Globalization: East and West*, London, Sage, 2010.

ver Eecke, Wilfried, 'The Relation Between Economics and Politics in Hegel', in Donald Phillip Verene (ed.), *Hegel's Social and Political Thought: The Philosophy of Objective Spirit*, New Jersey, Harvester Press, 1980, pp. 91-101.

Walton, A.S., 'Economy, Utility and Community in Hegel's Theory of Civil Society', in Z.A Pelczynski (ed.), *The State and Civil Society: Studies in Hegel's Political Philosophy*, Cambridge, Cambridge University Press, 1984, pp. 244-261.

Wartenberg, Thomas E., 'Poverty and Class Structure in Hegel's Theory of Civil Society', *Philosophy and Social Criticism*, vol.8, 1981, pp. 169-182.

Westphal, Merold, 'The Basic Context and Structure of Hegel's *Philosophy of Right*' in Frederick C. Beiser (ed.), The

Cambridge Companion to Hegel, New York, Cambridge University Press, 1993, pp. 234-269.

Williams, Robert R., (ed.), Beyond Liberalism and Communitarianism: Studies in Hegel's Philosophy of Right, Albany, State University of New York Press, 2001.

Winfield, Richard Dien, 'Hegel's Challenge to the Modern Economy', in Robert L. Perkins (ed.), History and System: Hegel's Philosophy of History, Albany, State University of New York Press, 1984, pp. 217-253.

Winfield, Richard Dien, 'Postcolonialism and Right', in Robert R. Williams (ed.), Beyond Liberalism and Communitarianism: Studies in Hegel's Philosophy of Right, Albany, State University of New York Press, 2001, pp. 91-110.

Wood, Allen W., Hegel's Ethical Thought, Cambridge, Cambridge University Press, 1990.

Žižek, Slavoj, Less than Nothing: Hegel and the Shadow of Dialectical Materialism, London & New York, Verso, 2012.

www.ingramcontent.com/pod-product-compliance
Lightning Source LLC
Chambersburg PA
CBHW030109170426
43198CB00009B/550